WIND IN MY W

Fair winds &
best wishes
Fran Taylor

WIND IN MY WINGS

Running Away to Sea in the 20th Century

Fran Taylor

Albatross Press

First published in 2008 by
Albatross Press, PO Box 104, South Perth WA 6951, Australia
email: albatrosspress104@yahoo.com

National Library of Australia
Cataloguing-in-Publication data:

Taylor, Fran
Wind in my wings:
running away to sea in the 20th century
1st edition
ISBN 978 0 64 649522 4 (pbk)
Bibliography

Women sailors – Biography
Endeavour (Ship: Replica)
Sailing ships

910.45092

Consultant editor: Allan Watson
Cover image by John Warburton
Printed by Everbest Printing, China

To all tall ships volunteers everywhere, particularly the "Endeavour Family".

Without volunteers' endless enthusiasm and dedication most of these wonderful ships would not be sailing the seven seas.

FOREWORD

In the romantic and challenging world that is sail training and the operation of great wind-driven "tall ships" on the world's oceans, as diverse a collection of personalities may be found as can be imagined. They are drawn to the sea, and the very physical business of crewing a sailing vessel and its thousands of square feet of canvas, for very many reasons. Collectively they are a fraternity – and, equally, a sorority – of adventurous souls who keep alive the traditions and skills of a vanished age, and in doing so often go on voyages of self-discovery. Rarely are they particularly literate about their experiences, but Australian Fran Taylor is someone who has been to sea as a blue-water square-rig crewman, and can write feelingly and well about it.

In her book, Taylor relates not only the day-to-day events in the seagoing life of a diminutive but lion-hearted woman who will not say "No" to the challenges in her life, but also the deeper thoughts and feelings that occur to her as she joins other men and women in the precarious business of crewing a square-rigger across half the world. In particular, her book deals with the dramatic voyage of the Australian replica of HM Bark *Endeavour* from England to Australia in 2004–2005. Taylor knows and loves *Endeavour*, and, as the ship wends its way homeward after three years of wandering to a more sedate existence at a Sydney museum dock, one can feel her empathy for the ship and a sense that her sailor's heart beats along with the heart of the vessel itself.

Others have written in more erudite style about the sea, but few have written with such direct honesty and engaging freshness as does Fran Taylor. For everyone who has gone to sea, or anyone who merely dreams of it from the safety of an armchair, sailing along with this very brave and passionate woman of the sea on her remembered voyages is a delightful experience.

Captain (N) Victor JH Suthren, CD, MA
Honorary Captain to the Chief of the Maritime Staff, Canadian Navy Reserve
Former Director General, Canadian War Museum, Ottawa
Author, Edward Mainwaring series of naval adventures
Voyage crew member, HM Bark *Endeavour*, October–November 1999

ACKNOWLEDGEMENTS

Captain Chris Blake, OBE, AO, for putting up with me many times.

All of my shipmates on various ships, who provided me with much of the material (wittingly or otherwise) for parts of this book. Apologies to those who are not mentioned specifically, but you all know who you are.

Endeavour Volunteer Guides in many parts of the world, but particularly the Fremantle, Western Australia, Division, who have harassed me for years (nicely) to write a book about my experiences.

Victor, Heather and Kathy, for taking the time to proofread my drafts and provide me with valuable feedback. Ross Shardlow for permitting me to reproduce his renderings of sail plans. The photographers individually acknowledged in captions.

And of course, my long-suffering land-lubber partner Ken; without his blessing and encouragement, my wings would probably never have been spread and I would not have experienced the joy of fulfilling my dreams.

CONTENTS

Foreword   vii

Acknowledgements   viii

1   The North Pacific Ocean   1

2   Hawaii   15

3   The South Pacific Ocean   27

4   In The Beginning   36

5   Dreams Coming True   47

6   Maiden Voyage Around Australia   60

7   Tall Ships Pilgrimage   73

8   Sydney to New Zealand   92

9   Short and Sweet X 2   108

10   No-One Told Me   117

11   Halifax to Amsterdam   134

12   The Prodigal Daughter Returns   156

13   The Winds of Change   171

14   Madeira and the Atlantic   182

15   Stand Aside, Boys   189

16   The Caribbean   194

17   Panama   208

18   The Galapagos Islands   224

19   Shipmates and Shenanigans   238

20   French Polynesia   247

21   Cook Islands   260

22   On to New Zealand   267

23   Homeward Bound   278

24   Epilogue   288

Glossary   291

Sail Plans   296

Maps   298

Selected References   300

I am the albatross that awaits you at the end of the earth.

I am the forgotten soul of the dead sailors who cross Cape Horn from all the seas of the world.

But they did not die in the furious waves.

Today they fly on my wings to eternity,

in the last trough of the Antarctic winds.

Sarah Vial

1

THE NORTH PACIFIC OCEAN

"Get up here", yelled the disembodied voice from above. Richard, my captain o' tops, was calling to me from much further up the rigging. It was two o'clock in the morning, pitch dark, and I was on board HM Bark *Endeavour*, having not long before joined the ship as a voyage crew member in Vancouver. We were heading for faraway New Zealand, it was pouring with rain, and the ship was rolling heavily in the swell.

I was a member of mainmast watch, and that night we were the duty watch on the "graveyard shift", from midnight until 4 am. We had just sailed down through the Inside Passage and Juan de Fuca Strait between the Canadian mainland and Vancouver Island, dropped off the pilot and cleared the lee of the island. The wind was starting to pick up, so we were being sent aloft to bring in and furl the t'gallant sail on the mainmast. This is the highest sail on the ship, some thirty-five metres above the deck.

I had sailed on the *Endeavour* before, and it wasn't the first time I'd been called on to climb up to the t'gallant. So I knew that I could do it, albeit with a little trepidation. On previous voyages I had made do with what clothes I already had, to my detriment occasionally, but for this voyage I had decided to kit myself out with some proper wet-weather gear, including sea boots.

Sea boots are a bit like glorified Wellingtons, with non-slip soles and a lace that can be tied around your leg at the top of the boot. Mine were roomy enough to accommodate good thick woollen socks, so I knew that even if I got wet my toes would stay nice and toasty warm, which would make a huge difference to my comfort level during a four-hour watch on deck. What hadn't occurred to me was that the very size of my lovely new boots might be a problem while climbing the shrouds.

Shrouds are ropes or wires that run from high up on the masts down to the deck, usually in pairs, basically to help hold the mast upright. Tied between the shrouds are lengths of rope, known as "ratlines", which serve as rungs for climbing up to the higher levels. As the rigging gets higher up the masts, the ratlines inevitably become shorter, until there is barely enough room for a toehold at the very highest points. No doubt this is why sailors of old used to go barefoot – no luxuries like sea boots for them.

We are taught to climb safely on these ships, always using what's referred to as three points of contact. This means that instead of progressing upwards the way you might climb a ladder, with one hand and one foot moving up at the same time, you always have either two hands and one foot, or two feet and one hand, firmly connected to the rigging. And you always climb on the windward side of the ship so that the wind is at your back, blowing you in towards the rigging rather than out from it. This all makes perfect sense, even to an amateur. Together with having a safety harness, such knowledge helps to dispel the fear of going aloft.

Well, there I was in my new gear climbing up towards the t'gallant sail when, about halfway there, I found to my dismay that I was stuck. One of my boots was jammed in the rigging. None of the teaching I'd received or the drills I'd done had prepared me for this. The wind was picking up still more, making the job at hand more urgent. The rest of my watch members had overtaken me on the rigging and were now up on the t'gallant yard. "Get up here Fran", cried the voice from above again. By this time I was starting to panic. I pulled and heaved, trying to free the boot from the rigging, to no avail. Finally something gave – but it was my foot extricating itself from the boot. Now I was hanging on like grim death, with one foot on a ratline, two white-knuckled hands clinging to the shrouds and the other foot waving about in the air as the ship went on rolling. This was not good! I decided the only thing to do was try and unwedge the boot, get it back on somehow and make my way back down to the deck, even though this would mean letting down the rest of my watch.

I let go one hand from the shrouds (which at that moment I was thinking were well named) to reach down and tackle the boot. This now meant that I had only one hand and one foot connected to the rigging. Of course this was against the rules, and indeed it proved to be a very bad move, as just then the ship rolled again and I found myself pivoting around on the rigging some twenty metres off the deck. If I'd been starting to panic before, I was definitely in panic mode now. "Take some deep breaths and calm down", I told myself. I also clipped my safety harness on to the ratlines, which we don't normally do while climbing, as it impedes one's progress. This reassured me a little, and I reached down and had another go at the boot.

After much puffing, panting, muttering, cursing and wriggling the boot around, I finally managed to free it, only to drop it immediately to the deck below. By this time I was beginning to think the purchase of sea boots to keep my feet warm and dry had not been a particularly good idea. Previously I'd worn deck shoes when climbing and, although they don't necessarily keep your feet dry, they most definitely suit the purpose of climbing much better.

At least the shouting from above had stopped. Richard had obviously given up on me, or perhaps the rest of the watch had been able to tell him I was stuck. Soon they'd finished furling the sail and were on their way back down the rigging again. By this time my breathing had returned to something like normal and my heart had stopped pounding, and there was nothing for it but to climb back down with them, one foot in its boot and the other clad only in a very wet sock. Hopefully I could retrieve the other boot once I got back down on deck. The rain continued to pour down.

We reassembled in our little group on deck, with the rest of the watch – every one of them, like me, an amateur – feeling elated that they had accomplished what they had set out to do in quite difficult conditions. While high fives were going around I stood there feeling very silly and ashamed that I hadn't been able to pull my weight, particularly as I wasn't a new hand on this ship: I had already done several shorter voyages on her.

Much to my relief, however, they were all very kind and supportive – even Richard, although I did get a mild telling-off for not having my

3

three points of contact at all times. They were so kind, in fact, that I burst into tears. You're not supposed to cry like a girl when you're a roughie-toughie sailor on a square-rig ship. In hindsight I think it was delayed shock setting in – I'd given myself a hell of a fright – but it was their kindness that triggered off the emotion.

Nothing more was said about the incident apart from a lot of teasing from my watch-mates, who were inclined to burst into short choruses of "These boots are made for walkin'" at every opportunity. One of the team, however, seemed to realise just how much of a fright I'd given myself. For the next few days, whenever there was a need to go aloft (minus the sea boots of course), Rob seemed to be always at my side making sure I was all right. He did it in an unobtrusive way, and I don't think anyone else noticed, but I was very grateful. It was a few days before I got as high as the t'gallant yard, and when I finally made it there was Rob's quiet voice beside me: "Fran's back on the horse again".

It was October 1999, and I had flown from Perth, Western Australia, where the *Endeavour* was built and where I live, to join her in Vancouver for this trip of a lifetime. At that time she was owned and operated by the HM Bark Endeavour Foundation, a non-profit organisation that had been formed some years previously. It would take approximately three months to sail from Vancouver to Wellington in New Zealand via Hawaii, Kiribati and Fiji. This was the stuff of dreams for me, and I'd resigned from my job, sold my house and put my belongings into storage so that I could do it. I was going to move in and share with my partner Ken upon my return. So it was that I headed off with a backpack and holdall, technically jobless and homeless, with no responsibilities and a huge grin on my face.

The *Endeavour* carries around fifty people in several different categories on voyages. First there is the professional crew, which comprises the captain, first and second mates, bosun, engineer and chef. Other paid crew normally include a shipwright or carpenter, bosun's mate, cook's mate, captain's clerk/steward/curator and a "captain o' top" for each of the three masts: fore, main and mizzen. Sometimes there is a guest navigator or watch officer. This configuration changes from time to time, depending upon the voyage route and duration.

4

Voyage crew, which was the capacity in which I was on board, generally number around thirty-five to forty. They are split up into three groups, or watches, that are supervised, taught and generally become the responsibility of one of the captains o' top. In other words, they give us our orders, after having received their orders from the mate or second mate, who in turn has received theirs from the captain. It might be the 21st century, but ships still operate in the time-honoured hierarchical naval fashion. No room for democracy here!

The third category of the ship's company is the supernumeraries. Both voyage crew and supernumeraries pay to be on board, with the latter group paying much more than voyage crew. Because of this, they are afforded the "luxury" of a cabin, albeit sometimes a cabin not much bigger than a broom cupboard. The rest of us scurvy dogs sleep in hammocks in one large communal area of the 18th-century deck, just like in the old days. Occasionally the ship also carries some volunteers, who virtually work their passage as deck hands, also just like in the old days. They don't get flogged, however, and we're all fed very well – hard tack and weevils are no longer on the menu, thank goodness.

HM Bark *Endeavour* is a replica of Captain James Cook's famous ship, and she has been described as the most authentic replica sailing vessel ever built. The weather deck, the lower or 18th-century deck and the ship's masts and rigging are virtually the same as on the original *Endeavour*, although constructed from different materials. What would have been the hold on the original ship is called the 20th-century deck on the replica vessel. Here there are an electric galley, comfortable mess, showers and toilets ("heads"), fridges and freezers, and an engine room. While every effort was made to keep her as authentic as possible, modern maritime safety regulations required that radar, satellite navigation and all the other technology available to 21st-century ships were incorporated. She also has engines, required for insurance purposes, which were used only when necessary.

The ship is basically run in an 18th-century manner, with watches of four hours being stood at a time, twenty-four hours a day. Everyone is required to take their turn at carrying out the variety of tasks needed to keep a ship (particularly a wooden one) well maintained and working safely, and generally being a useful hand. One of the best of these tasks is helming – steering the ship. Of course this is done under supervision and after training.

Supernumeraries are not required to go aloft, help with the daily cleaning and other more menial tasks, or stand night watches, but most of them pitch in with the rest of us. It always impresses me enormously how such a variety of modern people of such disparate ages, backgrounds, nationalities and personalities willingly and happily subject themselves to the order and discipline necessary on board a ship, and pay for the privilege of doing it. Not to mention forgoing many of the creature comforts available to us these days. But we do, and we love it. Many of us have sailed on the *Endeavour* a number of times – the captain calls us "repeat offenders" – and we never seem to get enough of her. Maybe we are escaping life ashore in the 21st century, or fulfilling a long-held desire to run away to sea, or trying to capture what it might have been like in our great-grandfathers' day. Who knows?

I had flown into Vancouver a week before I had to join the ship in order to visit my cousin Helen and her husband, Tommy, and family, whom I hadn't seen in about thirty-five years. The day after I arrived they took me down to the ship to deliver the crew mail that I'd carried from Australia, plus some Aussie goodies like Tim Tams, Cherry Ripes and Vegemite that I knew the crew wouldn't have had for some time. I hadn't seen the ship since October 1996 when she left Fremantle for Europe and America, and could hardly contain myself. I'll never forget Tommy's reaction when he saw her sitting at the dock: "You're not going to sail all the way to New Zealand in *that*", he exclaimed. He was appalled at how small she was. I was overwhelmed at seeing her again and couldn't wait to get on board.

When I joined the ship I was put into mainmast watch, shown the locker where I was to stow my gear and allocated a spot on the 18th-century deck, which would be where I was to sling my hammock. Every person in each watch is given a number, which corresponds with the point where his or her hammock gets slung. This avoids the wrong people getting woken up during the changeover of watches in the night. (It's still possible to make this mistake, but it's a cardinal sin that you only ever commit once – sleep is precious on a square-rig ship.)

On this occasion my watch comprised Terry, an artist from California; Rob, a surfie-cum-mobile-mechanic from Texas; Jack, a professional musician and actor from Vancouver; Axel, an engineer (I think) from Germany; Victor, a maritime historian and author of some note from Ottawa; Chuck and Laura, a couple from Hawaii on their honeymoon; Bob, another American who was an acupuncturist; Kristen, who had come on board as a young trainee for six months, from California; Paul, yet another American who had been a rocket scientist with NASA; and myself, a contracts engineer from Australia. Richard, who was English and a plumber by trade, was in charge of us lot. As I said earlier, very disparate ages, backgrounds and personalities sign on for these shipboard adventures.

I discovered that my "hammock mate", i.e. the person whose hammock was slung next to mine, was Victor, the maritime historian. We were allocated spots in the marines' area, the deck head (ceiling) of which is much lower than the rest of the 18th-century deck. The deck immediately above it was added specifically for Cook's first voyage – it had not been part of the original ship when she was the *Earl of Pembroke*. Our location had its advantages and its disadvantages. In cold weather it's a warmer spot, as it's not adjacent to hatches; and if you happen to fall out of your hammock, or the knots holding it up come undone, you don't have so far to fall. In hot weather it becomes a pretty unbearable hole, as there's no ventilation. It's also an area where people passing by during watch changeover often bump you. Being woken this way can get very tiresome.

In total the crew comprised the usual motley company of some fifty-odd souls ranging from teenagers to some in their mid-seventies. We had all been required to obtain a medical clearance and demonstrate a certain level of fitness. Sometimes supernumeraries join the ship in that capacity because they don't quite pass the medical at the level required for voyage crew.

We were issued with hammocks and safety harnesses, shown where our muster stations were and put through various safety drills. These would be ongoing during the voyage, and general alarms – such as would be raised if there was a fire on board, man overboard or collision/grounding – would also take place fairly regularly. The permanent crew

7

members are the main participants in these drills, as they have been trained in fire fighting and so forth, but we all have a role to play, and it's impressed upon us how very important the drills are.

With the basic safety aspects of the ship covered, we were taught how to don our harnesses properly and how to "buddy check" one another to make sure they were firm enough and fastened properly. Then it was time for the first climb aloft. I don't care what some people say: your very first climb up wobbly rigging on a square-rig ship is heart-pounding stuff. I've already mentioned that safety harnesses cannot be used on the *Endeavour* while you are actually climbing, as they would impede your progress. Once you get to the yard, however, you clip your harness onto a jackstay or other permanently attached piece of rigging before you begin the task you have climbed up to perform. When you're in position it's amazing how secure you actually feel. You are standing on a footrope, preferably with your belly hanging over the yard so that your weight is distributed evenly, holding on to a sail and attached to a jackstay, so you're not going anywhere.

The climb up, however, is another matter until you begin to get used to it and your confidence develops. The major area that perturbs most people is when you have to go over the futtocks. This is where the rigging from the lower section of the main mast goes into the top mast, the mast being in sections. That's just below what's called the fighting top platform. From there, the rigging comes back out again to continue on up to the next section of the mast. A futtock is like a cliff overhang, so you have to climb out backwards and then up and over its edge.

It's especially difficult if you're female, only 160 centimetres in height, bottom heavy and middle-aged. With not a lot of upper body strength and short legs, I had to develop my own way of getting up and over, hooking in on the shrouds by locking an arm around at the elbow joint rather than depending on a handhold. My hands are simply not big enough to fully enclose the shroud and get a proper grip. The captain told me it looked as awkward as hell from the deck, but after he had watched me a few times he realised that it was quite safe, and in my case probably better than trying to depend on a handhold. Just as well he didn't see me the night I got my sea boot jammed.

8

With the ship under way we settled into the sea routine. The day is split into watches of four hours each, except between 4 pm and 8 pm when two "dog watches" of two hours each are the norm. This allows each watch to be rotated throughout the twenty-four-hour day so that no one watch always stands the midnight to 4 am, for example. It can be a little confusing at first, but it seems a fair system to me.

The other thing that gets rotated by the dog watches pushing you through into the next block of time is the cleaning duty associated with whichever watch you are in. For example, if you are in the morning watch (8 am to noon) it might be your job to clean the 20th-century deck, which includes the heads. Because you don't work the morning watch permanently, everyone takes their turn at cleaning the heads. Again, this seems eminently fair to me, although there are always those who will grumble at having to clean toilets.

Everything gets cleaned every day and, for reasons that I've never quite figured out, the whole process is referred to as "happy hour". The supernumeraries more often than not take over the deck duties of the duty watch, standing lookout and taking the helm to steer the ship. This latter is always done under the close eye and/or supervision, where necessary, of the watch officer at the time.

This frees up the three watches to be split throughout the ship to attend to the cleaning, which generally takes an hour or so each day. We always tried to make it fun, to take the laboriousness out of it. It seemed to work, as there was always a lot of laughing at the same time as the scrubbing and polishing and sweeping and mopping. Once a week there are Captain's Rounds, when the captain will come through and inspect everything. You might be a paying volunteer on board, but heaven help you if something hasn't been cleaned properly – you have to do it again, and you have let down your watch badly. Standards of cleaning, how fast you can furl sails and how well you do a myriad other tasks on the ship become very competitive between the watches. Peer pressure is an amazing thing.

While the whole business of cleaning was taken seriously, and the captain, Chris, was very fastidious about the standard to which it was carried out, in my experience he made a bit of a game of it as well. He climbed up on things to reach impossible places, and stuck his fingers into air vents and nooks and crannies that our mothers would only clean once a year during the annual spring-clean of the house. We would try to catch him out by doing such things as hiding sweets wrappers and the like in spots where he just *might* look, and if he didn't find them we'd let him know with great glee that he'd missed something.

We once put chocolate sauce under the rim of a toilet bowl to test him, but he called our bluff beautifully! Of course he found it, but he then proceeded to sniff it, and even taste it before he burst out laughing and said, "Good one guys, but it didn't work!" We were all cringing at the very idea of what he was doing, but, as someone pointed out, it was testament to his faith in us that he knew there was no way we would have left a mess in the toilet bowl. I still squirm when I think of it, though, and have a laugh to myself every time I clean the toilet at home.

On another occasion, when we had been cleaning the showers, heads and locker-room area, he had the last word again. Just as he was coming down the stairs to inspect our area, someone decided it would be fun if one of us hid in the storage area at the bow of the ship, then leaped out and surprised him when he came through. These cupboards are known as the breast hooks, an appropriate name as it turned out. There wasn't a lot of room inside, so I, being the smallest in the watch, got volunteered to hop in.

When he came to the appropriate place, one of the watch said in a loud voice full of feigned dismay, "Oh, I forgot to clean in the breast hooks". Of course, the captain immediately pulled the door open, whereupon I popped out, lifted my tee-shirt and "flashed" him with a cheery "Good morning Captain!" Once he recovered himself and stopped laughing, he responded with, "Get that woman out of there and put her on the bow where she belongs … and take the tee-shirt and bra off first!" Like the original *Endeavour*, the replica ship doesn't have a figurehead. If it had, it could well have been a bare-breasted lady. As I said, the captain always has the last word …

A number of people were seasick for a few days initially, and they joined the "lee-rail club". Poor Chuck was so badly afflicted as to claim his own blue plastic bucket for his exclusive use. He carted it with him as he moved around the deck but, to his great credit, still managed to haul lines and pitch in with the rest. This is often the best remedy for seasickness: being busy does take your mind off other things. I make particular mention of the blue bucket because it takes on some importance later on.

Over the next few weeks we all settled in to the routine, with the weather getting progressively warmer as we sailed further south. Victor and I had become good mates by this time, partly due to the fact that we were both stuck in the marines' area. He teased me about how I looked upon waking up, rolled up in so many layers of blankets plus my sleeping bag when we left Vancouver that all he could see in the hammock next to him was a huge pile of bedding and a nose poking out. As it got warmer, and the layers started to get discarded, he said it was like something emerging from a chrysalis. I don't think I quite achieved butterfly status though.

We had also become "partners in crime" mostly due to the bumping in the night. If someone bumped him on the way past, his hammock would swing and bump me, and we would both wake up and curse. We cursed a lot, quietly between ourselves, and seemed to manage to apply the ƒ word to just about everything and everyone, while secretly loving every minute of it. It became a huge semi-private joke between us. We both agreed what an extremely useful word this ƒ word was: it could be used as an adjective or a verb or a noun and it could be applied to just about anything. Indeed, you could even split a word up and put it in the middle of it, as in "un-ƒ...ing furl the sail". We both enjoyed playing silly buggers with the language, and I think we even invented a few new swear words of our own. Our respective loved ones at home would have been horrified if they'd heard us, I'm sure.

As well as taking our turns at the chores, we also learned about helming the ship, sail handling and all sorts of other wonderful 18th-century skills, like splicing rope, tarring rigging and doing something called "worming, parcelling and serving" lines. I now have some wondrous new skills, all from the 18th century, to add to my CV when next I apply for a job in the 21st century. It could turn out to be an amusing interview… "You can what? Worm and parcel and serve? What on earth is that?"

As is often the case in particular occupations, a square-rig ship seems to have a language all of its own. We learned about buntlines, clew lines, leech lines, reef lines and halyards; t'gallants, topsails, courses, staysails and headsails; hauling, flaking, belaying and coiling; robands, earrings, cringles and grommets; fids and seizing mallets; cleats, belaying pins, blocks and bits. I could go on ...

I mention this only to relate how one day, while Laura, Victor and I were standing by a line waiting for instructions, he commented on how many new words he'd learned since coming aboard. Given that he is a writer, and extremely articulate, Laura and I were interested to hear what these new words were, expecting him to say "cringles" or "grommets" or something similar. Nothing of the kind. Instead he came out with some of the more colourful phrases that he and I had been practising in our little world in the marines' area. We cracked up laughing – it was *so* unexpected and out of place coming from such a gentleman.

We also had sailing lectures and navigation classes from the mate and other members of the professional crew. Navigation covered both coastal and celestial, and many people were able to learn how to use a sextant to take sun and star sightings. I must admit to getting beaten by the trigonometry involved in celestial navigation, but it was still wonderful to have the opportunity to try it and to understand a little bit about it. Voyage crew members with particular interests gave us various other talks on a variety of topics ranging from meteorology to surviving the sinking of a tall ship!

Victor gave us talks on maritime history, particularly about Captain Cook and the Royal Navy in King George III's time. He also demonstrated how to fire the muskets on board. These are among the ship's artefacts that are shown when she is on display in museum mode during port visits, and are normally stowed away when she is at sea. It was a bit of a treat to be allowed to have a shot (literally) with them. Not very successfully in my case, but I did have a go.

We also carry cannons, replicas of those on the original *Endeavour*, which a foundry in Western Australia made for us. I believe the original idea was that they were to be on board as artefacts, but very early in the ship's sailing life it was discovered that they work. We would fire them at every opportunity, and take great delight in startling entourages of small boats as they welcomed us into port. The barrels were stuffed with newspaper, which shreds beautifully when the charge goes off. No harm done, just a bit of a mess created. On very rare occasions, and only if it's safe of course, we have even fired off a cannonball or two.

The days rolled by, one into the next, and became weeks. It took about a month to sail from Vancouver to the Big Island of Hawaii. We sailed, we learned, we stood our watches and we became good friends. We carried out seemingly endless maintenance – sanding and painting and chipping rust and oiling and tarring. We laughed and we cried sometimes. We entertained ourselves with chess and domino tournaments, card games, musical evenings, funny skits and old 16mm movies projected onto the sails.

And we fished. Oh yes, we fished. Richard got a big hit on the troll line one day, and it turned out to be a huge yellow fin tuna. It was so big that we had to slow the ship down to haul it in. Even then it took ages, with four of the lads hanging over the side rather precariously to get it gaffed and on board. It was "guesstimated" to weigh about fifty kilograms – a real beauty that fed the whole crew for two days and was absolutely delicious.

We got the opportunity to go over the side and swim occasionally, on one occasion in water that was around six kilometres deep. As a precaution in these situations, the fast rescue craft (fizz boat) is put in the water and people are posted aloft as shark spotters. I couldn't help but be a bit concerned about what other sea creatures might be underneath looking at all those legs splashing about and contemplating a nibble or two. It was too wonderful to miss out on though.

On a tall ship you get to know one another incredibly well, especially the members of your own watch, as you eat, sleep and work together. You also get to know yourself very well, and find strengths and weaknesses that you didn't realise were there. Life on a ship is very routine and ordered, and in many ways very simple. That, and the camaraderie that develops are, I find, hugely appealing. It's something that rarely happens "shoreside", particularly in this day and age of ever-expanding technology and the faster pace of life.

One of the guys in my watch, who had been in Vietnam during the war in the 1960s, said it was the closest thing he had experienced to the camaraderie that existed among his unit when they were under fire. We all felt quite humbled and honoured when he told us that. In fact we had a "group hug" and wept when he had to leave the *Endeavour* in Hawaii.

Saying goodbye to some of these people when the ship gets to the next port is extremely emotional. While we all promise to keep in touch (and many of us do), the chances are you will never see many of them again. I was to endure many of these heart-rending farewells over the next few months.

2

 HAWAII

We arrived at Hawaii on 30 October. We knew we were getting close when we began to see aircraft in the distance. For about ten days we had seen absolutely nothing except the sea and some of its creatures. Not a ship or a seabird and certainly not land. There was a competition going on to see who sighted land first – there's an inescapable urge to shout, "Land ho" after days of seeing nothing. Perhaps we've all been reading too many books or watching too many movies. The first aircraft that was spotted brought forth a shout of "Plane ho", and everyone burst out laughing. It was nice to think that we were getting close to civilisation again though.

We were to visit three of the islands in the group – Hawaii (The Big Island), Oahu and Kauai, and spend some time on each. Mixed emotions prevailed. This *Endeavour* had never been to Hawaii, and that, of course, was where Captain Cook had been killed in February 1779 during a skirmish with the Hawaiians. Several of the locals had also been killed, so we weren't entirely sure how welcome we would be. The other reason for the mixed emotions was that some of the voyage crew would get off here, so we would have to say goodbye to many buddies, for that was what we had now all become.

We dropped anchor off Hapuna Resort on the Big Island, and it was decided to hold the traditional SODS Opera that evening. This is an acronym for "Sailors' Operatic and Dramatic Society", but over the years it has taken on something of the other meaning of the word as well. It's normally held on the last night of a voyage, but we knew the next couple of days would be very busy, so we held it that night while we

15

were at anchor. No-one could go ashore yet, of course, because we still had to clear all the customs and immigration formalities.

Sods Operas often turn up a huge variety of unexpected talent among voyage members, and are always a good laugh. Recurring features are skits that poke fun at the crew, with the captain inevitably a target, or that grossly embellish some event that's taken place on the voyage. Taking a well-known song and "Endeavourising" the words often accomplishes this. That was what our watch did, and it turned out that we had some talented lyricists among us.

We performed a medley of different songs, but the one that has stuck in my mind ever since was to the old Rolling Stones number "Paint it Black". Because everything had been getting painted in readiness for our arrival at Hawaii, it lent itself to the occasion. In our version it went something like, "I see red primer and I want to paint it black; the main companionway is closed to paint it black; my bladder's bursting but the mate don't give a damn; he doesn't care at all, he's such a nasty man …" and so on. Judging by the volume of laughter from the audience, it went down well. Occasionally, the original still gets played on the radio and I can't stop myself from breaking into the *Endeavour* version … I've long ago forgotten what the real words are. Even my partner, Ken, sings our version now, and he wasn't even on board the ship at the time.

Next morning there arrived a flotilla of small boats loaded with customs and immigration officials. They were to come aboard and clear all of us, and the ship. This turned out to be less straightforward than I had expected. We were a "foreign" ship, flying a "foreign" flag, and we had about a dozen different nationalities on board. Some of us had needed to get visas for the USA and some of us hadn't. The US Consulate in Perth had told me I didn't need one on my Australian passport, but the CEO of the Endeavour Foundation had insisted that I did, in his experience. Thank goodness I'd listened to him.

When the customs officers climbed up the manrope and over the rail to come aboard, I was quite taken aback to see that they were openly wearing formidable-looking handguns. I hadn't encountered this in Canada, and Australian customs officers don't wear handguns, so I found this quite confronting. Laura said my jaw dropped noticeably. I got chatting to one of the customs guys and asked him why they wear guns. His comment was, "Well ma'am, we get some pretty bad dudes come through here on boats." I'm sure he wasn't referring to us, but I had to have a bit of a chuckle to myself, given what a scruffy lot we looked at the time.

My paperwork was all in order as things transpired, but some of my shipmates had a bit of bother. They *should* have had visas but didn't. However, in his usual diplomatic manner, the captain managed to sort out all the problems, his clerk attended to the paperwork, some money changed hands for last-minute visas and we got our clearance for Hawaii. What we didn't realise at the time was that we would have to go through the same procedure all over again at Oahu and Kauai. Bureaucracy is alive and well all over the world it seems.

After the officials left, we motor-sailed around into Kealakekua Bay and dropped anchor virtually at the same spot where Cook himself had anchored during his voyage on the *Resolution*. It was a very spooky feeling to think that we were here, in his replica ship, in the same place where he and his men had been all those years ago. We had attracted a bit of attention by then, and a small flotilla of boats had escorted us around, including a couple of wonderful Hawaiian sailing canoes.

Our stay here would be brief but memorable. A working party was sent ashore to the Captain Cook Monument, which marks the spot where Cook fell, to carry out some gardening and painting. It's the only piece of British land in the United States and, by tradition, only British seamen are allowed to tend the site. One or two of the Aussies and Kiwis on board became "honorary Poms" for the morning so that we could do this. We unwittingly left evidence of our visit behind too, as a little gecko fell into the bucket of whitewash and got stuck on the obelisk. Very unobtrusively I might add.

Another group of us went ashore to attend a memorial service at the Kahikolu Congregational Church, which was absolutely unforgettable. The service, readings and hymns were conducted in both Hawaiian and English, and our hymn sheets were printed in both languages. While the words may have been different, I knew the tunes of many of the hymns and it certainly took me back to childhood Sunday school sessions. We were all in our best uniforms, and everyone else was dressed in their Sunday best, Hawaiian-style, which was very colourful. We were all

17

wearing beautiful leis of fresh flowers, mostly frangipani, that had been presented to us when we arrived.

The exception to this riot of colour was about half a dozen splendidly dressed Hawaiian ladies in the front pews, who were clad completely in black – hats, dresses, shoes, stockings, gloves and handbags – except for a small necklace of tiny bright orange feathers. We were told later that these feathers come from the tail of a species of bird endemic to the Hawaiian Islands. One or two feathers are harvested at a time, before the bird is released again. It takes years to make a necklace, and wearing one has great significance. These ladies were direct descendants of the ancient chiefs – Hawaiian royalty. It would have been wonderful to photograph them, but we had been asked not to.

When we returned to the ship, the captain declared the swimming pool open and we all went over the side for a quick dip before weighing anchor and motor-sailing around from Kealakekua Bay to Kailua-Kona, where we would spend the next five days open to the public on exhibition in museum mode. This would be the pattern in other ports. The ship earned her bread-and-butter money this way, and many thousands of people from all over the world have visited her. They got a tiny taste of what life would have been like on an 18th-century ship and learned something of the history of Captain Cook and his voyages.

We quickly unpacked the artefacts that get stowed away while we are at sea, got the museum set up and had a last-minute rehearsal of the sea shanty that Jack had taught the "Endeavour Choir". This had been formed during the voyage because we'd been warned that a large welcome awaited us at Kailua-Kona. And indeed it was so: several hundred people were waiting for us with more leis, dancers, bands, dignitaries and a contingent of locally recruited *Endeavour* volunteer guides. There were even a couple of the original volunteer guides from Fremantle among the crowd. I could hardly believe my eyes when I spotted Roy and Sue. They were holidaying in America, and had deliberately planned to be in Hawaii when we arrived. Such is the interest in and allure of this magic ship. It was lovely to see familiar faces from home.

And there were children, lots of children. Needless to say they thought this "pirate ship" was just fantastic, but couldn't quite understand why we weren't dressed like pirates. We were all on our best behaviour, what with so many VIPs in attendance, not to mention TV cameras and reporters everywhere. After the formal speeches had been delivered and national anthems sung, the "Endeavour Choir" sang the shanty we had learned, with some appropriate changes to the original lyrics to "localise" it. The welcome party on the pier went on well into the night, and we all fell into our hammocks exhausted. It had been a very long day, but one indelibly etched into my memory. It was such a privilege to be a part of this.

Some of the voyage crew got off at Kailua and we would take on new crew for the short leg to Honolulu. Laura and Chuck were among the group who left us, as they were flying back to Honolulu to return to work. They live aboard a boat there, and said they would come out and meet us as we sailed in. This meant we would see them again in about a week's time.

Some of us who were going all the way to New Zealand took the opportunity to sign off the ship for a few days and go and stay in hotels. Oh, the luxury of a proper bed that didn't move and an en-suite bathroom where you could indulge in long, long, hot showers and even perhaps have a bath. On board ship we have thirty-second sea-showers: you turn on the tap to get wet, then turn it off after ten seconds before soaping up and turn it back on to rinse off for the remaining twenty seconds.

Sometimes, if the fresh water is getting a bit low and the weather is clement, we don't even have those. Deck showers using the fire hose and seawater become the order of the day. These are actually quite fun, but are inclined to leave you a little sticky if you can't at least have a quick rinse off with fresh water. The ship has a reverse-osmosis machine, which turns seawater into fresh, but how efficiently it works is largely dependent upon the temperature of the sea. We ration water very strictly of course, so if it's getting a bit low the fresh water is kept for drinking and cooking, and we make do with seawater for washing.

The first full day in Kailua-Kona dawned, and the ship would soon be open to the public for exhibition. Many of the enthusiastic locals who had been recruited as volunteer guides and who had welcomed us the previous night arrived for duty. They would be showing people around and telling them about this ship, and about the original *Endeavour*. A few of the permanent crew stay aboard on duty during these port visits, but quite a number of the rest of us were free to go and have some rest and recreation.

Prior to the ship being opened to the public, however, there arrived a Hawaiian elder and his entourage, resplendent in traditional capes. They wanted to see the captain. He had stayed ashore the previous night, so he was sent for hurriedly. Then, with the crew assembled on deck to form a guard of honour, Victor piped them aboard. The senior member of the party was an elder from the local tribe. He inspected the ship, spoke with a number of the crew and welcomed us warmly. All was well. Now that we had his blessing, any misgivings about our reception dissipated.

Quite a few of us spent the day doing a bus tour of the Big Island, taking in many of the sights, including Kilauea Caldera, orchid and macadamia nut plantations, black and green sand beaches, spectacular waterfalls and a lava tube, which we walked through. At the same time we learned much about Hawaiian history. After a leisurely evening meal and a couple of drinks, it was time to fall into those wonderful beds back at the hotel room. It was magic to go to sleep once again secure in the knowledge that we wouldn't be getting wakened to go and stand a watch during the night or early in the morning.

In fact we slept right through until midday, when a raucous siren of some sort wakened us. We quickly phoned reception to find out if there was a fire. "Oh no," said the young voice, "it's only the tsunami warning." *What?!* Talk about being instantly awake! It turned out that, at midday on the same day every week, the tsunami warning sirens are tested. No-one pays any attention to them, however. It begs the question as to what would happen if there really *was* a tsunami at this particular time.

The next few days flew by with sightseeing, including a helicopter flight over a section of Kilauea that still had lava erupting from it, walking across the actual caldera itself, swimming and resting, as well as necessary tasks like phoning home, catching up with laundry and doing bits of shopping. It's amazing how quickly you seem to run out of things like toothpaste and shampoo when you can't just pop down to the shops to replace them. It was also lovely to be able to do "girly" things again, like shaving your legs and getting your hair and nails done. We get a bit scruffy on board ship: no-one bothers about things like make-up or nails, and every day is a bad hair day. We use lashings of sunscreen and moisturiser, but that's about it.

Soon it was time to rejoin the ship, meet the replacement voyage crew and get allocated to new watches. Many of the new adventurers were mainland Americans and expatriates from other countries who now live in Hawaii. Unfortunately, because it was such a short hop to Oahu, we didn't have the opportunity to get to know one another well. They all seemed to enjoy their experience, however – particularly a couple from the local historical society who joined as supernumeraries and spent the whole time between the Big Island and Oahu in period costume. I thought it was very brave of them in the tropical heat. Pantaloons and petticoats are not exactly practical clothing on board an 18th-century ship.

There's a stretch of water between Hawaii and Oahu called the Alenuihaha Channel, which we were told is one of the worst ten stretches of water in the world. In local dialect, it roughly means "The sea who laughs at you". It turned out that the conditions were unusual but very favourable that day. We had 30 knots of wind and got up to 11.4 knots, so it was extremely exhilarating sailing. This is very fast for the *Endeavour*, her average speed being more like 4 or 5 knots.

A local photographer was in a light aircraft taking shots of the ship as we went through the channel, which, as we discovered later, were absolutely spectacular. We had all the sails up, and she looked nothing less than majestic. Later, in Honolulu, we met up with a fisherman who was out in his boat that day and saw "this pirate ship flying down the channel" and couldn't believe his eyes. He thought he'd had too many beers. Most of us ordered pictures from the photographer: they are shots we would not normally be able to take ourselves.

If we thought we'd had a welcome into Kailua-Kona, it was nothing compared to what was in store for us coming into Honolulu. A veritable armada of small boats, outrigger canoes, sailing canoes and sea kayaks came out to escort us in. Including, of course, Laura and Chuck in their boat. The problem was that no-one knew the name of their boat or even what colour the hull was. How could we possibly find them among this flotilla? Then we spotted it: a blue plastic bucket hanging off the spreader

21

bars of their mast. We laughed and laughed, then had to explain the joke to the newcomers, who hadn't been aboard when Chuck was carrying around his blue upchucking bucket. The boats all sailed along with us as far as they could, until we had to turn for the harbour entrance and they had to bear away. It was an awesome sight.

While this was taking place there were half a dozen helicopters overhead filming our arrival for local and international TV stations. One of them was carrying a huge quantity of flower petals, which they dropped onto the ship, completely covering the deck. Although we didn't know it then, things were being put in place on a grand scale at the dock at Aloha Tower as well.

The dock was a riot of colour, and as we approached we could see hundreds of people crowded on and around the pier. There were bands, about 150 hula dancers from different dancing schools and young men blowing conch shells as well as lots of VIPs. There were more speeches and formalities, and more leis got presented. When the captain went ashore to formally accept the welcome on behalf of the ship, he randomly picked two of the voyage crew to accompany him. It happened to be Jack and me. Months later friends back home told me that they had glimpsed me on the TV news when shots of the *Endeavour*'s arrival in Honolulu were shown locally. Fame at last!

During the three days I had off in Honolulu I took a hotel room again and set about doing a number of things that I'd planned. I had a couple of rides in a huge outrigger canoe, which was fantastic fun, and of course went to the famous Waikiki Beach. There I discovered to my amusement that its golden sand was imported from Australia some years ago. (Along with most of the natural beaches in volcanic Hawaii, its original sand was black.) The Aussies on board thought this was a hoot, of course, and had great fun teasing the locals about it.

There's a wonderful maritime museum in Honolulu, and tied up at the pier is a four-masted full-rigged ship called *The Falls of Clyde*, which was built in Port Glasgow in Scotland in 1878. I went on for a look around, partly because it's a square-rig ship, partly because it was built near where I grew up, and partly because it was where Laura and Chuck had been married just prior to joining the *Endeavour*. She's been restored beautifully, and is a real credit to the museum and to the volunteers who put thousands of hours of work into restoring her. She doesn't sail any longer, but was still very much worth a visit.

Pearl Harbour was also on my "must visit" agenda, and it was so interesting that I went twice. The memorial to the USS *Arizona* is extremely moving. She was bombed and sank at her berth on 7 December 1941 during the Japanese attack and is the resting place for many of the 1177 crewmen who lost their lives. Sixty years on, the outline of the ship can be seen clearly, and little traces of oil that still seep from it are visible on the surface of the water.

The USS *Missouri*, the battleship on which the instrument of surrender ending World War II was signed, is also at Pearl Harbour. She is quite awesome: almost three football fields long and with massive gun power. I noticed with great interest that, even on a mighty iron warship like this, her weather deck is wooden. It was fantastic to stand on the spot where the official signing to end the war took place.

After my days off I was on duty back at the ship selling visitors their boarding tickets. It was during this time that I met Eric, a retired Irish seaman who now lives in Honolulu. What a character he turned out to be. His business card says, "Authentic Irishman for Hire … Storytelling and Singing, Dancing and Carrying on. Available all Hours. Experienced Drinking Companion." Once I got to know him I realised this said it all.

The lines of people waiting to visit the ship were very long – of course we could only take on board a certain number of visitors at a time – and he got chatting to me while he was waiting in the queue. He thought I was someone local who had got involved with the ship during her visit, as is the case with the volunteer guides. "No," I said, "I'm one of the crew".

"You mean there are *women* sailing on that ship?" he declared with some amazement. "I never heard of such a thing." He didn't entirely believe me, and that was when the fun began. He started by asking me about the flag we were flying. When the ship is in museum mode, we fly an 18th-century English Royal Naval ensign, which doesn't have the cross of St Patrick on it. Very few people recognise it. He was impressed with my reply, but far from satisfied. Then he quizzed me about the names of sails and lines and various other items on board. This having gone on for about an hour, amidst a fair bit of laughter, he decided it was taking too long to get aboard and he'd come back the next day. He did, with more questions, which of course he'd had time to think about. Three days later he was finally convinced that I must, indeed, be a part of the crew.

He told me he'd been one of a family of thirteen, and had run away from home aged fourteen to join the Merchant Navy. At least on a ship he'd be sure of getting fed. He'd started as a stoker, shovelling coal on the old steam ships for fourteen hours a day. The conditions sounded absolutely harrowing, particularly when you take into account that he, like many others no doubt, was really just a boy at the time. He had spent all his life at sea, and worked his way up to being a chief steward on "fancy passenger liners" before retiring at age sixty-five. He never went back to live in Ireland.

On the day we sailed from Honolulu he came down to see us off – and to bring me a gift. It was his seaman's knife, which he'd had for many years. "I've never married and have no sons to pass it on to", he said. "I'd like you to have it, because you are obviously a real sailor." I was overwhelmed – I didn't feel worthy of it. Needless to say I treasure that knife as if it were the crown jewels. I already had a knife – not as good as the one I'd just been given, I might say – and I passed it on to one of the young trainees on board. What goes around, comes around …

Honolulu was also where we had to say good-bye to Victor, which was very sad. He and I had become great buddies, all of our mutinous mutterings and blasphemous cursings having created a special bond. We had shared lots of experiences and emotions, and lots of laughs at ourselves. A night out at the pub was arranged with almost all of our watch present. Chuck and Laura had secretly organised to have a bosun's call (whistle) specially engraved as a present from the watch. I'm sure he treasures it just as I treasure Eric's knife.

The new crew embarked, and we discovered to our delight that Laura had talked her boss into giving her more time off work, so she was coming with us to Fiji. Her boss had been one of the guides during our stay in Honolulu, and had also fallen under the spell of the *Endeavour*. He'd gone on to join up as voyage crew for the short hop to Kauai.

Unfortunately Chuck wasn't able to come along also. There was another huge send-off from Honolulu, with more bands, dancers, leis, escort boats and hundreds of people. Again, many of the new crew were only on for the short hop to Kauai, our next port of call and only a couple of days' sailing away, but a few would be with us until we got to Fiji.

Our next stop was supposed to be at Port Allen in Kauai, which is the most northerly of the Hawaiian Islands. The captain had discovered, however, that the tidal surge there is very strong, and it would more than likely not be good for the ship – we had already snapped off two timberheads at the Kailua-Kona dock because of tidal surge. So plans were changed. We went instead to Nawilliwilli, a smaller port, but we were still made very welcome – with a very formal, traditional welcome rather than hula girls. It was very solemn and moving, with the head woman of the district blessing the ship and her company and giving us permission to be in their territory.

The ship was open to the public again, with just about every school child in Kauai coming aboard, or so it seemed. Children are always fascinated to hear about how "the seats of ease" had to be used by ordinary sailors to go to the lavatory, and dissolve into fits of giggles at the very idea of it. They almost seem disappointed when we are able to tell them that our heads are not so primitive and we have a few other creature comforts that the original sailors didn't enjoy.

As this was our last port of call before another long haul, those of us staying with the ship took the opportunity to experience a few last shoreside luxuries, and booked into small hotels and hostels nearby. I stayed at a little inn close to a small beach about ten minutes away from the ship. Walking along this beach one day I came across the Kauai Marriott Resort and Beach Club, with grounds that go right down to the beachfront. This place looked *really* swish, way beyond my budget, but I decided to be bold, wandered in and had a lovely swim in their pool. I looked just the same as the guests there, wearing a swimsuit, sarong and sandals, so no-one paid any attention to me.

As I looked around it became apparent that if you ordered a drink from a passing waiter no money exchanged hands, no hotel key was needed as evidence that you were staying there, and you just signed for the drink. Hmmm … I hadn't brought any money with me, as I was originally just going for a swim in front of my motel, but the temptation was too much to resist. A very belated thank you to the occupant of Room No. 103, who would have found an extra pina colada on their bill when they checked out. I think it's the best pina colada I've ever had – mostly because it was illicit I suppose. I must confess, though, that I heaved a sigh of relief when I'd left the Marriott grounds without a heavy hand clapping itself on my shoulder and a voice saying, "Just a minute, madam".

A few of us took another helicopter trip so that we could fly over the Napali Cliffs and the Weimea Canyon. Both were absolutely awesome. Weimea, in fact, is referred to as "the Grand Canyon of the Pacific", with good reason. Helicopter is virtually the only way that you can see it, as there are no roads, just one or two tracks for very experienced bush-walkers. We flew over countless waterfalls, amazing cliffs and canyons, sugar and coffee plantations, and down into the crater of Mt Waialeale, some 1700 metres high and another dormant volcano. This area is reputed to have the highest rainfall in the world: they get about 10,000 millimetres per annum, hence the copious waterfalls.

Kauai is the oldest of the Hawaiian group in geological terms, and is where scenes for many famous movies such as *Jurassic Park*, *Blue Hawaii* and *South Pacific* were shot. It's an incredibly beautiful place, and much quieter and less "touristy" than Waikiki or Honolulu. It's definitely on my list of places to visit again.

Following a wonderful *luau* hosted by the local community at Waimea in our honour, it was almost time to bid farewell to the Rainbow State of Hawaii. Waimea was Captain Cook's first landfall in Hawaii and it was a coincidence that it was this *Endeavour*'s last. Having it happen meant, however, that the full circle of destiny had been completed. The locals told us that, because our *Endeavour* had returned to Waimea, they believed that the souls of the Hawaiians who had been killed during Cook's time had now been returned to their homeland. I rather like that belief, and feel somewhat privileged to have been allowed to play a tiny part in making it come about.

We sailed off into another spectacular Hawaiian sunset and headed out to sea again, with Captain Ted in command for this next long leg of approximately 2800 nautical miles to Fiji. Captain Chris was taking some well-deserved leave, after going on ahead of the ship to make all the necessary port arrangements for our arrival in Suva.

3

THE SOUTH PACIFIC OCEAN

We settled into seagoing routine again, with watches, sail-handling lectures, navigation classes and the never-ending maintenance. The shipwright had a difficult but interesting job ahead of him trying to repair the snapped timberheads, and a few of us volunteered to help him, as it would be a very challenging job to undertake while at sea. The permanent crew had become very competent at fixing things while the ship is under way, and it was always an education watching how it was done and learning some new skills.

I was in foremast watch for this leg of the voyage, with a different captain o' tops and quite a few new crew. Amazingly, perhaps, one of them was the son of a woman I used to work beside back in Perth. Talk about a small world. Our supernumerary was a retired English university professor called Martin, a wonderfully interesting gentleman whose wife, Ruth, was also on board but in a different watch. They took part in everything, though they didn't have to, and Martin and I had many long conversations during the night when we were on bow watch together. While bow watches and stern watches are always kept at sea, sometimes there's not a lot to see except the sea, so deep and meaningful discussions take place. Although we didn't know it then, our paths were to cross several times over the next few years.

Sailing along pleasantly at around six knots, we often found ourselves being accompanied by huge pods of dolphins, particularly the spinner dolphins that inhabit this part of the Pacific. We estimated the number in one pod to be upwards of two thousand. Leaping and spinning and frolicking around and past the ship, they took about half an hour to pass us. What a spectacle it was. Other creatures that were absolutely fascinating to watch were the flying fish – hundreds of them at a time, some seeming to be able to "fly" for several metres across the waves with little or no effort. It's times like these that it's a joy to be at sea. Not to mention the awesome sunrises and sunsets that we got to see regularly.

During the run to Fiji we would be crossing the equator, so of course plans were being made for the inevitable "Crossing the Line" ceremony, which all "pollywogs" (landlubbers) need to undertake the first time they cross the equator at sea. Once you have been initiated into King Neptune's domain, you become a "shellback" and remain a shellback forever. An announcement was made at the morning meeting that all those who claimed to have crossed the line at sea previously had to go before King Neptune's Court the next day and prove it. In my case this was going to be quite a challenge. I *had* crossed the line at sea many years before, when I emigrated to Australia, but I no longer had my certificate to prove it.

I racked my brains that evening and consulted the big map on the wall of the mess, so that I was able to figure out pretty well exactly where I was when I had originally crossed the line. I knew what date it had been, the name of the ship that I was on and what had happened to my certificate. I didn't mind at all the idea of getting dunked in buckets of nasty goo (or whatever it was the crew was cooking up in the engine room in preparation for the ceremony), but it's supposed to be bad luck to be a victim again when you are already a shellback. My story must have been convincing enough for Neptune's Court, as I was excused. That, by default, meant that I would be one of Neptune's helpers, dunking the pollywogs! Out of the fifty or so on board, there were about sixteen of us who had previously crossed the line. The captain, I might add, stayed well out of all this, and left us to do the plotting and planning ourselves.

Various members of the crew took on the roles of King Neptune, Queen Aphrodite, Sweeney Todd the barber, the surgeon and the executioner, ably assisted by the rest of us shellbacks, who became Neptune's nymphs and policemen. Having been hauled up on deck in ones and twos, the victims were paraded before the court and accused of trespassing into Neptune's domain. They had to beg forgiveness and pay homage to the king, which entailed getting doused with the nasty fermented mixture that had been brewing for a week or so. They were then hosed down with the fire hose. All in all it was a pretty hilarious carry-on, with everyone getting very wet. It's a centuries-old tradition at sea, so who were we not to abide by it?

Although on this occasion I wasn't one of the "victims", I still received a wonderful certificate, made up on parchment paper with a ship's seal on it, dated 2 December 1999. It reads as follows:

> Be it now proclaimed that while aboard HM Bark *Endeavour* on her maiden world voyage you crossed the fine line separating north and south. It is further proclaimed that you have paid due homage and accepted with good humour, grace and fortitude the most rigorous initiation of our Equatorial Court making the transition from Pollywog to Shellback.

It's signed by King Neptune himself and, together with a number of photographs of the ceremony and our celebrations afterwards, is another treasure among my memorabilia of this trip of a lifetime.

We were hoping to go ashore for a little while when we arrived at Kiribati a couple of days later, but the weather conditions and the swell in the harbour were such that it wasn't possible. Captain Ted in particular was disappointed at this, as he had spent some time there many years ago and was looking forward to revisiting. There was nothing for it but to weigh anchor and keep on sailing towards Fiji, where we were due on 15 December. Occasionally we had to put the engines on to maintain our schedule. Unlike Captain Cook, we have crew members getting off and having to catch planes, and there are deadlines to meet with regard to berths and other arrangements that have been put in place in particular ports.

The legendary doldrums of this area sometimes used to take weeks to get through on the old sailing ships, but we were able to use the "iron topsail" (engines) when necessary. Still, we experienced the same conditions that would have existed then, inasmuch as there was stifling heat and no wind. We encountered several severe squalls and sudden monsoon-type downpours between Kiribati and Fiji, which made sail handling very demanding and interesting, but no-one seemed to mind the rain: it was a welcome relief from the heat. Most of us ran below to grab shampoo and soap, then have a long fresh-water shower on deck, albeit with swimming costumes on for the sake of modesty. The rain was warm, and it was a treat to be able to stand under it for more than the standard thirty seconds.

By the time 13 December came we were beginning to sail past some small islands in the general area of the Fijian group. Geoff, the mate, who had lived and worked in Fiji for a couple of years, told us to keep a good watch, as many of the small local fishing boats in those parts fish at night and don't use lights. We didn't have any mishaps, thankfully, and docked the next day with the help of a local pilot. There is a nasty reef that has to be negotiated on the way into Suva, and the remains of shipwrecks clearly visible through the water were evidence that it's claimed some victims in the past.

This was a short stopover to take on fresh food and change over some of the crew again, so there were more sad farewells to buddies and greetings to new crew members getting on for the leg from Suva to Wellington. One of the girls who got on was a Kiwi called Donnamarie, who subsequently became another of the *Endeavour*'s "repeat offenders". She is a real character, and lots of fun. Because she often used to mix up her right and her left, she wore a red sock on her left foot for port and a green sock on her right foot to remind her that was starboard. Apart from being very funny, I also thought it was quite sensible, and said to her one day, "I like your socks: good idea!"

"Thanks," she said. "I've got several more pairs just like them."

Captain Chris rejoined us too, with bags of mail that got devoured as though we had been at sea for years instead of weeks. The ship didn't open to the public on this stopover, so we didn't have to go into museum mode. This left us a little time to have a quick look around some local markets, have a raid on the supermarket and phone home before we headed off again.

Calling home took a little more figuring out this time around, as we had crossed the International Date Line between Kiribati and Suva and were now something like five or six hours ahead of Western Australia instead of eighteen hours behind, which was the case when we were in Hawaii. I had a lot of trouble getting my head around these time differences, and poor Jason, the second mate, spent ages trying to explain it to me until finally the penny dropped. No doubt the black spot in understanding was in the same section of my brain that refuses to understand celestial navigation and trigonometry.

He was exceedingly patient about it, and indeed his attempts were well and truly "beyond the call of duty". We had become buddies during the voyage, partly due to discovering that we had both spent part of our lives in the Middle East and partly because we had a unique experience while on watch one night. We were on duty and chatting in bright moonlight when I spotted what looked like a waterspout forming in the distance. I drew it to his attention, as he was the officer of the watch. We watched carefully, then he went below to check the radar. After pondering the matter for a little while we concluded that it wasn't a waterspout but something else altogether: a *moonbow*. It looked exactly the same as a rainbow does in the daylight except that it was in varying shades of grey, silver and white, as it was lit by the moon. Jason entered the sighting in the ship's log and we reported it to the captain the next day. Chris reckoned we must have been under the influence of *moonshine*, as he'd never seen such a thing. Jason and I were very indignant.

By Monday 20 December, with about nine hundred nautical miles to run until Wellington, we were starting to get back into warmer clothes and needing blankets or sleeping bags in the hammock at night. Given the stifling tropical heat we had been experiencing for several weeks, this seemed really strange, but it was actually quite nice to be able to snuggle into bedclothes again. I'd been sleeping with a wet, wrung-out sarong over me in the hammock and had enjoyed the benefit of some evaporative cooling. This method was used in the Australian goldfields in the 19th century to keep meat fresh, and the Aussies on board thought it was hilarious that I had set up a "Coolgardie safe" to sleep under.

As we would still be at sea on Christmas Day, the captain was planning on trying to find an anchorage somewhere on the east coast of New Zealand so that we could all have some downtime and enjoy Christmas dinner together as a whole crew rather than eat in watches – and, of course, so that Santa Claus could find us. We had all bought a fun gift of some sort in Suva or Hawaii to put into the Santa bag so that everyone would have a present on Christmas Day. It was still a few days away at this stage, but the preparations had begun and much giggling went on as things were wrapped up in secret.

The next day all thoughts of Christmas Day were put on hold, as the wind was back with a vengeance and it was all hands on deck to get sails furled as a sudden squall brought fifty knots with it. Too late: we blew out the main topmast staysail before it could be brought down. Within an hour the winds had eased to around twenty-eight to thirty knots and things were well under control again, although we still had lifelines strung all over the weather deck and were rolling a lot. It was all pretty exciting in hindsight.

We "rocked and rolled" in the wind and the swell for the next couple of days, to the point that no real maintenance work could be done and handwriting in journals became very squiggly and strange looking. The upside to the wind was, however, that a small flock of sooty terns and a couple of wandering albatrosses were following us, and it was just magic watching them. They were putting on the most fantastic aerobatic display and were really entertaining to observe. One of them landed in the water while I was watching and, after bobbing about for a few minutes, decided to get airborne again. What an effort! It looked like a B52 bomber trying to take off, it was so cumbersome. Hard to believe it was the same bird wheeling around with such grace and aplomb a few minutes later.

The North Island of New Zealand was sighted at 6.15 am on Christmas Eve. Needless to say the "Land ho" call was heard again. We sailed down the east coast as the day progressed, passing East Cape, Gisborne and Poverty Bay, the plan being to anchor at Kidnappers Cove in Hawkes Bay. Well that was Plan A, but it wasn't going to work out as the winds were gusting forty knots again. The anchor won't hold the ship steady in winds as high as that, so the captain had to switch to Plan B.

Christmas morning dawned and we discovered that it had snowed in the night. Well, sort of. A phantom painter had been at work in the hours of darkness and the two carrick heads on the foredeck now sported some embellishments. Carrick heads are heavy wooden end pieces to a windlass, often elaborately carved; the *Endeavour*'s are in the form of two olden-day sailors. Eyebrows, moustaches, beards and bobbles on their hats had been made out with daubs of white paint, looking for all the world like snow. As the *Endeavour*'s carrick heads are painted red, it looked quite festive. A couple of coils of rope had been hung on them to look like earmuffs, too, which was very amusing.

While the captain was figuring out what Plan B would actually amount to, we managed to get the 18th-century deck festooned with lots of home-made Christmas decorations, mostly made from aluminium foil (pinched from the galley) and old charts and posters, which we'd fashioned into paper chains. We even had a little wooden Christmas tree, courtesy of the shipwright, that got decorated with some fairy lights. Joanna, the cook, had produced these from a secret stash of Christmas goodies.

In the end Plan B entailed the ship being hove to in Hawkes Bay. This is a manoeuvre that square-rig ships can carry out by allowing the wind to blow onto the face of some sails while keeping others trimmed to catch it from behind. It's called backing the sails, and the end result is like putting brakes on. This allowed the ship to ride smoothly enough for Christmas dinner to be served and enjoyed. And the cook certainly did us proud with a wonderful meal, followed by some superb cheeses that had been brought on board at Fiji by one of the joining crew from Melbourne (affectionately known thereafter as "Will the Cheese Man").

There was a ripe Camembert, I remember, that positively oozed when it was cut. As one of the girls in my watch said, "It kind of orgasmed out of its skin!" She was a bit of an actress, and had colourful and imaginative language at the best of times. We shrieked with laughter at that one. I still refer to it as "orgasmic cheese" when I write my shopping list out. We were even allowed some wine with the meal – a rare treat – although it was rationed because of safety concerns.

Following the dinner, Santa Claus (in the form of the captain) visited us and handed out all the silly, fun presents. The evening was rounded off by lots of carol singing. Apart from the fact that our respective families were not there, it was a very happy occasion. We made one big happy family by ourselves. It was a truly memorable, if different, Christmas Day, and it seemed fitting to celebrate the last one of the millennium in such a unique way.

The next day was back to normal with a vengeance, as we were now only a couple of days from Wellington and had much to do before docking at Queen's Dock on 28 December. The ship would be open to the public again, and we still had lots of sprucing-up to take care of.

The majority of the voyage crew would be getting off at Wellington, and we could hardly believe that the trip was almost at an end – particularly those of us who had sailed all the way from Vancouver, as we had now been on board for the best part of three months. Life on board an 18th-century sailing ship had become our "norm". It was going to be hard to revert to the 20th century – indeed almost the 21st-century – mode of living again.

Wellington has a wonderfully sheltered harbour in a big bay, but at its entrance there are a couple of nasty reefs and rock outcrops. We had a pilot on board to take us in, and as we passed a particular spot he pointed out where the *Wahine*, one of the inter-island ferries, had come to grief in 1968 with the ultimate loss of fifty-eight lives. It's so close to the shore that such a tragedy seems inconceivable, but the weather was so horrendous that rescuers were unable to do very much at the time. We struck our bell and had a minute's silence on deck as we passed the monument to honour those who had died. It's solemn moments like these when you are reminded of the power and unforgiving nature of the sea.

The solemnity soon passed, however, as we neared the waiting crowd at the dock and were all excitedly looking for family and friends who had come there to meet us. I was looking forward to catching up with my friend Adelia, who lived in Wellington at that time and who I hadn't seen for a couple of years. She was an *Endeavour* soul mate from a 1996 voyage, and we had kept in touch in spite of the distance separating us in the hope that somehow we would see one another again. And indeed we did.

The whole crew went out to party that evening knowing that we had to say our farewells the next day and go our separate ways. I was planning on spending a few days with Adelia and her family before flying out back to Perth, but ended up staying longer. Because it was the first country in the world to see the dawn of the New Millennium, New Zealand was full of visitors and I couldn't get a flight out for three weeks. So I ended up seeing in the New Millennium with Adelia and her family in Wellington.

I grasped the opportunity to take myself on a tour of the South Island and visit Milford Sound and Dusky Sound, spectacularly beautiful isolated places that Captain Cook had "discovered" and charted in 1769. Although I was, of course, travelling on modern-day conveyances, you could still experience a sense of awe at the beauty and majesty of the areas that presented themselves to Cook and his people. You couldn't even begin to wonder at the bewilderment the local Maori people must have felt upon seeing this square-rigged ship entering their domain.

Before I flew home, the *Endeavour* left Wellington with her new crew on board to continue with her visits to many New Zealand ports before returning to Australia some time in 2000. Those of us who were still in town went down to the docks to see her off and wept as she sailed away without us on board. Our "home" for the last three months disappeared beyond our view; my trip of a lifetime was over. Or so it seemed at the time.

4

IN THE BEGINNING

So where did it all start, this obsession of mine with ships and the sea? I don't come from a family with a long sea-faring tradition or anything of that nature – although my brother did go off and join the British Merchant Navy when I was about fourteen or fifteen – so I can only speculate that it evolved from personal experiences that influenced my development.

I grew up in Helensburgh, a small town on the West Coast of Scotland, situated on the River Clyde. The Clyde used to have a huge shipbuilding industry, not to mention the docklands of Glasgow and Govan. Also nearby, at Faslane, was a Royal Naval base. From my earliest childhood I can remember watching, from my bedroom window, ships of all shapes and sizes, even submarines, regularly going up and down the river.

They were mostly naval and commercial ships rather than sailing vessels, but even those fascinated me and used to send me off into wild daydreams. Where had they come from? Which country's flags were they flying? What were they carrying? And, most interestingly perhaps, where were they going and who was sailing in them? So the seed was sown. I never tired of watching them and wondering about them. At that time the closest I had got to being on a ship was going on day trips on the old paddle steamers that used to ply the Clyde, usually on a Sunday school picnic. Even they were enthralling, and it gladdens my heart to know that one of them, the *Waverley*, is still sailing today.

And then in 1961, when I was aged fourteen, I was given the chance to go sailing in a *real* ship for about two weeks. The Scottish Education Department at that time had chartered three fairly old converted troop ships to use for adventure excursions for school children. These were the *Dunera*, the *Uganda* and the *Devonia*, each of about 10,000 tonnes.

Schools had to apply to the department to be considered, and names of the schools were drawn by ballot. If a school was one of the lucky ones, pupils then had to apply to be considered for one of the places, and there was another ballot. I couldn't believe my luck – my name came up! I was going to join a ship and go off to magical places that I'd been dreaming about for years as I watched shipping going up and down the Clyde.

In due course I caught the ferry from Helensburgh with about twenty of my schoolmates (and most of our mothers – we were only kids) across the water to Greenock to embark on the MV *Dunera*. (Although I didn't know it at the time, this was the same *Dunera* that, during World War II, had transported German Jewish refugees to Australia for internment because they were suspected of being spies.) There was roughly five hundred children altogether, from schools from all over Scotland, together with two teachers from each of the schools. We were heading off to Spain, Portugal and Gibraltar and were all terribly excited. Most of us had never been outside Scotland before.

Interestingly, I've got absolutely no recollection of saying goodbye to my mother, although it was the first time I was going to be away from home and there should have been some butterflies in the tummy at least, and maybe even a little sadness. I suspect I was so excited that I couldn't wait for her to go so that we could get on with our adventure.

The ship's officers were mostly British, as I recall, and the majority of the rest of the crew were Lascars, from India. Growing up in our sheltered little environment, we'd never seen such handsome and exotic men. This was looking better and better. We were housed in dormitory-style accommodation with about twenty kids in double bunks in each dormitory, and our ages were all in the fourteen-to-sixteen-years range. We still had to do our normal lessons, as it was term time, and we had additional language, geography and social studies lessons relevant to the places and people we were going to visit. It was such a change from my normal life that it excited and challenged me beyond anything I could previously have imagined.

There were lots of interschool deck competitions and movies and quiz games and things of that ilk in the evenings to keep us occupied and out of trouble – and to tire us out I suspect. There were also illicit dormitory raids between different schools, pillow fights and other unofficial activities normal to a bunch of teenagers. In hindsight I'm not entirely sure how the teachers managed to keep control of us at all, or to stay sane. Times were more innocent then, however: there certainly wasn't any drug-taking or hanky panky. It was all just boisterous high spirits.

Corunna in Spain, Lisbon in Portugal and Gibraltar were all fascinating places, where lots of sightseeing, plus visits to museums and art galleries and other such venues, had been organised for us. It was a school excursion, of course, and we were all a bit too young to be let loose in some foreign port anyway I guess. That still didn't stop some of the girls flirting with Spanish and Portuguese boys we met – all of them to our eyes stunningly good-looking in a Mediterranean sort of way. None of the local boys at home looked like that. There were even one or two marriage proposals, for goodness' sake, which we giggled about in classic teenage fashion.

On the way home we encountered a force ten gale going through the infamous Bay of Biscay, and were confined to below decks. This was the first really rough weather we had experienced, and most of my dormitory buddies were seasick. I, on the other hand, was as well as I could possibly be, and thought it was absolutely fantastic – quite the most thrilling thing I'd ever experienced. The ship rocked and rolled, and pitched and yawed, and did things I don't think there are words for. No stabilisers on this boat! There were safety lines and things to hold on to all over the place, and we weren't allowed on any of the open decks at all. Waves were breaking and spraying spume up onto the highest of the decks, though I have to add that it was a small ship.

Every now and then the propeller would come out of the water as we crested the top of a big wave, and the whole ship would shudder as the prop kept turning. It was as though you were using a jackhammer – absolutely brilliant if you weren't seasick! One of the junior officers with whom I'd become friendly seemed to be intrigued with my reaction to the weather. I wasn't in the slightest bit frightened, although in hindsight perhaps I should have been.

Classes were suspended, as we were being tossed around so much there was no way you could hold a book steadily enough to read it, never mind write anything down. Most of the schoolchildren, many of the teachers and even some of the crew were seasick anyway. The few of us who were still upright were skulking around looking for things to do, and trying to stay out of the way of the poor souls who were vomiting everywhere.

My officer friend invited me up to the bridge. "Would you like to come and see what the sea looks like ahead of us?" Would I! We could get only a fleeting impression of what it was like through the portholes or windows from the decks to which we were confined. He got the captain's permission, and four of us lucky kids were allowed into the hallowed area. Two of them left almost immediately, as they freaked out when they looked out of the bridge windows. My remaining companion and I were mesmerised. You could see properly from here, and what could be seen was awesome: huge waves of varying colours of green, blue and grey with white crests, heaving and churning all around us for as far as we could see. Every now and then the bow would bury its nose in a wave, the window would get obliterated with spray and we could feel the shuddering as the prop came out of the water again.

We were holding on to ledges and other handholds for dear life, and shrieking with glee as each huge wave swamped the ship. The officer of the watch didn't really appreciate this interruption to his duties and told us to clear off. It wasn't really the time to have navigation aids and so forth explained to us, but if we wanted to we could come back to the bridge at another time when the weather was less violent. "With the sea-legs that you two have got," he said, "You would make good sailors." What prophetic words they turned out to be. While most of my classmates were falling in love with junior officers, good-looking Lascars, hunky Spanish or Portuguese boys or even the gym teacher who accompanied us, I fell in love with the sea.

When we docked back in Greenock, all of our mothers were there waiting for us. I can remember crying my eyes out and my mother being very touched. She thought I was overwhelmed at seeing her again. I finally told her some thirty years later that wasn't the reason at all – I didn't want to get off the ship! I felt I had found my passion in life. I wanted to become a sailor.

My declarations of this wish got dismissed as silly, whimsical teenage notions. "Just a passing fad", everyone said. Fourteen is such an impressionable age. I guess that a large part of me probably agreed. Life went back to normal, school resumed with ordinary classes and I continued to daydream about going to sea. When the time came for us all to discuss possible options for our futures with the school vocational counsellor, I raised the subject of "going to sea" again. But at that time – about 1962 – there were very few occupations that a female could undertake at sea. In Britain, the notion of a girl wanting to be a deck officer was so out of the question that it got laughed at. This was long before equal opportunity laws had been devised and enacted. I felt the counsellor wanted to pat me on the head and say, "Go away little girl; you're just being silly".

I investigated the possibility of joining the WRENS. Lots of job opportunities were available, but none of them were on ships. It would have to be the Merchant Navy, then. That afforded some options, although none of them were as deck officers. I thought about trying the communications avenue, as many Scandinavian ships had female radio officers. My brother, in fact, had trained at the Glasgow Radio College and had joined the Merchant Navy as a radio officer not long before this, but I wasn't allowed into the college to train because I was a girl. My father wouldn't let me go to Norway or Sweden to train (well, I was only fifteen), and there would have been the language barrier to contend with anyway.

He also wouldn't entertain the idea of me going to sea as a stewardess or taking up one of the few other possible female options like children's nurse. This was all proving to be much harder than I thought. Then I hit upon the idea of going to sea on a cruise ship as a hairdresser! That was acceptable (although only just) to my parents, so that was the direction I took when I left school. A hairdressing apprenticeship was secured and I spent the next few years training, ultimately becoming a qualified ladies' hairdresser. The job didn't particularly fire up my interest, but I saw it as a possible means to an end.

Somewhere in the early 1960s two wonderful sailing ships, the *Winston Churchill* and the *Malcolm Miller*, were built and launched in Scotland and much was made of them in the media. My ears pricked up. They were primarily built for the purpose of sail training, and young people aged from sixteen to twenty-five years were encouraged to apply to undertake ten-day voyages around the Scottish coastline. I asked my dad if I could go. To my joy he said, "Yes." By this time I think my parents were beginning to realise my penchant for the sea was more than just a passing fad.

I made enquiries about getting on to one of these wonderful ships, and had all sorts of pictures, brochures and other information about them hoarded in my bedroom. I had left school and was working by then, but something could be done during my annual holidays, or so I thought. The Outward Bound School operated them at the time, and to my dismay I discovered that they only took boys. I was beginning to think that I had been born the wrong gender at the wrong time.

I went back to concentrating on my hairdressing and made enquiries with shipping lines like P&O and Cunard about joining a ship. Alas, I was stymied again: you had to be twenty-one years of age to join a passenger ship's crew in those days, and I was just nineteen. What could I do with myself to fill in a couple of years? I didn't relish the thought of "just" hairdressing in Glasgow for two years. Apart from the job not thrilling me that much, I hated the weather.

That was when I decided to emigrate – I would go to Australia under the "Ten Pound Pom" scheme, which meant paying only £10 for a sea passage provided I undertook to stay for at least two years. My plan was to work and gain more experience in Australia, then go back to Britain and pursue the ship's hairdresser career once I was twenty-one. I had no idea then that I would spend the rest of my life in Australia – and neither did my family, or I don't think I would have been allowed to go. As well as being before the days of equal opportunity, it was also still a time when you didn't disobey your father.

So that was how it came about that in 1966 I left home, headed for the "land down under" and spent four memorable weeks on board a Greek ship called the RHMS *Ellenis*. At 28,000 tonnes she seemed huge after the *Dunera*, but I was just as enamoured of her as I had been five years previously with the old troop ship. I was back on the briny, albeit with some 1800 other souls and as a migrant. The *Ellenis* also seemed to have an alarming number of extremely handsome, mostly Greek, crew, and happy memories of my time on the *Dunera* with my schoolmates came flooding back.

We'd left from Southampton on 14 April. This was a somewhat auspicious date in contemporary maritime history, being the anniversary of the day the *Titanic* hit the iceberg that would end her maiden voyage so tragically in 1912. After sailing across the English Channel to the Hook of Holland and picking up some more passengers, it was back down through the Bay of Biscay, in calm seas this time – which was perhaps just as well given the number of people on board. It would not have been pleasant if that many people had been seasick.

The biggest bulk of the passengers were families migrating to Australia, but there were about thirty or forty of us travelling as singles. Within a couple of days we had all found each other and chummed up into a big group, and we set about having a good time for the duration of the voyage. Most of us didn't have a job lined up in Australia, so the attitude was, "Let's have a good time, because we have no idea when we might get our next holiday".

Our first proper port of call was Piraeus, the port for Athens, when we were allowed to get off and have a look around for a day or so while the crew changed over. This was the ship's homeport, so there was almost a complete turnover of personnel, those on board having already done the round trip from Piraeus to Australia to Britain and back to Greece. We visited the Acropolis and the Parthenon and some of the other famous sights, and couldn't believe how much smog there was in the city. Even as long ago as 1966 it was starting to have an impact on the integrity of the old buildings.

On down through the Mediterranean, we headed to the Suez Canal. To traverse the canal it's necessary to get into a convoy, as there is only one place where the northbound and southbound ships can pass each other. This is an area located roughly in the middle of the canal called the Bitter Lakes. So we had a short time at Port Said, at the Mediterranean end of the canal, while the convoy of southbound shipping was formed. *Ellenis* was to be the last one to join this particular convoy and, strangely enough, the oil tanker that my brother was on was the first ship in this same convoy.

I can't remember his ship's name – he has been on many ships over the years – but he knew which one I was on and he called me up on the radio. I was sent for to go to the radio room, next to the bridge, to speak to him. I was most impressed. So were the officers, and I got the chance to have a tour of yet another ship's bridge, normally pretty much off limits for passengers. This one was more sophisticated than I remembered *Dunera*'s being, but just as fascinating.

We traversed the canal without anything untoward happening and, to be honest, I have very little recollection of it, so I guess it couldn't have seemed that interesting at the time. I do remember being astonished at how narrow sections of it were, as on both sides of the ship there seemed to be nothing but miles and miles of desert sands. It was a rather strange feeling, as though you were sailing through a desert. We had become used to seeing a lot of water and little or no land whenever we went on deck.

Aden, in Yemen, at the bottom of the Red Sea, was another port of call, and indeed was going to be our last port prior to arriving in Australia. We all got off again – for a look round of course but also to buy some duty-free goods, as it was a very, very cheap place in those days. We came back on board loaded with transistor radios, portable record players, cigarettes, booze and perfume, and settled down for the long haul across the Indian Ocean.

Somewhere on this leg we would "Cross the Line" and enter the Southern Hemisphere, an event I've already mentioned. The crew was beginning to make supposedly secret arrangements for the ceremony and looking for volunteers from among the passengers who hadn't yet been initiated. Of course most of my friends and I put our hands up: we wouldn't have missed it for the world.

We were all duly allowed to enter King Neptune's domain after paying him homage in the appropriate manner, which entailed kissing his feet. You were blindfolded and led onto the deck by his cohorts (some of the crew); then, at the last moment, Neptune's feet were replaced by a very cold, very smelly, very dead fish, much to the merriment of the watching passengers. Then you got led across to the "operating table" where the executioner, the barber and the surgeon got to work on you. Strings of sausages and various other pieces of offal got flung off into the crowd, supposedly removed from your innards. It all ended up with everyone being "baptised" in buckets of nasty stuff (this seems to be obligatory at Crossing the Line ceremonies) before getting flung unceremoniously into the swimming pool.

It was great fun. We received certificates to testify that we were now shellbacks, and I have some wonderful photos of the event taken by the ship's photographer. The girls were all treated to a hairdo in the ship's salon afterwards, as we couldn't get the goo out of our hair. Perhaps it was just as well I never did find out what was in the buckets ... Years later, when I was called upon to explain my status to Neptune's Court on the *Endeavour*, I could tell my tale of the *Ellenis*, giving them the date and location of when it occurred convincingly enough to be spared the experience again. Sadly, that original certificate has long ago been lost, but the memories remain vivid – and I do have the photographs.

The first port of call in Australia was Fremantle, where many people got off, but I was going on to Sydney, where I had relatives with whom I was going to live initially. No-one at that time had any idea that I would end up back in Perth/Fremantle some years later, and indeed spend the rest of my life in that part of the country. More passengers, including most of my pals, got off in Melbourne.

Nearing Sydney, we sailed past the entrance to Botany Bay, which of course was the original *Endeavour*'s first landing-place in Australia, where Captain Cook and his officers spent some considerable time mapping and cataloguing the native flora and fauna. Joseph Banks first referred to it in his journals as "Botanical Bay". There was great excitement as we went through Sydney Heads into Port Jackson, where Captain Cook had *not* ventured. It was, however, where the First Fleet later anchored and started the new British colony. Cook had had no idea that such a magnificent safe harbour was hidden inside the Heads.

Our new lives were about to start. Amid the excitement we also felt some trepidation. We were a long, long way from "home" and committed to staying for at least two years. Soon we got our first glimpse of the famous Sydney Harbour Bridge and the Opera House. The Opera House was still under construction then, but it looked as though it was going to become the eighth wonder of the world even at that stage. Then the moment came for those of us who were still aboard to disembark at Sydney and go our separate ways, although a number of us stayed in touch for many years. My relatives were at the dock to meet me, and off I went to live with them in Sans Souci, a pleasant suburb of Sydney near both Botany Bay and the Georges River.

A number of years passed as I went about the business of settling down and making a new life for myself. Caught up in all the novelty of life in Australia, which I loved, changing jobs and earning a living, thoughts of going to sea faded into the background. There were new friends and a new career, as I'd given up hairdressing by this stage and was working as a secretary. A new boyfriend, a new flat and flat mates, marvellous weather and a new lifestyle completed the picture. Homesickness was something that only affected me occasionally, and even then I realised I had no desire to go back to Scotland to live. Life was just fine the way it was. Suddenly, it seemed, almost three years had gone by.

And then one day, as part of one of Sydney's many maritime festivals, some "tall ships" came to town. Two of them I remember in particular were the navy training ships *Esmeralda* and *Libertad*, from Chile and Argentina respectively. The newspaper said they would be coming through Sydney Heads at 8.30 am, and I took a day off work to go and watch – as did half the population of Sydney I think. There were thousands of us lining the North and South Heads to see the spectacle. Eventually these two absolutely glorious square-rig sailing ships emerged out of the morning mist with their crews "dressing the yards" – up the rigging standing at attention on all of the yards. It was one of the most awesome things I had ever seen. My desire to go to sea was back with a vengeance. How can I get onto one of *those*, I thought. Forget working as a hairdresser on a passenger liner.

Esmeralda and *Libertad*, along with other ships that were part of the festival, were open to the public for a number of days during the celebrations, and my day off work turned into a week's leave. I visited everything that I could get onto, lapping up the atmosphere, talking to crew and generally loving every minute of it. Sadly, however, the majority of these ships were training vessels for naval cadets, so my only chance of sailing on them would be to stow away! My dreams went into the too-hard basket again but my appetite had been whetted.

Life went on busily and happily enough. I did some sailing with friends on yachts around Sydney Harbour and in the Georges River, which was pleasant – but they were boats, not ships! I had a trip back to Scotland to visit my family and travelled fairly extensively throughout Australia with various sets of friends before finally settling down in Perth in 1973. Happily, too, my parents and brother decided to emigrate to Australia when my father retired, and they all took up residence in Perth in 1974.

A number of years later, in 1986 in fact, things began to look up as far as getting involved with a sailing ship was concerned. STS *Leeuwin II* was getting built in Fremantle, and it didn't belong to the navy or to another country. Furthermore it was *here* – and so was I. Perhaps there would be the possibility of getting on to her. Indeed that proved to be the case, although it was to take another three years.

More encouragement followed in 1988, when Australia celebrated its bicentenary. There was a re-enactment of the First Fleet voyage from Britain to Australia, with other tall ships joining with the official vessels for the journey. Many of them called in to Fremantle on the way to Sydney, so I haunted the dock during their stay. Chatting with several of the voyage crew members, I discovered that amateurs like myself could, indeed, get on to some of these ships. It was relatively simple in fact. You had to be reasonably fit, which I thought I was, and be prepared to pay for the experience. If you could fulfil those criteria there wasn't really anything to stop you. Yee-ha! Things were definitely looking up!

5

DREAMS COMING TRUE

STS *Leeuwin II* was launched in 1986 with the intention of her being operated in a similar fashion to Scotland's *Malcolm Miller* and *Winston Churchill*. Her primary focus would be involvement of the youth of Australia, in particular Western Australia. Some twenty years later that remains her *raison d'être*, her mission statement being "To challenge and inspire the education and development of our youth and wider community in terms of leadership, team skills, community spirit and environmental awareness".

The *Leeuwin* is a steel-hulled, three-masted barquentine, that is to say she is square-rigged on her foremast, while the main and mizzen masts have fore-and-aft-type sails. She is some fifty-five metres long with a nine-metre beam, and her highest mast is thirty-one metres. I understand that she is the largest "tall ship" in Australia – and she's quite lovely. She is owned and operated by the Leeuwin Ocean Adventure Foundation Ltd, a private not-for-profit organisation based in Fremantle.

For the first year or two of her operation there was very little opportunity for me to get aboard her, partly due to the emphasis on youth and partly due to my work and family commitments. And then, in 1989, I booked to go out on her on a whale-watching weekend. This was ideal for working folks, as it left Fremantle at 6 pm on the Friday and got back at 6 pm on the Sunday, so it could easily be fitted in with work schedules. With great excitement, and some trepidation, I joined the ship at the appointed time. When I stepped on board I felt like I had come home; the most overwhelming sense of belonging swept over me. It was almost as if I had been here before – in a past life maybe?

We were allocated into watches, issued with wet-weather gear and safety harnesses, and shown where to stow our belongings. The *Leeuwin*'s accommodation is a great deal more comfortable than the *Endeavour*'s, as there are actually bunks rather than hammocks. There are six cabins, some six-berth and some eight-berth, in the forward section of the ship for the trainees. Together with separate male and female heads, and a beautifully fitted out trainee mess lined in jarrah, a lovely West Australian native wood, things looked very comfy. I found out later that the ship had been privately chartered for a few weeks during the 1987 defence of the America's Cup, which had been held off Fremantle, and this was one of the reasons she was so nicely fitted out. It was the community's long-term gain after the excitement of the America's Cup had petered out.

There was also a small saloon off the main mess, a well-equipped electric galley, an engine room, chart room and crew's accommodation aft, and various working areas known as the Lazaret and Les' Locker. These contained such items as spare sails, ropes, the reverse-osmosis machine and the sewerage system. On a very short weekend voyage such as this we wouldn't get too involved with these latter areas, but it was good to know where everything was and get the overall feel of the ship.

On deck there was an absolutely bewildering assortment of standing and running rigging: some 160 lines (ropes), each one with a different name and a different function. At this time I was having enough trouble remembering the names of the masts and the sails, never mind where all the lines that operated them were belayed. And I had little or no notion of how they might all work. All would be revealed in the next couple of days, I was sure, and we would be taught and supervised by our watch-leaders and professional crew, who all seemed to be very competent.

The professional crew on the *Leeuwin* normally comprises the captain, first mate, bosun, engineer and chef, assisted by volunteer crew on each voyage – usually four watch-leaders, cook's mate, bosun's mate, watch officer and purser. These volunteers are generally ex-trainees of previous *Leeuwin* voyages who have been invited back by the organisation. Obviously they all love what they do, or they wouldn't be there. The captain in this instance was Chris Blake, who later became the permanent master of the *Endeavour* and with whom I would sail many times over the ensuing years.

We cast off our mooring lines from Victoria Quay and motor-sailed around the corner of the harbour to drop anchor off Port Beach, where we would stay the night. Among other things we were briefed on the safety aspects of the ship, told where our muster stations were and shown how to don our life jackets and use our safety harnesses. Later we would have an evening meal and play a few "icebreaker" games to get to know one another, but while there was still some light we were invited to have a practice climb up the rigging, which seemed like a good idea, as the ship was barely moving. That was when I discovered I had a fear that I didn't know about.

As is always the case on these ships, my watch was made up of an interesting mix of people of different ages, personalities and backgrounds. Our watch-leader was a lad called Allan, a vet by profession, aged about twenty-eight at the time. He had been on the *Leeuwin* many times before and was very patient with us as he explained things. He was also very supportive and encouraging, particularly to those of us, including me, who were a bit anxious about going aloft. Actually I didn't see myself as being a particularly nervous type – after all, I'd been one of those kids who used to climb trees and shimmy up walls without any fear.

The *Leeuwin* at the time used a different safety system from the one it has now. In today's much more safety conscious climate there is what's called a static line running the whole way up the mast from the deck, and crew members wear full-body harnesses similar to those used for abseiling. This type allows you to clip onto a "shunt" that runs up the static line with you before you leave the deck, and you are therefore attached to something the whole way up the mast.

On the harness there are two lines that end in clips, which allows you to "cow-tail", i.e. to clip onto another point before unclipping from the first one, so that at all times you are attached to a piece of the standing rigging or a jackstay or some other point that has been rigged for the purpose. Theoretically at least, it is impossible to fall. In 1989, however, the safety harness consisted of a waist belt with one clip coming from a piece of rope spliced to the harness, and there was no static line running up to the top of the mast. Instead, you "free-climbed" up to the yard or wherever you were going and clipped on when you got there.

Along with other members of my watch, I started to climb up the foremast after being briefed by Allan on how to hold on and what to hold on to, and instructed to always have three points of contact. We were to wait for him when we got to the first platform. He also emphasised that it wasn't a race: there was no pressure, and we should take our time depending upon how comfortable we each felt individually. That all sounded fine to me.

Some of the younger ones shot off up the rigging like proverbial mountain goats, supremely confident and a lot fitter than I was. Another one or two of us started making our way up behind them, with Allan following all of us, keeping a close eye on everything. There was a bit of a logjam of people waiting to get over the futtocks onto the platform, so those of us at the back of the group had to stop where we were and wait for that to clear. It was at that point I made the classic mistake – I looked down. And I absolutely, completely froze with a fear that was so paralysing I'll never forget it. It was also totally unexpected, as I'd never been aware of a fear of heights before.

I'm not sure if my face was so drained of blood that it gleamed in the twilight, but Allan picked up on my plight immediately and climbed over beside me. "What's up, Fran?" Though privately a little nervous, on the deck I'd been one of those brimming with enthusiasm, so he hadn't been expecting this. I was trembling so much my teeth were chattering, and I couldn't string two words together to answer him. He clipped my harness onto a ratline, and told me to wait for him while he saw that everyone else was all right. Wait for him? I wasn't going anywhere! I clung there for dear life while all the rest of my watch plodded their way onwards and upwards, and safely made it onto the platform. Then they climbed back over the futtocks and made it down again. After a round of high fives they turned their attention upwards and started calling encouraging comments to me.

By this time my heart wasn't pounding quite so hard and I was beginning to feel a bit foolish. Nevertheless, every time I tried to unprise my fingers from their grip around the shrouds they seemed to have taken on a mind of their own and simply wouldn't let go enough to

50

allow me to move. Allan came back and reasoned with me. There was no question of me going any further up at this stage, but at the very least I had to come down, or else he'd have to lash me to the rigging and I would have to stay there all night.

Common sense began to permeate through my brain but it didn't overcome the fear. Allan got behind me and positioned himself so that he was straddled with one leg on a ratline on either side of me, holding on to the same shrouds as I was. I was kind of "tucked in" between him and the shrouds, and wasn't going anywhere – if I fell I would have to take him with me. About forty minutes had passed, and the rest of the watch had been sent below to square away the last of their gear and make up their bunks for the night. It was dark now, and somehow that seemed to make it better – I couldn't see the deck so clearly! "OK Fran, we're going to do this together, and just take it one ratline at a time", said Allan. "But you have to let go with one hand, and move your hand further down the shroud". It was about then, I think, that I wet my pants. Oh God, I was so embarrassed.

Allan was brilliant. He said nothing, and he didn't move until I was ready to move. Talk about "above and beyond the call of duty". He must have realised what had happened, but there was no way he was leaving me or making me feel any worse than I already felt. It took another twenty minutes or so, but he finally got me back down and onto the deck, where I promptly burst into tears. There was virtually no-one else on deck by this stage, so he just gave me a comforting hug and let me sob until I got my composure back and was ready to face everyone again. I felt such an idiot, but he knew that my fear had been very real. "Don't worry about it", he said. "If you want to, we'll tackle it again tomorrow, but only if you want to." Of course I wanted to – I couldn't be on a tall ship and not go aloft. I'd been dreaming about it for years.

The next day we had another go. To my amazement I discovered the fear didn't hit me again until I was much, much higher up the rigging than the point at which I'd been overwhelmed the previous night. Everyone was encouraging – not one person made me feel inadequate or foolish. That's one of the fantastic things about the people you meet on these ships: they really help you to push your boundaries far beyond what you think you may be capable of, and the sense of accomplishment when something is achieved is almost indescribable.

By the time we came back alongside the quay at Fremantle two days later I was dancing the can-can on one of the yards! That's the *Leeuwin's* version of dressing the yards – it looks much more fun for the waiting loved ones on the dock. (It *is* much more fun!). Ken could hardly believe it, as he knew I'd been a little apprehensive about the whole thing. He told me afterwards that, as he watched the ship coming into the quay, he thought to himself, "Look at all the young ones up the rigging – that looks great", and then to his astonishment realised that one of the "young ones" was me.

I'd had an absolutely fantastic weekend, and yes, we *had* seen whales, and the experience had just been so great that I couldn't wait to do it again. I was hooked. Work commitments were such, however, that it was a couple of years before I could do a full-on ten-day voyage, but every time there was a weekender on offer I went. On each occasion I learned more and got a bit more confident about what I was doing. Then I got to the point of being able to help others overcome their fears and stretch their boundaries. It's the old "what goes around comes around" syndrome again.

In due course I was invited back as volunteer crew, and some eighteen years later I'm still involved with the *Leeuwin* and still sail as volunteer crew from time to time. It's very rewarding working with the young people particularly, as it's great to see them gain confidence and blossom during their time on the ship. Many of them have gone on to professional studies and made the sea their chosen career. Even quite a few of the girls have become professional seamen (should that be sea persons these days?) and three female ex-*Leeuwin* trainees now hold their masters' tickets. One of them is the captain of a very large vessel involved in the oil industry – things have certainly changed since my young days.

The *Leeuwin* sails mostly up and down the extensive West Australian coast, in voyages of five to twelve days' duration. I've now been fortunate enough to have covered pretty well the whole coast over the years, sailing from Esperance in the south to Darwin in the Northern Territory at various different times – in all sorts of weather conditions and with a myriad of people. My dreams had certainly begun to come true. Even if I couldn't satisfy them in a professional capacity, I had found an outlet for my passion.

And then in 1993 HM Bark *Endeavour* was launched. She was also built in Fremantle, and there was terrific local interest in and support for her. I hadn't been involved with her during the construction phase, although I had gone to see her being built several times and was getting pretty excited about another tall ship being around in my home town. Immediately after she was launched at Fishing Boat Harbour, she was towed around to Victoria Quay where she would be tied up for three months or so while her masts were stepped and she was rigged. A call went out for local people to become volunteer ship-keepers and general helpers during this period. I couldn't get on the phone fast enough.

Ship-keeping is a little like baby-sitting a vessel. It entails sleeping aboard during the night and standing a watch of around two hours' duration. During the watch you are required to be on deck most of the time and you have rounds to do – checking things like the mooring lines, the gangway and the depth of water in the bilges and generally making sure everything is in order. There were a number of us who had volunteered to carry out these duties and we were organised into watches, most watches doing a stint on a once-weekly basis. There was always a professional on board to whom we reported, usually a member of the rigging/construction crew or a watch officer.

During this time the ship was open to the public for inspection on weekends when rigging wasn't in progress overhead. Volunteer guides, who had done such a fantastic job in the construction shed when she was being built, showed the public around and told them about Cook and the original *Endeavour*. It didn't take me long to join their ranks as well, so I now had "two hats" on with regard to the ship.

It took about three months for the rigging to be completed, and then she was required to undergo sea trials to ensure that everything was working as it should and to satisfy the requirements of the Australian Maritime Safety Authority. This meant that she would need crew to sail her. To be considered as volunteer crew you had to either have had considerable "blue water" experience as an open-ocean yachtsman or have had twenty days at sea on a square-rig ship.

I was about three days short of the required twenty days, but had another two days booked on the *Leeuwin* before the commencement of the *Endeavour*'s sea trials, leaving me only one day short. Surely they wouldn't deny me the chance because of only one day! I started doing all sorts of extra volunteer duties and grovelling like mad to the man in charge of recruiting in an effort to get more brownie points. I can still remember saying to Ken, "If I can just get to sail on her once, I'll go and meet my Maker happily". He still reminds me of that at times.

The big day of her first sail came on 16 March 1994. She was going out just for the day, primarily to test her engines. She would do several day sails during the rest of that week, and I had managed to get myself on as a volunteer deckhand. I've never been sure whether I was accepted because of my *Leeuwin* experience or my enthusiasm or my grovelling, or whether it was just because I was in the right place at the right time. I had taken a week's leave from work so that I could be on call for whenever they wanted me, and was down at the dock every morning to see what was happening.

I wasn't lucky enough to be on her very first day sail, as that honour was kept for VIPs, people who had been involved with her building and rigging, and their families. I *was* lucky enough, however, to get onto the chase boat that was organised to follow the *Endeavour* just in case anything went awry. As things transpired, it was the most magical place to be. It was a glorious day, and the captain and crew decided to try out one or two of her sails. As the morning passed they got a bit carried away, and kept putting up more and more sails until all seventeen were up. This afforded those of us on the chase boat the most fantastic photo opportunity, and I have some glorious pictures gracing my photo albums. Perhaps it was as well I hadn't got onto the *Endeavour* herself.

On the next day and several subsequent days I did get on board, and found it quite different working the *Endeavour* from my experience on the *Leeuwin*. This was especially so during these shakedown days, when everyone was still finding out how she really sailed. Her rigging is harder to climb than the *Leeuwin*'s, as it has rope shrouds (newly tarred at the outset) rather than steel guys. Her masts are higher too. Thankfully, I didn't have a repeat of the incident of my first weekend on the *Leeuwin*

– that would have been too much. We all got home in the evenings very tired, very dirty, very tarry and very satisfied.

Chris Blake, the captain, remembered me from my first sojourn on the *Leeuwin* back in 1989 and, if he'd ever learned about my panic up the rigging, in true diplomatic fashion he never mentioned it. Many years later I referred to the wet-pants incident, but he claimed not to have known about it. He did have a chuckle when I shared my "secret" with him, and kindly reminded me that I had made huge progress since those days.

Following the successful sea-trials programme, some short voyages were undertaken to Mandurah and Busselton, to the south, and Geraldton, to the north. The *Leeuwin* accompanied the *Endeavour* on the sail down to Mandurah, where both ships would anchor overnight in the new Dawesville Cut prior to its official opening. The two locally built tall ships anchored there together was a grand sight, and as luck would have it there was the most spectacular sunset that evening. There are some glorious photographs from that night, with the two ships in silhouette against that sunset. One of them was used as a *Leeuwin* Christmas card later that year.

By September of 1994 the *Endeavour* was almost ready to set off on her maiden voyage to Sydney, the run up the coast to Geraldton being her last local foray. I was fortunate enough to be selected as volunteer crew again. This trip would be a little different inasmuch as we had on board a film crew that was taking some footage to be used in a docu-drama about the Dutch VOC (East India Company) ship *Batavia*, which was wrecked on the Abrolhos Islands in 1629. So at times we flew the Dutch flag, and those of us who couldn't be made to look like 17th-century sailors and used as extras had to stay below while filming was going on.

One of the actors hadn't been aware that the *Endeavour* is a non-smoking ship and, by the time we dropped anchor at Geraldton a few days after leaving Fremantle, he was absolutely dying for a cigarette. It was a balmy afternoon, and the captain said we could go over the side for a swim once the anchoring was completed. When most of us were in the water, and much to everyone's amusement, his mate carefully lowered down a packet of cigarettes and lighter on the end of a piece of string so that he could have a smoke while treading water. He wasn't on board, so he was complying with the regulations. The stratagem wasn't successful, but we had to give him ten out of ten for trying. It was only another couple of hours until we were allowed to go ashore anyway, so he didn't have too much longer to wait.

Later on, when we started putting the rescue boat in the water during swimming sessions, we could stand on it to get to the "man steps" on the side of the ship's hull when we wanted to get back on board. But, as things were on this occasion, one went about it by grabbing the manrope and swinging your legs up to the bottom step. This proved impossible for me to manage, as the step was far too high out of the water for my short legs to reach. A couple of the guys climbed down from the deck to try and help haul me up while another one who was still in the water was trying to give me a push from behind – *on* the behind – apologising profusely because of where he had to put his hand. I got the giggles; in fact I was just about helpless with laughter at the mental picture of what this debacle must have looked like. So were those who'd already got back on deck. Eventually the combined pushing and pulling efforts managed to get me to the point where I could help myself and climb on up the steps. I slithered over the rail onto the deck and was sure I must have looked like a mini beached whale. Everyone else said the swimming episode had been the entertainment of the day – the actor trying to have a smoke and me trying to get back on board.

Also on board that trip were Rod, a professional photographer from Perth, and John, a book publisher from Sydney, who were involved in the production of a book titled *Sailing Endeavour*. They were both in my watch and the three of us became quite friendly during the voyage. John, the publisher, was along in the capacity of a supernumerary, so he didn't have to stand night watches with us. He did say, however, that he would like to do one of the early-morning watches, from 4 to 8 am, so that he could see the sunrise.

One morning when there was promise of a nice sunrise I went down to his cabin and wakened him to come up on deck. By the time he arrived it was my turn to be on bow watch, and I was sitting out on the end of the bowsprit in one of my favourite spots. When the spritsails are set it's difficult to see beyond them. We used to do bow watch in twos, and if the weather was clement one would climb out to the end of the bowsprit and the other would stay inboard as the runner. The runner's job was to convey to the officer of the watch, back on the poop deck, whatever the watcher called back in the way of report from the bowsprit. The sense of solitude when sitting out on the end of the bowsprit is just wonderful, particularly because there is virtually no private space anywhere on the *Endeavour*.

When John appeared on the deck he thought this looked like rather a good spot to be, so I climbed inboard to help him come out and join me. It took a little careful manoeuvring but we ended up fairly comfortably settled, with me astride the bowsprit holding on to a stay and John holding on to me motorbike pillion-passenger style. We were both clipped on with our harnesses too. The sea was dead flat calm, the sky was just starting to lighten, the ship was still quiet and it was glorious.

And then we heard these odd noises – some slight splashing, great sighs and what seemed like nasal sounds. What on earth could it be? As the light became a little stronger we realised that we had a pod of humpback whales for company. They were swimming alongside the ship, and even diving underneath the bowsprit, right below us. There was a beautiful sunrise as well. Overcome with the awe of it all, we clung to each other and wept. It would have to be one of my most memorable experiences at sea. You really felt that God was right there, allowing you to see some of His wonders.

There were very few people on the ship who had the privilege of seeing this – just those who were the duty watch on deck that morning. By the time we woke people up to turn to, most of the whales had either dived down or swum off and the sun was well and truly up, so the whole magical effect had passed.

John and I referred to that day as "the morning of the whales" for a long while afterwards. We kept in touch after the voyage ended and he went back to Sydney. He promised that once the book was published he would send me a copy and, true to his word, a few months later a copy arrived hot off the press. When I opened the package I discovered a card inside containing a beautiful poem he'd written about that morning. It has become another of my treasured possessions, but I'm sure he wouldn't mind me sharing it with others. It was just such a special moment.

> Twas the night near Abrolhos
> When all those on board
> Not a crewman was stirring
> In hammocks they snored.
>
> When out off to starboard
> We heard a great sigh
> As two hump-back whales
> Surfaced right by.
>
> With glimmer of dawn
> Dole shadows arose
> On lovers on bowsprit
> Watch-keepers? – Who knows?
>
> Sunrise on the staysails
> An emotional tear
> For the world's natural beauty
> Was never so near.

Many times over the past few years people have asked me why I like to go to sea. I can't think of a more eloquent way of putting it than that.

Another story from the same voyage concerns the "scram bag" auction. I understand this used to be an old Royal Naval tradition. Items of lost property were auctioned off, usually at a very modest sum, so that people could reclaim their own belongings – buy back their own lost jocks or socks or whatever. We tried this on board the *Endeavour* but didn't quite stick to the rules, and people ended up bidding against one another just like at a normal auction. It was all very funny, and ended up raising far more money than had been envisaged.

What should be done with the cash? A vote was taken among the crew and it was decided that a ship's library should be started. As I had been acting as the auctioneer's clerk, scribbling down all the names and bids and subsequently collecting the money, the captain charged me with the responsibility of buying an appropriate book when we got back to Fremantle. So a copy of *Ashley's Book of Knots* at a nicely discounted price was sourced and donated to the ship on behalf of the crew from Voyage No. 29A/B, Fremantle–Geraldton–Fremantle, September 1994. It was with great pride that I handed it over to Captain Blake – what had started out as a bit of silly fun had resulted in something really worthwhile.

We approached Fremantle in time to dock on the Friday, but it was decided to drop anchor for the night just off Port Beach so that we could sail into the harbour with the *Leeuwin*, which was due to dock on the Saturday morning after one of her voyages. This would make a grand sight for the anticipated spectators. The *Leeuwin* arrived shortly afterwards and dropped anchor nearby. That was when I discovered that there is a well-established raiding tradition between tall ships. Whenever there is more than one in the same area, you need to double your deck watch because it's likely you will be raided.

Many of us on the *Endeavour* had also crewed on the *Leeuwin*, so we knew exactly where flags, *Leeuwin* smocks and so forth were kept. A raid was planned, and four of our lads snuck across to the other ship in the fizz boat. They did very well, arriving back with four watch-leader smocks, the bell rope and the *Leeuwin* commissioning pennant. Now that *really* was a prize. They didn't think any *Leeuwin* crew had seen them, so we were looking forward to some reactions the next day.

Next morning both ships set some sails and weighed anchor. Captain Chris was watching the *Leeuwin*'s captain through his binoculars to gauge his reaction when he saw the *Endeavour* flying the *Leeuwin*'s pennant from the top of our mast. "Not a happy chappie" was the verdict. We were gleefully jubilant. Then they noticed some of our deck crew wearing their watch-leaders' smocks … and then they saw their bell rope hanging on the *Endeavour*'s ship's bell. Oh the ignominy of it all. It was wonderful! We gave everything back once we were both alongside Victoria Quay, but we'd certainly thrown down the gauntlet. The *Leeuwin* crew would get their own back in due course.

6

MAIDEN VOYAGE AROUND AUSTRALIA

The *Endeavour* was scheduled to leave Fremantle for her maiden voyage to Sydney on 2 October 1994. Competition for voyage crew places for this auspicious journey was pretty fierce, and naturally I was one of the applicants. I made a great nuisance of myself by repeatedly ringing up to see if the crew had been selected yet. After about my tenth phone call I was told that I was on the stand-by list. That was a little bit encouraging, but I didn't really hold out much hope of getting on. Just in case, however, I negotiated some time off with my boss in the event that I was lucky enough to be selected. And then I got the phone call: I was on! I couldn't wait to tell Ken. By this time he had nicknamed me "The Albatross", as I was fast turning into a wandering, seafaring bird.

I'd been allocated a spot only for the first leg of the voyage, from Fremantle to Albany, but what a privilege anyway: only a handful of people would have the honour of crewing on the maiden voyage. We had to join the ship a few days before departure, as there was much to be done before we left. All the spare sails, lines, blocks and other pieces of equipment had to be loaded, and the food and other supplies had to be taken aboard and stowed. This would be the longest journey the ship had yet undertaken, and there was quite a lot involved in getting everything ready.

The ship also had to be sparkling clean and gleaming, as the Governor and many other VIPs were coming on board for a visit before seeing us off – not to mention the thousands and thousands of spectators, the television cameras and the flotilla of small craft that were expected. One television crew was to join us on the ship, and they took some fantastic footage that we all got to see a few weeks later.

As the ship hadn't encountered any particularly rough weather during all of her day sails and sea trials, there was an element of uncertainty about this much longer voyage. As it happened the weather forecast for the next week or so wasn't looking too favourable, so this voyage was going to be the *real* test for young "Miss Endeavour". As John Longley, the Project Manager, said at the time, "Our girl's grown up; she's leaving home".

"Farewell to Fremantle" day dawned very stormy and gloomy, but nothing could dampen the air of excitement that permeated the ship and the crew. People had begun to gather on the docks and all around Fremantle to gain good vantage points. A large contingent of the *Endeavour* volunteer guides formed a guard of honour and there were bands from various organisations including the Royal Navy and the Fremantle Sailing Club. The local football team had just won the grand final the day before, and all the leftover blue and yellow balloons and streamers from the match got a second life, as those were also the *Endeavour*'s house colours.

It was decided to loose the gaskets on the square sails and have them "hanging in their gear", ready to be set, prior to the arrival of the VIPs. We therefore got sent aloft to carry out this task before all the formal pomp and ceremony started. When we shook out the sails, pounds and pounds of rice fell to the deck like snow! The *Leeuwin* crew had got us back for pinching their bell rope and pennant on the return from Geraldton. To this day I've never been able to find out how they managed to pull it off, but it was brilliant. Fortunately we'd made the discovery before the rice christened the Governor, and had time to clean up. We did have a good laugh about it though. The score was now even.

Following all the formal speeches, the bestowal of good wishes and the last of the visitors going ashore, the gangway was taken up, mooring lines were let go and we began to pull away from the dock. A "Made in WA" sign was unfurled and rolled down the rigging to a huge cheer from the watching crowd. Streamers by the hundreds were thrown across the ever-widening void between the quay and the ship, just like in the old days when passenger liners used to frequent Fremantle. It was all very emotional, and many of us were struggling with our composure while clearing the streamers away from the blocks and running rigging. I was barely hanging on to mine when the band started to play "Auld Lang Syne". Then the tears started.

They didn't get the chance to last long, though, as the minute we left the shelter of the harbour we were out into pretty rough weather and had to get on with the business of setting and trimming sails. No time for tears here. We turned right and did a lap of honour up the coast towards the Perth suburb of Scarborough, and could hardly believe the sight. West Coast Highway was at a standstill, with cars pulled over everywhere to watch our passage. It seemed like every balcony on every house had blue and yellow balloons tied to the railings, and behind them people waving. It was an amazing send-off, and certainly did the people of Perth and Fremantle proud.

We turned towards the ocean and headed off into the wide blue yonder – except that it was anything but blue. It was grey and black, and getting more and more threatening by the minute. We had all got into wet-weather gear even before we left the dock, and with the wind picking up it looked like we were going to need it. We were sent aloft to furl and gasket some of the sails. The rough rule of thumb as the wind picks up is that you start at the top and work down, and at the furthermost point out on the bowsprit and work in.

We were rocking and rolling pretty well by this stage. The ship has a very bluff bow and a very round bottom with not much keel. Consequently she rolls a lot. This soon tested everyone's stomachs and sea legs, with some interesting results. One of my watch mates, who shall remain nameless in the interests of not embarrassing him *too* much, had the most gentlemanly bout of seasickness that I think I've ever seen. Our wet-weather smocks had a pocket in the front, and in the pocket were our sou'wester hats. While aloft he was suddenly stricken with the urge to throw up, without having the time to climb back down to the deck. He turned and apologised to me (I was next to him), pulled out the sou'wester, threw up in that, and then quietly and unobtrusively climbed down, carefully carrying his hat full of spew. He emptied it over the side, washed it out and went about his business. What style! I still tease him about it when I see him.

62

On the way to Albany we would be passing Margaret River, an area where many Perth people take weekend breaks. The family of one of the shipwrights, Nick, was going to be there, and this particular day happened to be his young daughter's birthday. He asked the captain if we could possibly fire the cannon in celebration as we passed Margaret River. "Certainly," came the reply, "great idea. In fact, we'll fire off a cannonball." Nick called his family on the ship's phone to let them know where and when this was planned so that they could be on the lookout for it. What excitement the idea sparked as word spread through the ranks!

The company that had made the cannons for the ship had also made some cannonballs, primarily for display when the ship was in museum mode. Now that we had tested the cannons a few times, the captain thought it would be appropriate to try one of them out properly. Everything was prepared with due care by Nick, who was also the gunner. "Fire in the hole", came the shout as the fuse was lit. Whoosh … off flew the cannonball in the direction of the cliffs of Margaret River. Those of us who were watching very carefully thought we could see the splash as it fell into the sea; the people in the charthouse tracking it on the radar could tell us it travelled more than a kilometre. I think I'd be safe in saying it would be the first cannonball fired off the West Australian coast in about three hundred years. What a fantastic "show and tell" story Nick's daughter would have had when she went back to school. "It was my birthday last week, and my daddy fired a cannonball for me out of a real cannon!" I'll bet there weren't any other kids in Western Australia who could claim that.

The weather grew progressively worse over the next couple of days, and gale-force winds were predicted. Not good. The ship was, however, performing brilliantly. We went about our business as best we could, although there wasn't a lot of cleaning getting done. It was a bit too uncomfortable below decks, especially when you started working with cleaning products that smelled. Although we use only biodegradable cleaners, some of them do smell. If you were remotely queasy, the combination of the smell and close confines was enough to make you race up on deck and head for the lee rail.

We slung our hammocks for the night and tried to eat some tea. How the cook managed to cook anything was a bit of a miracle, as everything was crashing about in the galley. He had all the fiddles up on the stove, but still managed to produce a reasonable meal. It's a definite challenge trying to keep peas on a plate on a rolling ship.

The wind was still picking up and we now had a swell of about seven metres. All the hammocks were swinging in unison as the ship rolled from side to side. I wasn't sure whether to be amused or alarmed. In hindsight I think I was a bit of both. I climbed into the hammock with most of my clothes on – I was pretty sure we would get called out in the night to furl more sail. Once I was settled in my hammock, one buttock cheek would get bumped against the bulkhead as we rolled to port, and then the other buttock cheek would bump against the galley stove chimney as we rolled back the other way. I didn't get much sleep that night.

As I had suspected, we ended up being called up on deck to furl more sail. By this time there were lifelines strung around the weather deck, and you had to clip on to something all the time – there was a real danger of going overboard if you didn't. Not a good idea at the best of times, but certainly not at night in this weather. The wind got clocked at fifty-three knots across the deck and the bubble in the inclinometer was off the scale at times, meaning we were rolling more than forty-five degrees. Indeed at times the lee rail would dip right into the water before the ship would come back up, right herself, and then roll the other way. I was pretty scared, though interestingly enough still not seasick.

Over the howling of the wind as it screamed through the rigging we could hear the bilge pumps going constantly. That was a bit of a worry. Every time we heeled over, the ship would shudder before she began to right herself and then heel the other way. And every time she shuddered, sawdust came out of nooks and crannies that we had been unable to clean. The problem with this was that the sawdust was clogging up the bilge pumps, which were therefore having to work twice as hard. And I had volunteered, nay *paid*, to come and do this?

I had to convince myself that nothing untoward was going to happen. I kept thinking of Captain Cook's famous quote "No Sea can hurt her laying too under a Main Sail or Mizen ballanc'd". But that was the other, real *Endeavour*. This one was a relatively untested replica, built from different woods. And she hadn't been in the water long enough for the planking to have swelled properly. Would she prove to be as seaworthy as the original *Endeavour*?

One of the guys who realised I was pretty scared painted me a "worst-case scenario". In contrast to Cook's situation, the Maritime Safety Authority, Coast Watch and half the country knew where we were. If the ship went down, we would all end up in the life rafts, probably very seasick, but would only be there for a few hours at most before being rescued. That wasn't too horrific a prospect, was it? In reality it probably wasn't, but I preferred not to think about it and kept myself busy.

Of course my fears were unfounded and probably a bit melodramatic, but nevertheless real at the time. In fact our *Endeavour* handled the heavy seas beautifully. She probably handled it better than the crew did, truth be told. We had lots of new members of the lee rail club by this time, and many of those who hadn't been sick had at least been frightened. And the television crew was wondering how soon they could get off. Neither seasick nor frightened were the two shipwrights who were on board. Two of the lads who had been on the construction crew and were sailing with us went around below decks continuously "sounding" the ship to check watertight integrity. They kept reappearing on deck with big grins on their faces – all was well. When this was pointed out to me I relaxed a lot more, and actually began to enjoy the wild weather. This truly was an adventure.

After a couple of days in this storm the wind began to abate a little, and we were able to put some sail back up. At one stage we had been down to little more than bare poles, with the engine going to keep us heading towards Albany. Once the wind had begun to ease, we were pretty surprised to see a light plane flying around above us. He seemed to be checking us out, which was reassuring. What we didn't imagine was that it was carrying a photographer from the local paper, the *Albany Advertiser*, who was shooting off rolls of film.

When we arrived in Albany to a very warm welcome, the photographer was at the pier with the most amazing shots, some with the *Endeavour* heeled over to such an extent that you could see half her bottom. We had had no idea what we looked like while we were in the big seas, and it was nothing short of spectacular. I couldn't help conjuring up the memory of some lines from John Masefield's famous poem:

I must go down to the seas again, to the lonely sea and the sky,
and all I ask is a tall ship and a star to steer her by...

The shots certainly illustrated how lonely the sea and the sky looked. The photographer did a roaring trade with the crew, never mind all the other uses his pictures have been put to since then.

What we also didn't realise was that half the people in the State had been following our progress down the coast very closely. This was especially true of Albany, a former whaling town where a considerable number of fisher-folk still live. They are very aware of the perils of the sea, and had been quite concerned about us until we arrived. When we went ashore we were literally unable to buy a drink in the town. As soon as locals realised we were from the *Endeavour*, drinks were propped up on the bar. People came up to us in the street and asked for our autographs, we got asked to pose for photographs and we were hugged incessantly. One woman tearfully told me she'd been lighting candles in the church and praying for our safety. These were total strangers. It was really humbling, and certainly restored my faith in human nature. We can all be a bit cynical these days, unfortunately. All this made me feel so warmed, so proud, and certainly very glad that I'd had the privilege of being on board.

After a few days in Albany, it was time for the *Endeavour* to continue on her way to Sydney for the rest of her maiden voyage. It was also time for those wretched farewells again: I was only one of many of the voyage crew who departed at this point. New crew joined for the next leg to Esperance and beyond, and those of us who had to get off and return to our "normal" lives went to see the ship off and wish everyone well. Our tears mingled with the pouring rain as the ship headed out into Princess Royal Harbour and disappeared off into the night. "See you in Sydney", I called out to those on deck. But I was really talking to the ship.

A contingent of the stalwart *Endeavour* volunteer guides of Fremantle was making arrangements to fly to Sydney to be there when she arrived, and I had already decided to join them. And so it was that, on 17 December 1994, when the *Endeavour* sailed triumphantly into Sydney Harbour, I was there to see her again – this time on a special harbour ferry that had gone out to the Heads to meet her and escort her in, together with many other tall ships and dozens of other craft. It was a wonderful spectacle. She would be on display for about four months at the National Maritime Museum in Darling Harbour before continuing on her circumnavigation of Australia. I flew home to Perth and my life returned to normal, for a while anyway.

Once the *Endeavour* started sailing again, heading north up the Queensland coast, it didn't take too long for my itchy feet and the call of the briny to set in. I contacted the office, now in Sydney, to see if they needed any voyage crew on any of the Queensland legs. To my delight the answer was affirmative. It seemed to be a bit easier for me to get on board this time: perhaps I had proved myself somewhat by this stage. Captain Chris teased me for a long time about only letting me on board when he wanted the heads *really* cleaned. It seemed I'd gained a bit of a reputation for being a very, very fussy cleaner, and had been nicknamed "The Queen of the Heads". I didn't much care *why* they let me back on; I was just happy to be going back to join my beloved ship again.

I didn't need to arrange time off from work this time as I'd taken a redundancy package from my job and now had a bit of spare cash and lots of spare time. I'd been almost due for long service leave, and thought I'd take a few months off before I looked for another job. I was, in fact, organising a big trip back to Scotland and beyond, as the 1995 Cutty Sark Tall Ships Race would be leaving from Edinburgh that year and would end up joining the fleet that gathered every five years in Amsterdam for a big maritime event there. These two events only coincided once in ten years. With that kind of incentive, this was definitely the year for a trip back to the old country, and plans were well under way for my "Tall Ships Pilgrimage", as Ken had christened it. But I had time to fit in another voyage on the *Endeavour* ... this had become a bit of an obsession.

So in mid-June I flew to Bundaberg in Queensland to join up as voyage crew again. The ship was working her way up the coast from Sydney in legs of roughly ten days, and I was going to do the Bundaberg–Mackay stretch, immediately followed by Mackay–Cairns. Doing the two legs one after the other helped me justify spending the airfare to Queensland, but it also meant I would get to sail through the Whitsunday Islands and the Great Barrier Reef. This was where the original *Endeavour* had gone aground, on what is now called Endeavour Reef for obvious reasons. Unfortunately I didn't have time to stay on board until the ship got up to Cooktown, which was where Cook stayed for about six weeks while the crew undertook repairs after the grounding.

I'd planned to have a few days in Bundaberg before the ship arrived so that I could catch up with old friends from my hometown in Scotland before embarking. Anne and Drew drove up from Brisbane with a boot full of old photograph albums, school pictures and the like, and we had a great reunion. We drank too much red wine and laughed and talked non-stop for a couple of days – not surprising, really, when you consider it had been more than twenty-five years since we'd seen one another.

When they took me down to rejoin the ship I discovered that many of the crew had been with her since she left Fremantle, so I knew quite a few people on board. They all thought my accent was considerably broader than it had been: just goes to show what three days with other Scots will do. The voyage crew coming on consisted of all new people, so yet another batch of friendships would be made.

I was in Main Mast watch this time, so had a completely different spot to sling my hammock, one well away from where I had been bumping my bottom on the galley stove when we were rounding Cape Leeuwin. The watch had nine members, most of whom were in the thirties-to-fifties age group, so it was a more mature band than I had previously sailed with. It turned out that it didn't make any difference: we got up to some mad escapades anyway and became good buddies.

We left Bundaberg in the late afternoon and headed out at sunset on a very calm sea. It was very pretty, but in those conditions we had to go out under motor, although we put some sails up anyway for the benefit of the public that had come to see us off. During the night we passed a tiny settlement on the coast called "1770" – of course named by Captain Cook, and reputed to have been his first landfall in Queensland. We also passed Bustard Head Lighthouse, so named because it was in that area that Cook's people shot and cooked a bustard. This trip turned up interesting historical snippets such as these that I hadn't previously known about.

It turned out we were to have a surprise stop for a couple of hours in a group of islands called "the Percys". They are in the Whitsunday Group, but are not developed tourist destinations. Middle Percy Island is, however, apparently well known to the "yachties" who frequent these waters, as evidenced by all the identifying souvenirs left by those who had been there before us hanging off the A-frame shelter on the beach. Blocks, sections of sails, tee shirts and other paraphernalia, all bearing their boats' names and dates of visit, were abundant.

The one that really caught my eye was a wooden leg, complete with sandshoe on the foot. The boat's name was painted up the shin, together with the statement that this was "the best leg of the journey". Then as we looked around a bit more we found the *other* leg and, yes, they were a matched pair. Someone obviously had a great sense of humour. Not to be outdone, we left a cannonball mounted on a small block of jarrah that had been knocked up by the shipwright, with the *Endeavour*'s name and the date we were there (21 June 1995) painted on it. Some thirteen years on, one wonders if it's still there or if it's been pinched as a souvenir by now.

The next day we arrived at Mackay, where we would be on exhibition for a few days. It was a very early start, with all hands on deck to get sails furled and everything looking shipshape before we docked. We also had to set everything up in museum mode, ready for the public to come on board. This had now been done many, many times by the permanent crew, so they had become pretty slick at it and it didn't seem to take as long as the last time I'd been involved.

A number of the voyage crew got off at Mackay, and it was a relief to find the goodbyes were not quite so painful this time, probably because we'd only been together for a few days. Those of us who were staying on for the next leg to Cairns got some time off and went into town to have a look around. Almost inevitably we ended up at the local yacht club for drinks and a meal and the telling of tall tales, which often happens when sailors get together. It doesn't seem to matter whether you're amateur or professional, young or old, 18th or 20th century, the wind gets stronger and the waves get higher every time the story gets told.

It was surprisingly wet, windy and cold in Mackay, but we still managed to have a few pleasant days off. We were looking forward to getting into more tropical weather, though, and hoped this would be the case between Mackay and Cairns. New crew joined, everyone got allocated watches and settled in, and off we headed again, farewelled by a small crowd, a band and a lone piper.

I was getting to be a bit of an old hand at this by now, and got called on quite a lot by my captain o'tops to help the new people with such things as names of lines and sails, which I found very rewarding. I also got called on quite often to take the helm, which has to be one of my favourite tasks on board, and to be the bow-watch lookout. Given the area that we were sailing in, especially at night, this was very challenging: there were islands everywhere.

We sailed through the Northumberland Passage past Kreswick, St Bees, Brampton Island and the St James group during daylight, and the whole area was just as picturesque as postcards and photographs suggest. We went through the Whitsunday Passage at night, which was a bit of a shame, but very exciting as you really had to keep your wits about you. While this area is further south than Endeavour Reef, there were lots of wisecracks being made about history repeating itself.

We were heading for a small settlement called Cape Upstart, about halfway between Bowen and Ayr, named – inevitably – by Captain Cook. His journals reflected that the winds had been really fluky in this area and the peninsular had been "an upstart of a Cape to get round". Our captain had been invited to dig up a time capsule that had been buried some twenty-five years before, when the local community had erected a cairn to commemorate the bicentenary of Captain Cook's visit there. The winds were still fluky, but we of course had the benefit of some engines to help us manoeuvre into the bay, where we dropped anchor.

We all went ashore in dress uniform, as we had been told there would be a bit of a ceremony. What a ceremony it turned out to be! The locals really did themselves proud, particularly as there are no roads in to Cape Upstart and everything had to be brought in by boat. Most of the people actually live in Burdekin, which is the nearest town, and come here at weekends. They have even built themselves a small sailing-club premises there. Just about the whole community had turned out, the Australian flag was up, and there were copious amounts of food and drink, including a huge chocolate cake with an image of the *Endeavour* on the icing. An exchange of gifts took place, speeches were made, the time capsule was unearthed and handed to the local mayor, the reporter from the local paper took notes – the whole thing was very professionally handled in spite of the isolation of the spot. We agreed the afternoon had been a real treat.

When it was time for us to leave, we got ourselves organised to sail off the anchorage rather than use the engines. This is very dependent upon the wind, and it took a bit of time. The local lads in their speedboats took the opportunity to circle around the ship, "mooning" us in the process, much to our amusement. We couldn't let them get away with that though, so we set up the fire hose and got them on their bare behinds the next time around. It was all good fun, and certainly contributed to the bank of wonderful memories that being on this ship constantly provided.

The weather by now had warmed up and the breezes were very light. This made for some very pleasant sailing, and we had even managed to put up the recently made studding sails (or stunsails as they're also known). These are extra square sails set on booms that extend out from the yards, only used in very light winds. We took turns at going out in the rescue boat to take photographs of the ship, as she looked majestic.

Our next unscheduled stop was at Hinchinbrook Island, where we dropped anchor at Zoë Bay and called in for a few hours. We had a lovely swim, though we did have people on the lookout for sea snakes and crocodiles. Not being too sure whether there were any crocs in this area, we decided we'd better play it safe. We had a picnic on the beach and even managed to have some fresh coconut water, courtesy of the shipwright's drill. We had wrestled and wrestled with a few of them but couldn't break them open, so John obliged by boring some holes for us. Modern technology to the rescue again.

All too soon it was time to leave this idyllic spot and head off for Cairns. We were due in on 30 June, and understood there was another large welcome organised for us. The downside to sailing this ship in today's world is the schedule that has to be adhered to, but the upside is the wonderful welcomes that she attracts virtually everywhere she goes. A veritable flotilla of boats usually appears, complete with water cannons, jet skis and helicopters – it's quite overwhelming at times. As we passed Fitzroy Island on the way into Cairns Harbour, we fired off the cannon to greet and salute all those welcoming us. Another *Endeavour* adventure was coming to an end.

I wasn't quite so sad at leaving her this time around, as my big trip to the UK to see the tall ships race was imminent and I was pretty excited about that. I'd also had some big hints dropped to me about perhaps joining the *Endeavour*'s crew again for her upcoming voyage to New Zealand and I would certainly be excited about that! It hadn't been entirely confirmed at that time, but it was looking promising and would probably eventuate around November/December that year. The timing was perfect: I'd be back from overseas by then. The few months off that I'd promised myself looked like becoming longer than I'd anticipated.

7

TALL SHIPS PILGRIMAGE

I had a couple of weeks at home with my partner and family before heading off to the UK and Europe on my "Tall Ships Pilgrimage", as Ken had christened it. While I wouldn't be taking part in any of the events as a crew member, I was still pretty excited about being able to see a Cutty Sark Tall Ships Race and, of course, the Sail Amsterdam event. I had only ever read about them.

The Cutty Sark races were started in the United Kingdom in the late 1950s by a group of enthusiasts who were afraid that graceful sailing ships of olden times would become a thing of the past, and that younger generations would never get the opportunity to see them. If some of the remaining ships could be gathered together in one place for a race, it was thought, this might generate some public interest and these ships might have a reinvigorated life.

As the name suggests, the Cutty Sark Scotch Whisky Company agreed to be the sponsor for the inaugural event, and it continued to do so until recently. The Sail Training Association has also been involved for many years. One of the rules of the race is that fifty per cent of the crew in each participating ship has to be under the age of twenty-five. This would guarantee interest among young people and also present new challenges to those who participated.

Initially these races were held every two years, but, as interest grew and more and more ships took part, they became more frequent and are now almost an annual event. They are nearly always held in the northern hemisphere, however, so I'd never had the opportunity to see one. Living in the Antipodes we often miss out on these types of events and, indeed, before the coming of the Internet and other modern forms of communication I sometimes didn't know about them until it was far too late even to think about taking part, as had been the case in 1992 when there'd been a huge event commemorating the five-hundredth anniversary of Christopher Columbus discovering America.

Sail Amsterdam is a gathering of tall ships and other sailing vessels hosted by the city of Amsterdam in Holland. This event had been held only once or twice when I became aware of it through sailing magazines, and it sounded as though it would be a fantastic sight. As I've mentioned, it was held every five years, so back in those days the two events only coincided once in a decade. The opportunity presented in 1995 was too good to miss.

Following an uneventful but very long flight I duly arrived at Heathrow. After Perth's relatively small airport I found it a bit overwhelming – in size and activity – and was heartily relieved when I saw the familiar sight of an English "bobby". As my intention was to catch a train up to Edinburgh, where the race was to start on this occasion, I approached the policeman to ask how to get from the airport to Kings Cross Station. He looked at me a bit strangely, as though I was perhaps taking the mickey out of him. And then it dawned on me: although I'd been away for many years, I still sounded Scottish. Quickly I explained that I'd been living in Australia since 1966 and things had changed a lot since then. I'd never actually been in Heathrow airport anyway, as I'd gone to Australia by ship.

He was very kind and helpful, and even found me a trolley for my luggage. Ten out of ten for London bobbies! Inevitably he had a Scottish cousin living in Melbourne, whom he thought I might know! It's amazing how people in the UK seem to think we might all know one another just because we were all British originally. They have no idea how big Australia is. He had a laugh when I explained that Melbourne was about three thousand kilometres from Perth. And, no, I didn't know his cousin.

Off I went to catch the train into Kings Cross Station. "How are you going to manage all that luggage on your own?" asked the policeman.

"Oh, I'll get a porter", I replied. When he stopped laughing he told me British Rail had stopped having porters years previously and wished me luck. It was about then that I realised I had far too much luggage with me. Not knowing what the weather was going to be, I had cold-weather gear for Scotland, hot-weather gear for Hong Kong, where I would be calling in on my way back, and my sailing gear, just in case I managed to get onto a ship. Plus I'd brought a load of *Endeavour* and *Leeuwin* badges and other bits and pieces to swap with other sailors I might meet.

Airport to Kings Cross was easily manageable, as I could take the airport trolley down into the underground station, but when I got to Kings Cross that would be another kettle of fish altogether. I would have to change levels in order to catch the Inter-City train that went up to Edinburgh. Sure enough, when I got off the airport train there wasn't a porter in sight. It was peak hour, and thousands of people were pouring off trains and hurrying off to work. Peak hour in the London Underground was something to behold.

I was standing to the side of the escalators out of the way of the scurrying hordes, contemplating how I was going to get all this gear of mine up two levels without a porter, when I was approached by a classic bowler-hatted, pinstripe-suited English gentleman, complete with rolled umbrella and newspaper tucked under his arm. "Can I be of some assistance, my dear?" he asked. I could have hugged him. Chivalry was alive and well. "Yes please", I replied, and told him I had to get up to ground level to catch the train to Edinburgh. "Are you going for some time?" he asked, looking at the luggage. My accent, again, had him fooled. More explanations about having just flown in from Australia ensued, and it transpired he also had a cousin in Melbourne!

Not only did he assist me up the escalators with the gear, he insisted on taking me for a cup of tea. While sharing our cups of tea and chatting, I learned that he was a barrister, no less, and loved to sail, so he was very interested in the reasons for my visit. Tea and toast consumed, he insisted on escorting me to the correct platform and helped me onto the train. I was very glad that I'd bought a Britrail ticket before leaving Australia and that I was in first class. (I had *never* travelled first class when I lived in Britain.) As the train pulled out he actually raised his bowler hat to me … what a positively charming English gent. If this was an indication of things to come, it augured well for the rest of the trip.

75

It's amazing what you forget when you've been away from somewhere for a long time. So many simple things that I would have taken for granted when I was a child, and which I had long since forgotten, presented themselves through the train windows as we travelled up to Edinburgh. The pitch of the house roofs was much steeper than I'd become used to in Perth, and many of them were shingled rather than tiled; then there were rows and rows of houses that all looked the same and all had chimneys, which is also unusual in Australia. Most of the sheep I saw had black faces; foxgloves, poppies, rosebay willow herb and convolvulus grew in profusion along all the railway embankments; and of course there were hills! Perth is a pretty flat place, so I hadn't seen real hills for quite a long time. Nostalgia had started to creep in; I'd forgotten how pretty British countryside can be.

At some stage on the journey, after we'd crossed the border into Scotland, a huge crater-like hole became evident at the side of the railway line. The steward happened to be in the carriage at the time, so I asked him what it was. He looked at me as though I'd been living on the moon and was some kind of inhuman creature. "Madam," he said, "this is Lockerbie." Oh dear, how could I not have guessed. I knew very well that Lockerbie was where a Pan American plane had been blown up in 1988 and had come down on the village, with dreadful loss of life. The explanation about living in Australia since 1966 had to be forthcoming again, or I'm sure I would have been chucked off the train at the first opportunity. I could see that my accent was going to get me into a bit of strife: people had no idea I hadn't been "local" for thirty years.

When I got to Edinburgh I phoned the woman with whom I was going to stay for a few days. She was the mother of a girl I'd previously had stay with me in Perth, so the favour was being returned although we didn't actually know one another. The hospitality she extended to me was absolutely fantastic, and furthermore her home was within walking distance of the town and the docks. My room even had a captain's bunk that had been made for her daughter many years before by a ship's carpenter. If that wasn't an omen of things to come, I don't know what could be.

I had a couple of days in town before the tall ships started arriving from all over the world, so had time to re-acquaint myself with the area and do a few touristy things such as visit Edinburgh castle and the Royal Mile. I discovered that there is a huge tourist market now for anything tartan or remotely Scottish, and that the buskers on most of the street corners are bagpipers in full Highland dress. I didn't remember any of that from my childhood. The town was in full swing, really gearing up for the arrival of the tall ships. The weather was absolutely glorious too, and no doubt that would have helped bring in the visitors. Scotland in the rain can be pretty miserable, as it seems to drizzle all day and it's grey and gloomy, dampening enthusiasm for outdoor activities. The word we used to describe it was *dreich*. I don't think I've ever found another that is quite so descriptive.

My hostess worked for BBC Scotland Radio. With all the excitement about the tall ships' imminent arrival, her colleagues were rather intrigued about the guest who had come all the way from Australia to see them, particularly when they discovered that I was Scots and had crewed on these types of vessels myself. Before I knew what was happening I found myself getting interviewed on the radio. "How to survive a force ten gale" was the topic, and I'm sure sailors who were about to board ships and head off into the North Sea didn't particularly want to hear about it. A bit like watching a movie about a plane crashing the day before you're getting on an aircraft.

The first of the ships to arrive at Edinburgh's port of Leith was *Kruzenshtern*, a large Russian full-rigged ship with four masts, the tallest of which, at 50 metres, was as high as a fifteen-storey building. She was 117 metres long and carried a crew of approximately four hundred, mostly cadets. I was absolutely agog. Over the next couple of days another hundred or so vessels would be berthing at Leith prior to the start of the race to Frederikshavn in Denmark. I was beside myself with excitement and looking forward to having a look over many of the ships, most of which would be open to the public before sailing.

Suddenly the weather took a turn for the worse, and a classic Scottish east coast *haar*, or sea mist, set in. We heard on the radio that there were dozens of ships held up in the Firth of Forth waiting for visibility to improve before they could get into their berths at Leith. In due course the *haar* cleared, and pretty soon all the ships were safely tied up. The whole dock area was a veritable forest of masts, but the most impressive in terms of size were the *Kruzenshtern* and another Russian square-rigger of similar size called *Sedov* – their masts towered over everything else.

My hostess and her daughter were working, and expressed some concern about me having to sightsee on my own. In fact it was probably just as well they *were* working: not being tall-ships fanatics they would have been bored silly after half a day, but I had a glorious time. First thing the next morning I was down at the docks. What a sight, well worth coming twenty thousand kilometres for – dozens and dozens of vessels tied up, most of them square-rig ships of differing rigs and sail plans, and many of them open to the public for inspection. I was like a child in a sweet shop: I didn't know where to begin.

I was deliberately wearing my *Endeavour* uniform – navy pants, cap and tee-shirt with the ship's logo emblazoned across the chest – and had a pocketful of cap badges from both the *Endeavour* and the *Leeuwin* to use as bribes or swaps. My thinking was that, if a particular ship, which I'd love to look around, wasn't open to the public, perhaps as a fellow sailor I could talk myself past the gangway guard. This worked beautifully, and I managed to get onto all sorts of ships that officially weren't open. Everyone was very interested in "my ships" and what they were doing in Australia. They also seemed impressed with the fact that I was interested enough in the whole scenario to have travelled all this way to see their ships.

Among the ships that were open to the public was the *Sedov*, and I joined a crowd of people boarding her. On the afterdeck was a group of young crewmen who looked as though they were about seventeen. "Gosh," I thought to myself, "these boys are all so young I could be their mother." I approached them to ask if we could have a photograph taken together. Alas, none of them spoke any English. I started trying to make myself understood, using Pidgin English and sign language. They got the bit about the photograph when I brought my camera out, but seemed at a loss to understand that I was trying to explain "This is my ship", gesturing at the picture of the *Endeavour* on my tee shirt.

Just then there appeared an older officer who spoke English. I explained to him about the *Endeavour*, and that I would love to have a photo taken with these lads. He turned and quickly translated to the boys, and they all smiled and nodded and gestured for me to get in among their group. Success! Then the officer explained how they had all been wondering why the *babushka* kept pointing at her bosoms. Oh dearie me, I was so embarrassed! I had been thinking I was old enough to be their mother and they referred to me as *babushka*! That's *grandmother* in Russian.

Some of the ships were selling raffle tickets to raise funds that would assist them with maintenance expenses. The first prize was a berth on the voyage from Leith to Frederikshavn. I bought heaps of tickets but wasn't lucky enough to win the prize. Never mind, the money would have gone to a good cause. These ships are very expensive to maintain, and one or two of them, particularly the Russian ones, were looking a little shabby. Since the collapse of the USSR their funding has almost dried up and it was very difficult for them to continue operating.

In contrast to *Kruzenshtern* and *Sedov* was a Portuguese bark called *Sagres II* that was absolutely magnificent. She belongs to the Portuguese Navy and is used as a training ship for naval cadets and trainee officers. Her complement is almost three hundred, so there were lots of willing hands to polish her brass, or "brightwork" as it is known on a ship. I'd never seen anything like it. All of her handrails, fife rails, stairs, ladders, cleats and belaying pins were brass, and they were gleaming! What a credit her presentation was to the crew. The almost eerie thing about being on this ship was that I already had a brass model of her, which I'd bought some years before in a little knick-knack shop in the Blue Mountains outside of Sydney – just because I liked it. I had no idea that it was a real ship, still sailing, and I certainly never dreamt that one day I would be on board her admiring all her brightwork. Life can be really strange sometimes.

The next few days I spent down at the docks, getting on anything and everything that I could and just drinking in the wonderful festive atmosphere. It was great to be able to talk to crews from the many different countries represented and share sailors' yarns. There were many static displays set up by the navy and other groups, photographic exhibits from previous Cutty Sark races and events taking place on the water, as well as sideshow tents, food stalls, samba bands and fireworks displays every evening. With the weather behaving itself as well, it was all absolutely glorious. The start day for the race was drawing nearer, however, so it would soon have to end. But first there would be a Parade of Sail on the Firth of Forth, involving all the vessels taking part.

As a thank-you for the radio interview I had done with BBC Scotland, my friend had managed to get me a ticket on a charter ferry that was taking a small group of people out to Inchcolm Island in the Firth of Forth, from where I could watch the Parade of Sail. The tiny island is home to the ruins of a 12th-century abbey and is under the management of the National Trust. Apart from the caretaker and his family it is uninhabited and generally fairly difficult to get to. I joined up with the group at North Queensferry and soon had a few companions with whom I could spend the day. They had heard my radio interview, so knew who I was.

The half-hour trip to the island was very interesting in itself, as we went under the famous Forth Bridge, built more than a hundred years ago. I used to throw pennies from the train window as a child when we went over that bridge. It was supposed to be lucky, and meant that you would come back again. All the times I'd done that I had never dreamt that I'd be back under these conditions, having come all the way from Australia. Nostalgia crept in again. It was refreshing to see that there were seals and puffins in the river, as I remember it being rather polluted. The environment had obviously improved since my childhood.

We had an hour or so on the island before the commencement of the Parade of Sail, so there was time to have a look around the ruins. They were in astonishingly good condition, given their age, and of course there's nothing like them in Australia. It was fascinating. I noticed a television crew heading up into the bell tower to set up their cameras to film the parade, and thought to myself, "If it's safe enough for them, it's safe enough for me". I went after them in hot pursuit. The spiral staircase we had to climb was so narrow that we had to ascend the steps sideways! I don't think there could have been any fat monks when the abbey was in use. From the next level there was a ladder leading up to the roof of the bell tower – not a problem to someone used to negotiating rigging on a moving ship.

What an incredible position from which to watch the parade. There were 360-degree views from up here, and even Edinburgh could be seen in the distance now that the earlier clouds had cleared. In the opposite direction was the Forth Bridge, which we had just come under and which was the limit of the route the ships would take before turning and heading back down the Forth towards the open sea. Not too many of the others seemed to want to venture up into the bell tower, so I had a completely clear view of the area where the ships would pass. This proved to be a great advantage when I started taking photographs.

To my great delight, I discovered that the ships would pass by only about two hundred metres away from Inchcolm Island, which no doubt was why the TV film crew had chosen it. There were other vantage points on both sides of the river but none of them would have afforded a view to match this. I silently blessed the radio interview, which I'd been a bit reluctant to do in the first place.

And then they started to appear, in the distance at first, having just negotiated their way out of the docks at Leith. They were led by the mighty *Kruzenshtern*, which, due to lack of wind and manoeuvring constraints, didn't have all of her sails up, but she was a magnificent sight nonetheless. Of course while the ships had been tied up at Leith all the sails had been furled, so it was fantastic seeing them under sail now. All the big ones I'd managed to have a look around were slowly passing by, interspersed with some of the smaller vessels. There hadn't been time to see absolutely everything, and I was planning to catch up with those I'd missed at Sail Amsterdam in Holland.

It took about five hours for them all to pass by, first heading for the bridge and then turning and going back down the river again. I was in seventh heaven, and shot off rolls and rolls of film. It was a little difficult to identify particular ships at times, but once I got the pictures back I was able to put names to most of them, as I could match up their rig or sail configuration with the literature I'd collected during the festival. *Alexander von Humboldt* was very easy to pick, as her sails were green, which is very unusual. I believe it had to do with Beck's Beer sponsoring her. It certainly made her very distinctive. Coming up at the rear of the parade was the other big Russian ship, the *Sedov*, and I thought about the young crew being unaware that the *babushka* was watching them from the bell tower of a ruined abbey. I related the story again to the TV crew, on the promise that they wouldn't include it in the broadcast.

It was quite late at night by the time I got home to my friend's house, tired but oh so happy. This had exceeded all my expectations a hundredfold. It had very definitely been worthwhile coming all the way from Australia for, and I still had Amsterdam to look forward to. I went to bed that night a very happy *babushka*.

The next day I said my farewells to Edinburgh and caught the train up to Aberdeen to meet up with some old friends and see where the *Malcolm Miller* and *Winston Churchill* were built. These ships, both of which I'd just seen at Leith, had ignited this craze of mine back in the 1960s, and it seemed appropriate that I should check out their birthplace. Then I headed back down the country again to visit an old school friend and her family in a little village called Alva in Clackmannanshire. No tall ships were involved in this part of the trip, but the tongues fairly wagged and old photographs got dragged out and much laughing and reminiscing went on. Her parents still lived in Helensburgh, the town where we grew up and went to school, and we drove across to see them. Unbeknown to me, my friend had already made tentative arrangements for us to visit our old primary school. This was literally where I'd grown up, as my father had been the school janitor and we lived in a house on the grounds. The building was no longer a school, however, being now used as a community centre.

It was nearly thirty years since I'd seen my old home, but it looked very much the same. The house was built in 1903, at the same time as the school, and was just as solid. The front door had been painted a different colour but the rest of it looked unchanged. Nostalgia really kicked in here. "Let's go into the school and have a look around", said my friend, pretending that she hadn't already arranged things with the caretaker. He made us very welcome and took us on a tour of the building. When he heard that my father had passed away in 1988 he insisted on giving me a horseshoe that had been in my dad's workshop to bring back to Australia for my mum. I was overwhelmed. Then he dragged out an old sled that had also been in the workshop and asked if it was mine. That was too much: I burst into tears. I didn't go into the house as my emotions were running so high by this stage that I didn't think I could have stood it.

We went back through to Alva and had another few days of talking, laughing, and walking in the hills in glorious weather. We even did a couple of touristy things like visiting Stirling Castle and the Wallace Monument. Thanks to the movie *Braveheart*, people other than Scots now know who the legendary William Wallace was. As kids we were taught about the Battle of Stirling Bridge in the 1700s and knew he was "the guardian of Scotland". The monument is some 180 metres high, with quite amazing views from the top and lots of interesting history within it. I saw Wallace's double-handed sword, the hilt of which was at the level of my nose. Wallace was supposedly over six feet according to the old measurement system , very tall for those days. I somehow couldn't imagine Mel Gibson wielding the weapon in the movie – perhaps they made him a smaller version. It was interesting that I viewed it all with different eyes now because I no longer lived in Scotland and because the movie had brought it to life for me. It wasn't just something to be tolerated in history class any more.

Then it was back to England to visit more old friends down in Manchester. We took the opportunity to spend a few days in the Lake District, an area that I'd never been to and so picturesque that I can scarcely begin to describe it. Again the weather was fantastic, which made the delightful villages full of hanging baskets of brightly coloured flowers seem even prettier. We stayed in a couple of classic English pubs with thatched roofs and ate steak-and-kidney pudding, and many of the little gift shops got raided for knick-knacks to bring home to Australia. My luggage was getting heavier by the week.

Another train took me down to Exeter to visit an elderly aunt and uncle in a village called Topsham. They had travelled to Southampton to see me off when I emigrated in 1966 and hadn't seen me since, so it was quite an emotional reunion. They remembered me as a teenager and had a huge laugh at the *babushka* story. When they realised that my interest in tall ships and maritime history was so strong, they promptly set about arranging visits to all sorts of interesting places in the vicinity. Among them were Sir Francis Drake's cottage, in the village of Topsham, and the Ship Inn, supposedly his favourite pub. It was built in 1587, the year before the famous Armada, so that could well have been the case. Its sign carried a picture of his ship, *The Golden Hind*. Although I had no way of knowing it at the time, I was to cross paths with Drake again much later – on the other side of the world and from an entirely different perspective. History can be very interesting, especially when the threads of stories go back as far as they do in Britain and Europe.

Many of the houses in Topsham village showed a distinctly Dutch influence, which I found especially intriguing given that I was about to head for Holland. Apparently, many years ago Topsham used to be quite a thriving port and much of its trade was with Holland. Many Dutch merchants had agents based in the village to oversee the cargoes, hence the flavour of the architecture. Thankfully, many of these houses are preserved for posterity under the auspices of the National Trust.

Next there was Portsmouth with its naval museum, one of the best maritime museums I've seen. There are dozens of ships' figureheads and other interesting artefacts, but the main drawcards are the ships. Among them are Nelson's *Victory*, which is still a commissioned ship of the Royal Navy, Queen Victoria's flagship, *Warrior*, and part of the remains of the *Mary Rose*, King Henry's flagship. Also on display is *Gypsy Moth IV*, in which Sir Francis Chichester did the first single-handed circumnavigation of the world – though she's a boat as opposed to a ship! Still worth looking at and marvelling at his achievement though.

Victory was absolutely overwhelming. A 74-gun ship of the line carrying a complement of over 860 men, she was much, much bigger than the *Endeavour*. We weren't allowed to wander around at will or take photographs on board, so I had to content myself with a formal guided tour and buy some postcards of below decks, including the famous spot on the orlop deck where Admiral Nelson died. You could take pictures from dockside, so I shot off a couple of rolls of film of all the rigging, carvings, figurehead etc. Not for the first time, I got a bit carried away.

HMS *Warrior* was the first and last ironclad battleship of Queen Victoria's time. To my eyes she looked a little strange – being both sail and steam propelled, she had masts *and funnels*. I had a special interest in her because I knew the historian who had been responsible for fitting out her interior – the same one who had overseen the fitting-out of the interior of the *Endeavour*. It seemed that our little ship had had one of the best in the world looking after her interests, ensuring historical authenticity with a relentless eye for detail. If it couldn't be authenticated from paintings or documents or some other source, it had not been included as part of the *Endeavour*'s museum mode, whatever the article might have been. I was very impressed with *Warrior*'s interior, and could understand now how lucky we had been to have this lady and her expertise involved with the *Endeavour*.

Mary Rose had been at the bottom of the Solent for over four hundred years, so had had to be treated very carefully when her wreck was raised in 1982 to avoid oxygenation occurring in the timbers. When I saw her she was in a special isolated shed where she was continuously sprayed with polyethylene glycol to keep her timbers wet. The danger if they dry out too quickly is that they would crack and disintegrate, and it was estimated that this process would need to be continued for another fifteen to twenty years in order to preserve her forever. There were drawings and schematics on the walls of the shed indicating what activity would have taken place in which bit of the ship, and you didn't need to use your imagination too much to get a picture in your mind's eye of how things must have been.

Another museum exhibit was a special display about the *Titanic*. Having sailed from Southampton on the anniversary of her sinking, I had a special interest in her beyond the interest that her brief tragic history has for everyone. Ironically, many of the exhibits from the display were on loan to the Maritime Museum of Western Australia at the time. The woman at the cashier's desk could hardly believe it when I told her where I'd come from and that the items hadn't been in Fremantle when I'd left a few weeks previously. It seemed that we'd crossed in transit, and I'd have to wait until I got home again to catch up with them.

My last "shippy" visit in the United Kingdom was to the *Cutty Sark*, one of the fastest and most famous clippers of her time, now on a hardstand at Greenwich. Like the *Victory* she is open to the public, but unlike the case with the *Victory* you do not have to join a formal tour. The guides are happy for you to wander around at your own pace. I ended up spending the whole day on her, as there was so much to see and absorb. She was built in 1869 in Dumbarton in Scotland, and I've always felt for her a special affection that comes from our both having been "born" in the same place. Her name comes from lines in the well-known poem "Tam O'Shanter" by Scotland's bard, Rabbie Burns, as does the image of her figurehead: a young woman with an arm outstretched clutching the tail of Tam's horse as he fled from the witches' coven.

We all learned this poem at school, so I couldn't stop myself from quoting the lines. "Her cutty sark, o' Paisley harn, that as a lassie she had worn, in longitude tho' sorely scantie, it was her best, and she was vauntie." The whole poem is in broad Scots so most people don't understand it, but the guide who heard me did and was most impressed. Inevitably we got chatting, and I told him of my involvement with the *Leeuwin* and the *Endeavour*, also that I'd been born in Dumbarton and had come all the way from Australia to see *Cutty Sark* (OK, among other things). Before I knew it I was taken below decks to the mess and introduced to the officers of the watch, and had a grand tour of all sorts of places that were normally off limits. They were all interested in hearing about the *Leeuwin* and the *Endeavour*, and asked me to come back the next day and bring the photographs and memorabilia I had with me. I was only too happy to oblige.

When I returned I discovered that a few phone calls had been made during the previous evening, with the result that a small but interested audience had gathered to hear my tales about the *Endeavour*'s construction and my experience of sailing on her. *Cutty Sark* has a small cannon on her weather deck that fires the one o'clock gun every day, an old naval tradition, and I was invited to ignite the fuse and fire the gun that day. A mouth-watering afternoon tea had been laid on in the mess, complete with the traditional scones and jam and cream: they couldn't have been more welcoming or hospitable. The *pièce de résistance* came after tea, however. They presented me with an original bolt from a section of the ship's hull that was under renovation at the time. I could hardly believe it. To most people it would just be a rusty old bolt, but it's now among my most treasured possessions.

My luggage by now was totally ridiculous. As I'd visited all these ships, maritime museums and other places of interest to me, I'd collected heaps of brochures and other souvenirs along the way. Now I'd just added to the weight with a huge rusty iron bolt – and I still had Amsterdam and Hong Kong to visit. I packaged up all my jumpers and heavier clothing, and the sailing gear that I hadn't had the chance to use, and sent them home in the post. Amsterdam, here I come.

I flew out from London on 10 August, in time to be in Amsterdam for the Tall Ships Parade of Sail up the North Sea Canal into the IJ Harbour. I'd booked myself into a youth hostel at Vondel Park for the time I planned to be there, but on arrival discovered there had been some mix-up and I didn't have a bed for that night or for the last two nights. And the city was full – some four million were in town for Sail Amsterdam, whereas it normally has a population of around 1 million. I had visions of sleeping at the airport or in Vondel Park itself, and was a bit anxious about it all given Amsterdam's reputation for drugs and hookers. I left the hostel people to see what they could sort out and went off in search of a coffee shop. That was my first mistake. In Amsterdam "coffee shops" are where you go to get marijuana. This one even had a menu of different varieties from which you could select. *Cafés* are where you go for coffee.

My anxiety must have been apparent to the hostel people. By the time I got back everything had miraculously been sorted out and I had a bed for the duration of my visit, albeit in a mixed dormitory. This was another interesting experience, but one that bothered me less than it would have before I'd got used to communal sleeping on board the *Endeavour*. With its four double bunks and its own shower and toilet, this dormitory was much more salubrious than any on board ship. I felt a bit like the "den mother", as I was by far the oldest one there. When some of my roommates discovered I had come for Sail Amsterdam, though, I became just one of the mob: they had also come for the event. The majority of us were sailors – and some spoke Dutch, which would obviously be useful.

We had a couple of days before the ships were due in, so had time to do a bit of sightseeing before getting immersed in "shippy" stuff again, although one of the places on the list of sights to see included the Maritime Museum, which is fabulous. They had a sail-loft set up there, and blacksmithing demonstrations, so you could observe how the old sails and fittings were made. They also had a wonderful Dutch musical group singing sea shanties and other songs, most of which I knew. They encouraged the audience to join in with clapping and dancing at appropriate places, and I was right into that. It didn't seem to matter one whit that I was singing in English and they were singing in Dutch. It

87

was a great afternoon, and an indication of the atmosphere that I would soon discover permeating the whole Sail Amsterdam event.

On the morning of the Parade of Sail I took myself down to the side of the North Sea Canal to find a good viewing spot. I was armed with sandwiches, fruit, coffee, water and camera, with rolls and rolls of film, and ready to spend as long as it took to see everything. The people at the hostel had told me where to go, and that it would take most of the day for all the ships to come down the canal and get tied up in the harbour. I thought they had been exaggerating, but when I bought the official programme I discovered there were over a thousand vessels taking part. I had thought that the Parade of Sail in Scotland was spectacular, but this was going to be in a league of its own.

The weather was perfect. Thousands upon thousands of people gathered all the way along both sides of the canal. Anything that could float was on the water to escort the ships during their passage into the harbour, and some of these craft were very amusing. Blow-up things that were really intended for use in swimming pools; all sorts of rafts with trucks, huge blow-up mobile phones, barrels of Heineken beer and other structures perched precariously on them; a craft made out of empty plastic drink bottles – imaginations had certainly been working overtime. I even saw a tiny one-man kayak with a plastic milk crate fixed on top of its "nose". A man was paddling the kayak and his dog was in the milk crate, and I got the distinct impression that it wasn't the first time the dog had been there. But the one that really took my fancy was a powerboat about five metres long, the hull of which had been made to look like a giant Dutch clog. It was brilliant.

A huge barge with a samba band and dancing girls on it came by. I was beginning to realise that samba bands had become something of a tradition at tall-ship festivals. They certainly livened up the crowd during waiting times. Dutch lee-boarders were plentiful, together with many tiny steam tugs beautifully decorated with hundreds of flowers. There was a competition among the tugs for the best decorated, and the owners vied for the honour with great flair. By the time the first of the ships were due to arrive the atmosphere had become quite electric.

And here she was – being towed by tugs, it's true, but nevertheless a wonderful replica of a 17th-century VOC East Indiaman called

Amsterdam. It was certainly fitting that she led the parade. She is normally tied up at the Maritime Museum, where I had been a couple of days before, so I had seen her already and been on board. (I was surprised to see her, though, as they hadn't told me she would be leading the parade.) Then many of the square-riggers I had encountered in Leith started to come through. They were interspersed with others I had not seen before, one of which was a Dutch barque called the *Europa*, which looked beautiful. I didn't know it at the time, but I was to cross paths with her again some years later. There were many other vessels that were not square-rigged, but still came into the "tall ship" category due to their size. There was even a replica of a 14th-century trireme, which I'd never seen before.

It took most of the day for all the ships to come by the spot I'd picked, and I truly had not known that there were so many of these ships in the world. The finale to the parade was the almost finished replica of the *Batavia*, which had been under construction for about ten years. Not all of her sails had yet been rigged, and she was under tow, but it was still amazing to see her. The original *Batavia*, wrecked off the West Australian coast during her maiden voyage in 1629, gave rise to one of the most extraordinary shipwreck stories in Australian history. Some of her hull and artefacts, which have been retrieved from the wreck site, are on display at the Shipwreck Galleries of the Western Australian Maritime Museum. While I was in Holland, and if I had the time, I had planned on going to Lilystaad to see the replica that I knew was being built, and now here she was, right before my eyes. It really had been the most incredible day. Indeed, it would turn out to be the most incredible five days, as most of the ships would be open for inspection and there were all kinds of activities taking place in, on and around the harbour.

There were fireworks displays every night, all choreographed to appropriate music. Even the barges from which the fireworks were let off moved – they *waltzed* for goodness' sake. There were buskers performing and street theatre happening all over the area, and lots of groups provided music for free-for-all dancing. At the food stalls I discovered *pofferjets*, tiny pancakes with butter and icing sugar, and *varmen hammen brodgievinkels*, or hot ham rolls, and learned that the Dutch put mayonnaise on their French fries. That was different. I had grown up with vinegar on chips, and in Australia lots of people put tomato sauce on chips, but I'd never come across chips with mayonnaise before.

I'd chummed up with a couple of ladies at the hostel by this time, and we spent several happy days wandering around the harbour drinking in all these festivities and enjoying the general camaraderie and good cheer that seemed to abound everywhere. The crowds were huge, and we often had to queue to get on board ships, but no-one seemed to mind. Amsterdam had really come alive, and the weather remained gloriously sunny all week. I had such a good time that I determined not to try and do it again in five years' time: I didn't think anything could top it. Past experience had taught me that sometimes when you try to recapture something the second time around you are disappointed. "The only thing that could beat this", I thought, "would be coming back as a crew member on one of these ships." That proved to be a very prophetic thought, as in the year 2000 I would indeed be back – crewing!

All too soon the ships sailed out again and headed off to continue their various voyages or return to homeports. I flew out to Hong Kong, my last stop before going home, where I had a cousin I hadn't seen for twenty-five years. My luggage by now was grossly over my weight allowance, but the KLM people at Schipol Airport were kind enough to overlook the excess, as the plane wasn't full. I had a fabulous few days in Hong Kong as a tourist rather than a tall-ship devotee. We still managed to fit in a bit of sailing on a Chinese junk, and I saw Hong Kong's tall ship, the *Ji Foong*. At that time the captain was a Canadian chap I'd already sailed with on the *Leeuwin*, and a few years later he ended up back in Western Australia as *its* captain. Looking back on my seafaring adventures now, it's interesting to notice how often I've crossed paths with the same people on different ships in different parts of the world.

My chickens came home to roost when I checked in at Hong Kong airport to fly home. Because I have dual nationality, I use two passports when travelling, either Australian or British, whichever is the more appropriate at the time. I'd flown out of Australia on my Aussie passport, which meant I would have to go back in on that one. I'd used my British passport to get stamped in to Hong Kong, as it was still a British colony at the time, so I had to leave Hong Kong on my British passport, but it didn't have a re-entry visa for Australia in it, which caused some confusion.

"I can't let you on the plane", said the little Chinese girl at the desk. "You no have re-entry permit for Australia."

"I don't need one. I have an Australian passport."

"Oooooh", said the Chinese girl. "No permitted have two passports."

"It is in my country."

"Let me see", she said. I handed over my Aussie passport. She spent some time examining both it and my British one. My heart was thudding a bit, and I started getting a bit anxious. The queue of people waiting to check in behind me was getting longer and more restless by the minute.

"One moment please", she said, and disappeared off somewhere to find her supervisor.

After some time she reappeared with her supervisor in tow. I explained the whole thing again as pleasantly as I could, though I must admit I was getting a bit rattled. Surely this scenario had presented itself before – I personally know *lots* of people in Australia who have dual nationality and two passports. Eventually the supervisor agreed everything was in order, and told the check-in girl to get me processed and onto the plane. By this time she was very flustered, embarrassed and unhappy.

"Baggage", she snapped, indicating that I should put it on the scale.

Oh dear, I thought, knowing full well it was very, very overweight. The KLM people had been kind to me, but this plane was full. I didn't get away with it here. All the stuff I'd collected ended up costing me $HK300 – about $A100 – in excess baggage. I learned a very important lesson that day: don't hassle a check-in clerk at an airport. Especially if they are Chinese and your actions could have them losing face.

I arrived back in Perth on 22 August very tired, very broke but very, very happy. I had rolls and rolls of films to get developed and memories to last a lifetime. It took me quite some time to get the photographs into albums, caption them and intersperse cuttings from newspapers and other literature I'd collected along the way. Rather than being a chore, however, it was a pleasant way of reliving everything all over again. The only problem was that the briny in my veins was stirring once more. I had a hankering to get back to sea, preferably on the *Endeavour*. I put my application in for the Sydney – New Zealand voyage, and found another job while I waited to see what would happen.

8

SYDNEY TO NEW ZEALAND

There were about four months between my return from the Tall Ships Pilgrimage and when the *Endeavour* was scheduled to undertake her voyage from Sydney to New Zealand, so I had time to work for a while. This would help to replenish my hugely depleted coffers. The three months off that I'd promised myself before looking for another permanent job had become much longer than that anyway, so perhaps it was time I settled down again. This proved to be more difficult than I had imagined, and I was really itching to get back to sea.

The trip to New Zealand would be the *Endeavour*'s maiden international voyage, so that was a huge temptation in itself, as I'd been on her maiden voyage out of Fremantle the year before. This voyage was being underwritten by TV New Zealand, and they had the rights to television footage, clothing endorsements and so forth. It had been agreed between the Endeavour Foundation and TVNZ that half of the voyage crew on this occasion would be Kiwis and half would be Australian. This meant that the number of available places to be allocated to the Aussies would be fewer than when I had sailed on her before. I wondered about the odds of getting on.

To my great delight I got a phone call from Sydney early one morning to tell me that I had been allocated a berth – if I was still interested. Of course I was still interested. There were only two of us from Western Australia going on as voyage crew, so I felt pretty honoured to have been chosen. I knew Simon, the other West Aussie who'd been selected, from previous voyages and ship-keeping on the *Endeavour*. There was one other West Australian joining as navigator in the professional crew.

I knew *of* him, as he had been the *Leeuwin*'s port warden in Bunbury for many years, but we hadn't actually met and had never sailed together before. At least that's what I thought at the time. It would prove not to be the case, although it took us quite a few days to figure out where our paths had crossed.

The phrase "trip of a lifetime" was beginning to wear a bit thin at home by now, but each time I went off somewhere I truly thought it would be *the* trip of a lifetime. When I went for that very first whale-watching weekend on the *Leeuwin* in 1989 I had no idea that I would still be "messing about in boats" years later. I've always had the attitude that when an opportunity presents itself it should be grabbed and maximised. After all, none of us know what may be around the corner in terms of breakdowns in health, changes in financial status or other dramas that life may throw at us, so I very much believed in "going for it". This was another one of those opportunities that just couldn't be passed up.

I flew in to Sydney a few days early so that I could catch up with friends and relatives before I headed off into the watery wide blue yonder again. Even they were beginning to tease me about the "trip of a lifetime" now.

On the appointed day I duly reported to the officer of the watch. I knew a number of the permanent crew already, as many of them had been with the *Endeavour* during the Queensland trip earlier in the year, but the voyage crew would all prove to be new to me, except for Simon, my fellow West Aussie. We were allocated into different watches though, so only saw one another at watch changeover times or occasions when more than one watch was working together. That was OK, as it meant we both got to make new friends in our respective watches.

I was in mizzen-mast watch this time, and my captain o' tops was a lad called Peter, with whom I hadn't sailed before. Sure enough, the watch was made up of half Kiwis, one of whom was Maori, and half Aussies. They all turned out to be great fun. There were four girls (I include myself in that category – loosely), and we became as thick as thieves during the trip. One with whom I "clicked" instantly was Adelia, the same Adelia I told of meeting in Wellington at the end of my *Endeavour* trip from Vancouver.

We all had to join the ship a couple of days before departure, as there was much to be done. She had been on display in Sydney for some time, and gear that would be needed for sailing had been taken off and stored in a warehouse while she was in exhibition mode. It all had to be put back on board and the stores and victuals had to be loaded for the voyage. We made many trips back and forward to this warehouse, which was more than a kilometre away from the ship, among other things humping lengths of heavy rope like giant snakes spread out across our shoulders. We got some very funny looks from passers-by. It was unseasonably hot in Sydney, and we were all sweating profusely and drinking gallons of water. The Kiwis, used to a somewhat cooler climate, were really feeling it.

Adelia was a journalist with the *New Zealand Herald* at the time, and had more or less been sent by her newspaper to cover the event. The idea was that she would write a daily column on board and use satellite technology to send it to her paper, which in turn would print it every day. By the time we arrived in Auckland, then, people would have been reading about shipboard events for ten to twelve days. It was assumed that this would generate a great deal of interest, encouraging crowds of people to come down to the docks and welcome us in, and ultimately visit the ship in exhibition mode. Good for Adelia, good for the paper, and good for the ship.

I can vividly recall poor Adelia just about passing out with the heat during our trips back and forth to the warehouse that day and, close to tears, saying to me "What the hell am I *doing* here?" It certainly wasn't what she expected when she left Auckland.

"Trust me", I said. "I've been on the *Endeavour* before. It'll get better." Needless to say it did. Eventually everything had been loaded on board and stowed, the exhibition artefacts had been dismantled and packed up, and we were just about ready to go. The excitement had been building for a day or so by now and exhaustion from the "warehouse humping" (as we had christened it, somewhat tongue-in-cheek) was already forgotten.

Before we left for Auckland there were a couple of other activities to be taken care of, one of them being a special corporate day-sail in Sydney Harbour scheduled for the day before we left. This looked like being quite a good thing from our point of view, as it would allow the new crew the chance to test their skills at line handling, going aloft and furling before we went out into the open sea. And it would give everyone the chance to settle in a bit more. It would also give some of the sponsors and other VIPs on board for the day a taste of what the ship was all about, which could only be good in the long run.

The other activity was something a little different. A book launch was taking place one evening at Government House and, because the book was about maritime events and early Sydney pioneering history, it had been decided to have the *Endeavour* riding at anchor in Farm Cove, near Government House, as a "background prop" so to speak. We motor-sailed around from Darling Harbour and dropped anchor at the appointed spot.

Having been invited to attend the book launch, the captain was rowed ashore in the ship's pinnace wearing his full dress uniform. The pinnace crew had to wait for him while he did the required amount of socialising and the rest of us stayed on board the ship. Before he went ashore, he'd left instructions about firing the ship's cannons as part of the launch formalities. When the appointed time came the cannons were fired, all four of them. We discovered afterwards, to our unmitigated glee I might add, that they set off all the alarms at Government House and the security people in the place got into a bit of a state. The captain realised it was probably the cannons that had been the culprit, but discreetly said nothing and quietly slipped off back to the ship. We loved it! The guns had often had the same effect on car alarms before, but setting off the security alarms at Government House was a new dimension indeed.

The morning of 28 November dawned bright and clear, deceptively bright and clear as it turned out. As the morning progressed, big black clouds began to gather, and it became obvious we were in for a downpour – it was just a question of when. The crowd that gathered to see us off included several Sydney VIPs, sponsors, the Town Crier, a band, all of the Sydney volunteer guides and a contingent of their Fremantle counterparts who had travelled over for the occasion, as well as many members of the public.

Notable among the crowd, however, was a contingent of the Sydney Maori community, in traditional dress, who performed a *haka* for us and sang a famous Maori farewell song, "Po Kari Kari Anna". Another striking group was a class of schoolchildren who were all in 18th-century costume. They had been studying Cook and the *Endeavour* that term, and had each taken on the role of one of the original characters from Cook's famous voyage. They looked absolutely splendid. I had a nasty feeling their costumes were at risk of being ruined.

Then the heavens opened. We rushed to grab our wet-weather gear and donned it quickly. Most of the people on the dock didn't even have an umbrella, and everyone got soaked to the skin. The Town Crier had trouble getting his bell to "dong" and had to abandon trying to read from his parchment notes. Anyway he managed to carry on very convincingly without them. The feather on his hat got very bedraggled-looking, though, much to my amusement.

The weather didn't seem to dampen anyone's enthusiasm, as most people stayed until we had the lines out to the longboats and had started to move. We were being rowed off the wharf, as used to happen sometimes in the old days, using the ship's pinnace and other boats from local rowing clubs. All the rowers were in 18th-century costume and it all looked wonderful. "Hang on a minute," I thought, "I know one of those blokes." It was Dave, with whom I'd sailed from Bundaberg to Mackay back in June.

He yelled up to me that he couldn't do the voyage, but that he "wouldn't have missed this for quids". Here was yet another individual who had travelled from their home interstate to take part in this historic occasion. The *Endeavour* was weaving her magic spell again.

Amazingly enough, Marian, one of the Fremantle guides who was there, hadn't planned on being in Sydney at this time. What happened was that she'd booked a "mystery flight" as a treat, and it turned out to be a flight to Sydney for two on the very day that the *Endeavour* was leaving for New Zealand. She couldn't believe her luck, and thoroughly enjoyed seeing my astonished face when she turned up at the gangway and asked for me. We have never tried to figure out the odds of that happening, but they surely must have been huge. She planned to see us off from Darling Harbour and then race down to the Opera House to watch us go by.

On a different occasion Marian booked another mystery flight that turned out to be a trip to Cooktown, where Captain Cook had careened the original ship to repair it after he'd run aground on the Great Barrier Reef. Not only was it a trip to Cooktown, it happened to be on the day that the local community was doing a re-enactment of Cook's landing. This is one lucky lady! We have since often speculated privately and very tongue-in-cheek over whether Captain Cook's spirit might have had a hand in these mystery flight arrangements.

Slowly we pulled away from the dock, threaded our way out of Darling Harbour and headed for Port Jackson proper. Inevitably we had to fire a few cannons off, and the bangs echoed off the city buildings gloriously. (We never did find out if they set off the Government House alarms again.) If there were some people who hadn't had the time to come down to see us off, they would certainly know by now that we were on our way.

We had a small flotilla of boats escorting us out and there were a lot of people on the Harbour Bridge waving and cheering as we went under it. I was on the helm at that point and waved back, thinking to myself, Is this a dream or what? Who would ever have thought that one day I'd be at the helm of Captain Cook's ship taking her under the Sydney Harbour Bridge and heading for New Zealand! I peered through the diminishing light trying to find my mystery flight friend Marian as we passed the Opera House, but wasn't able to pick her out in the thickening gloom. Anyway I knew she would be waving and wishing us fair winds.

As soon as we went through the Heads we got into the ocean swell and a few people started feeling a little green around the gills. Past experience had shown us that most of the people who become seasick get over it in a couple of days, and one of the best ways to handle it is to keep busy and stay on deck. I was OK – again! I've been very lucky in that regard: *mal de mer* has got me on only a couple of occasions, and then only very slightly. It must be the salt water in my veins I think.

The Tasman Sea has a reputation for being very rough at times, so we weren't quite sure what it would throw at us. Having been through the storm on the way from Fremantle to Albany, however, I wasn't in the least bit concerned. I had supreme confidence in the ship now, and always have had in the captain (particularly) and crew. I once told Chris I'd be willing to sail around Cape Horn with him, and he laughed and said, "You'd be going yourself, because I'm not", but he knew I meant it as a compliment. I came off the helm and off watch, and happily settled down in my hammock. With a bit of luck when we turned to the next morning, we would be out of sight of land. That's when I really liked being at sea.

Sure enough, when we got up on deck the next morning all we could see was the sea. My sailor's heart sang. We settled into the watch routines, got allocated some maintenance tasks, and began to get to know one another better. I discovered that I was in a watch with a real fun group of people, or perhaps mischievous might be a better word. As the trip progressed, it always seemed to be mizzen-mast watch that had initiated whatever fun and games had been taking place. Much of it was silly nonsense, really, but it was fun at the time.

One day, when we were the duty watch on deck, the relieving watch turned to on the poop and discovered all ten of us were gathered around the helm, each with a hand on it. "What are you guys all doing?" they asked.

"We're the steering committee", we said. Oh ho, very bloody funny! The next day, when they came to relieve us we were all there again. This time, however, the girls were sitting on the lads' shoulders and we were all standing at attention at the helm.

"All right, what are you supposed to be today?" was the question.

"We're the standing steering committee", we replied. Groans all round: the humour was getting worse.

A couple of days after that the watches had changed, and we would be taking over the duty watch around sunset. In the meantime we had found some balsa-wood pirates' cutlasses in the bosun's store during our maintenance work, and had commandeered them for just such an occasion. We got ourselves done up like pirates, with black eye patches and painted-on scars, and crawled along the deck on our bellies in the shadows, hiding behind whatever was available to avoid being seen by the duty watch.

Suddenly we leapt up out of nowhere, all "aaarghing" like pirates supposedly do, and took over the bridge. We had a cutlass to the throat of the helmsman, and one to the throat of the watch officer. It was great! We frightened the life out of them momentarily, not to mention a couple of other people nearby. And then everyone fell about laughing.

We became known as the "Mizzen Mast Mongrels" and our captain o' tops was "the Mongrel master". I understand that for a long time after that trip every mizzen-mast watch was nicknamed the "Mizzen Mast Mongrels" – but we were the originals!

One night the watch officer was the "other" West Australian, the man from Bunbury. We got chatting about how we'd both been involved with the *Leeuwin* for many years, but had never actually met one another, never mind sailed together. As the night progressed and we chatted a bit more, however, we came to realise that in fact we had sailed together, although it hadn't been on the *Leeuwin*. It transpired that, thirty-four years previously, when I had been a schoolgirl on board the *Dunera*, Clyde had been a junior officer! Neither of us remembered the other, but we had lots to reminisce and yarn about.

Next morning we all had a very rude awakening from slumber. Whichever was the duty watch between 4 and 8 am often had the privilege of selecting the music from the ship's CD collection that would be played over the loudspeakers to wake us up. Sometimes other things like bugle calls got played rather than music, and one morning there was the sound of someone snoring really, really noisily. Yes, we had a bit of fun with the wake-up calls. The morning after Clyde and I realised that we had both been on the *Dunera* in 1961 there came blazing over the loudspeakers an old rock 'n' roll number called "Reveille Rock". It was what had been used to wake us up on board the *Dunera*, so I knew this had been done for my benefit and just about fell out of my hammock laughing. Everyone else was wondering what I was chortling about and muttering, "Where on earth did they dig *that* up from?" As the day went on Clyde and I explained to others what it was all about, and they shared our incredulity that we should have met up again after so many years, and on the other side of the world.

We settled into our normal sea routine of watches, maintenance, eating and sleeping, with sail-handling talks, history lectures, knot classes and some sort of entertainment most evenings. Life on board a sailing ship is pretty simple really. While the captain still dealt with things like short-wave radios, GPS and satellite phones and weather faxes, we didn't have mobile phones or laptops with us (except for Adelia, who was writing pieces for her newspaper). I always thought that it was wonderful to leave all the paraphernalia of the 20th century ashore, where it belonged in my opinion. After all, Captain Cook wouldn't have had all these gadgets and gizmos.

New skills were learned, like how to patch and mend seams on sails using a curved needle, a sail-maker's palm and waxed thread. That was something I really enjoyed and seemed to have a bit of a flair for. It was to come in useful a few years later, in fact, at another time and on another ship. We also learned a lot about Maori culture courtesy of our shipmates.

Craig, who was in our watch, was a policeman from Gisborne, and Graham, in another watch, was from Auckland. His tribe would be the major welcoming group when we arrived, and they would be coming out to meet us in a thirty-metre *waka* or Maori war canoe. This sounded like it was going to be huge. The lads told us it was inevitable that a *haka* would be performed, and it would be nice if the *Endeavour* crew could reciprocate. Only men take part in a *haka*, so Craig and Graham took on the task of teaching the rest of the male crew the appropriate words and movements, much to the interest of the watching ladies.

Normally Craig was a joy to be around, as he had the wonderful ability to see humour in everyday things and generally had everyone around him laughing too. When it came to the *haka* lessons, however, he was very strict and very respectful of the solemnity of its proper performance. I'm sure some of the lads thought he was quite a hard taskmaster. The watching ladies could see it improving day by day and were getting quite impressed – although we didn't tell the lads that at the time.

Another chap who was a joy to be around was Slade, one of the crew with whom I'd sailed several times before. He had a nice touch with a practical joke, as the following story will reveal.

Sometimes, if it looked as though there might be a good sunset in the evening, for example, you would bring your camera up on deck in readiness for it. If you then got called upon to go aloft and furl sail, you would tuck your camera into a nook or cranny – some "safe place" – while you laid aloft and worked. Or you thought it was a safe place ...

Many a photograph of a paint pot or a blob of tar on the deck or someone's big toe or a close-up of an eye (but whose?) materialised

SYDNEY TO NEW ZEALAND

when films were developed later. The owner of the camera would have no idea how it got there. Slade would have quietly and unobtrusively removed the camera from its safe place, taken some whimsical nonsense picture and then equally quietly and unobtrusively put it back. The owners of the cameras, who were all busily working aloft and paying attention to what they were doing at the time, wouldn't have a clue until their films were developed. Obviously this was before the days of digital cameras: it wouldn't work now. Those of us who knew what he was up to thought it was hilarious, and had many a giggle together imagining the photographers' faces when they got their prints back. Even though I knew about the game he was playing, he had the last laugh: ultimately I found a close-up photo of deck-scrubber bristles on one of my own films. Good one mate!

The weather proved to be very kind to us on the crossing. We discovered later that we had crossed the Tasman in one of the highest high-pressure systems that had been recorded in years. Consequently, we had glorious sunrises and sunsets and some wonderful moonlit nights, and one night we even had fog – thick, thick fog, the likes of which I hadn't seen in years. We don't get much fog where I live in Perth, but I'd certainly grown up with it outside of Glasgow. "Pea-soupers" we used to call them.

I could remember being in Glasgow one day when you literally couldn't see the other side of the road, and all the buses and taxis had stopped operating. I'd had to feel my way along the street by running my hand on the walls of buildings. If you wanted to cross the street in such a thick fog, you would get into a big group with other pedestrians – a bigger group just might be more visible to the few cars and lorries still on the road.

This was like one of those. We had lookouts up the rigging and all over the ship in addition to our normal bow and stern lookouts. We blew our foghorn regularly. We were in the open sea with commercial shipping that travelled much faster than the *Endeavour* and was much bigger than her. Wooden ships don't show up on the radar quite as clearly as steel vessels either, so we were quite vulnerable. Interesting stuff, fog. Although there was no rain, when we went below we were all quite wet just from the moisture it contained.

101

While we were obviously vulnerable, when I came off watch and turned in I was mentally back in my little bed in Helensburgh recalling things I hadn't thought about in years. In winter months Mum used to light the coal fire in my room, and when the fogs were bad I would lie and listen to the foghorns of the ships on the Clyde. I would be all tucked in and warm and cosy and safe, with embers of the fire glowing and casting interesting shadows on the ceiling. I fell asleep (in spite of the foghorn!) with this image in my head and dreamed lovely childhood dreams.

We were about halfway across the Tasman by now, and so well on our way to New Zealand. We'd begun to notice the phosphorescence in the water, which was mesmerising and very pretty. One night when we were aloft furling sail, a huge pod of Pacific dolphins passed us by. As they frolicked and leapt out of the waves, the moonlight caught the phosphorescence of the water as it sprayed out behind their backs. If you ever saw the movie *Peter Pan* as a child, it will make sense if I say it looked just like the fairy dust that Tinkerbell used to wave around to enable people to fly. It was a magical sight.

The voyage continued pretty uneventfully, with light airs, fairly calm seas and more glorious sunrises and sunsets. Very often at night there would be lots of shooting stars, sometimes of different colours. It was great to be alive! Being on the helm was a wonderful experience and, in such light weather, she was fairly easy to steer. What is also fairly easy, however, is to lose your course due to the influence of the currents, so you need to pay close attention to what you're doing.

A fun "penalty" had been imposed if you were more than five degrees off course. One of the watch officers had a particular liking for chocolate frogs, which could be purchased from the ship's slop chest. If he came on deck and discovered you were more than five degrees off, the cost was a chocolate frog. (Plus a mild telling-off for not paying attention.) This came back to bite him – big time! – after we'd got into Auckland.

New Zealand was getting closer, and we discovered that the captain had on board a secret supply of red socks that were going to be issued before our arrival at Auckland. When the America's Cup challenge was being held off Auckland some years previously, it seems the Kiwi people really got behind their boat, *Black Magic*, and one of the sponsorship gimmicks was that everyone in the country should buy a pair of NZ-made red socks, some of the profit from which would go towards supporting the boat. The story goes that it was a huge success – red socks were being worn everywhere – so there would be no mystery about why we were wearing them when we docked. I liked it!

On 6 December we sighted Three Kings Islands and then Cape Reinga, the most northerly point of the North Island of New Zealand. When the watch officer sent me below to look at the chart to check something, I discovered to my amazement that we were using the chart that had been drawn up by Captain Cook. It's been updated and re-issued since our trip, but at that time the box containing the survey details and acknowledging the hydrographer still cited "Lieutenant James Cook". I was absolutely stunned. That was why the watch officer had sent me below to look at it – he knew he would get a reaction from me about it as I was so interested in Cook's story.

Once we'd rounded the Cape, we slowed down and hove to in the Bay of Islands, off Opua, where we had a bit of a reception committee in the form of several boats and another tall ship called the R. *Tucker Thomson*. She does trips of a few days at a time around the bay, which is a very pretty place. Customs and immigration came out to clear us through the formalities, and we embarked a TV crew from TVNZ, the voyage underwriter. They would be filming on board for these last couple of days as well as capturing the grand entrance into Auckland. This would be put together with some footage from the departure at Sydney and ultimately end up being shown as a documentary on New Zealand television and then distributed as a video.

We continued sailing down the east coast of North Island, with vistas of hills and very green countryside off to starboard. It all looked very pretty – the more so because we hadn't seen a blade of grass for hundreds of kilometres – and it was no surprise to find that there were a lot of sheep dotted about. There's a standing joke between Australians and New Zealanders about there being more sheep than people in New Zealand, and inevitably we Aussies started bleating at the Kiwis on board. They "haka'd" back at us at every opportunity, even using it as a wake-up call one morning. That was a good one – we all just about fell out of the hammocks in shock.

The night before the grand entrance into Auckland Harbour we anchored in Waitaranga Bay, off Brown's Head. We could now see lights twinkling in the distance instead of sheep. We were nearly there. The next morning we embarked several VIP's, including the Governor-General and her ADC, the Prime Minister and his wife, plus many other dignitaries and some reporters, before we made the grand entrance into Auckland Harbour. I'd been down below looking at the chart again and could see that it was a fantastic harbour, much bigger than I'd imagined and definitely a rival to Sydney's. This was going to be a very special entrance indeed.

We started making our way into Waitemata Harbour once all of the VIPs were safely aboard and everyone was issued with red socks. Even the Governor-General insisted on wearing them. I was very impressed: New Zealand really *had* got behind their boat in the America's Cup, from the top down. Because the Governor-General represents the Queen, we were given a twenty-one-gun salute as we passed the local Royal New Zealand naval base, which was a great experience. Naturally we had to respond, so fired off our four cannons with gusto.

The Governor-General was on the helm with the Prime Minister and seemed to really enjoy it. "Shall we do it again, ma'am?" asked the captain.

"Oh yes, Captain, I do like a good bang", she said, with such a twinkle in her eye!

Adelia and I were on the poop deck working nearby and couldn't help bursting out laughing when we heard her response. She must have known who Adelia was, as she laughingly threatened her with, "Print that and you're dead!" I decided I liked the cut of this lady's jib. The gunners had to quickly clean out and re-load the cannons so that they would be ready for firing off when we were nearer to the dock.

Our escort was led by an absolutely breathtaking Maori *waka* from Graham's tribe. At roughly thirty metres in length, she was bigger than us. It was manned by about eighty paddlers, all in tribal dress, who grunted appropriately every time they dipped a paddle into the water. I'd never seen anything like it. Also escorting us were the two New Zealand sail-training ships, *The Spirit of Adventure* and *The Spirit of New Zealand*, another beautiful old tall ship, the *Soren Larsen*, which is based in Auckland for part of the year, and the Maritime Museum's scow, the *Ted Ashby* – not to mention dozens of modern yachts with spinnakers flying, which passed us as we fired off the cannons again.

Quickly reloaded, they got fired off yet again as we went under the Auckland Harbour Bridge. The echo was fantastic. We were doing a lap of honour around the harbour before tying up at Hobson's Wharf in Princess Docks, which I found a very moving experience. As we passed various groups of spectators who had taken up vantage points all around the harbour, it seemed they weren't content to have just seen us – they began walking along to keep up with us. By the time we turned the corner to head into Princess Docks we not only had dozens of boats escorting us in a flotilla, there were hundreds of people "walking us in", so to speak. Of all the places I've been with the *Endeavour* before and since, I've never seen that anywhere else. I was very touched.

There was a huge welcome waiting for us on the docks as well, with the Mayor and many other dignitaries, heaps of journalists, thousands of members of the general public, a couple of bands and heaven knows who else all giving us a rousing cheer as we came into view. As we started going aloft to furl the sails, the red socks became visible and the crowd roared their approval. Most important, perhaps, was the welcome by Graham's tribe. The men who had not been paddling the *waka* performed the *haka* and the womenfolk virtually sang us in. It didn't matter that us *pakeha*s (non-Maori people) didn't understand the words: their meaning was pretty obvious. Graham and Craig were moved to tears by this time, with the rest of us not too far behind.

They went ashore first so that they could welcome us with a Maori *hongi* as we stepped onto their land. Again, it was all very touching and emotional. Once the formal speeches were over, and gifts had been exchanged between the city of Auckland and the captain on behalf of the ship, it was time for our lads to put their *haka* to the test. Led by Craig, they whipped off their shirts and got into it. The crowd seemed to really enjoy it, and Graham's people told us afterwards that it was the best non-Maori *haka* they'd seen. We all felt very proud.

TVNZ had organised a big reception for the *Endeavour* crew and the crews from the other vessels that had participated in the formal welcome. What a reception it was, too. Copious amounts of food and drink were on hand, people were asking for autographs, and journalists wanted to interview everyone. There were bands and singing and general merriment, which went on for several hours. It was absolutely marvellous.

Somewhere among all of these festivities I got tapped on the shoulder and a voice said, "Hello Fran. It was great to see you up in the rigging." Who on earth could know me here? He was in a *Soren Larsen* uniform, had sunglasses on, and had a beard. The penny didn't drop until he took his cap and sunnies off, when I realised that it was Allan, my very first watch-leader from the *Leeuwin* all those years ago – the one who had managed to coax me aloft after the embarrassing pants-wetting incident. He'd recognised me while he was watching us furl the sails and knew I'd be at the reception. He said he'd got a terrific buzz when he realised that indeed it *was* me up there, remembering how frightened I had been that first time I went aloft. He must have been conscious that, if he hadn't been patient and persevered with me, I wouldn't have been here on the *Endeavour*. He invited me to go over and visit the *Soren Larsen* before I left town.

After the reception everyone went to the pub and partied on. It was a memorable night. Most of us stayed on board that night, or what was left of it, before we had to think about packing up and going through the painful business of saying farewell again.

Firstly, though, we had to help set the ship up into museum mode, and we all turned to the next morning to get stuck into the tasks. At morning tea break, one of our Kiwi mizzenmast ladies' families turned up. They were bearing homemade scones and another, more mysterious, offering. It was a giant chocolate frog, which had been made in a jelly mould, for the watch officer. Our watch mate had phoned her relatives when we got into the dock and quietly organised the enormous frog. What a laugh. It was so big it could have fed about forty people. The joke then developed that Glennis's steering had been so bad that she was just paying off her debts, as the ship's supply had not been big enough. This wasn't true, but we all had a good laugh about it at the time, including the watch officer who was the target of the frog.

Later on I went across the dock to visit Allan and meet the rest of the crew on the *Soren*. She was berthed directly opposite the *Endeavour*.

It was then I discovered that they had managed to play a fantastic prank on us the night before. Protruding from each side of the *Endeavour*'s hull are small platforms called channels to which the standing rigging is fastened. When you are on the deck of the ship, you can't see the hull immediately below the channels as they obstruct your vision. Hanging there for all to see was a huge banner – "SAIL ON SOREN LARSEN". Talk about ignominious! They must have slung it there after the party, and no-one had noticed them skulking about below the channels in the dark. It was brilliant in its deviousness. One up to the *Soren* crew. The *Endeavour* would have to get them back!

Soon it was time for those wretched goodbyes again. The ship was going to be on exhibition in Auckland for a few weeks before a new voyage crew would embark. They would then tour both North and South islands of New Zealand over a period of several months. Simon and I chummed up again and decided to hire a car and do a little sightseeing around North Island before flying back to Western Australia, which helped to take the edge off the sadness of leaving the ship and our new buddies.

We had arrived in Auckland on 9 December, exactly two years after the ship had been launched in Fremantle. She certainly had grown up since she'd left home. It would be some considerable time before she would be in Western Australia again, but I was hopeful of being on board when next she came "home" to Fremantle. In the meantime, I had to fly home myself and get on with whatever the next stage of my life would be.

9

SHORT AND SWEET X 2

Back home in Perth life returned to some semblance of normality. I went back to work again, at my old company as it turned out, but on a contract basis this time rather than as permanent staff. In the back of my mind was the notion that this was more flexible, so that if I got the chance to get back to sea it would be easier to take whatever time off might be needed, or resign if necessary. The bug had obviously well and truly bitten.

There were no tall ships around to "play with" for quite some time. The *Leeuwin* was on her regular winter sojourn in northern waters and the *Endeavour* was sailing and on exhibition in New Zealand. I had to content myself with getting photographs of my *Endeavour* adventures printed and assembled into albums and watching the TVNZ video that Adelia had sent me. It was a bit of a shock when it turned up. It's an excellent video, but I hadn't known until I saw it that the film crew had managed to get a shot of me dozing while on watch early one morning. It's nothing short of a cardinal sin to fall asleep on watch, and there it was, captured for posterity. In King George III's Navy I would have been flogged. No wonder Adelia said in her covering note that I would be amused when I watched it.

A few months went by and I kept track of what the *Endeavour* was doing via the website that had been set up. She seemed to be doing very well in New Zealand, with many thousands visiting her when she was in port on exhibition and lots more people getting the opportunity to crew on her between the various towns. Then we heard that she would be heading back to Fremantle for a refit prior to going overseas to England and beyond. Excitement took hold again: my ship was coming home.

Adelia and I arranged to rejoin her in Albany for the last leg back to Fremantle in May 1996. I'd been on board when she sailed away so it seemed appropriate that I should be on board again to bring her home. It was a long way for Adelia to come from New Zealand for such a short trip, but the *Endeavour* had obviously got to her as well. Indeed, it seemed to get to everyone who ever had anything to do with her.

The bus that brought us to Albany from Perth arrived only about twenty minutes before the ship sailed in, so we just dumped our gear at the tourist bureau and hurried off to be at the dock to see her arrive. No, if I'm honest we *ran*, taking shortcuts across railway lines and up the embankment. Oh, the excitement and emotions at seeing her again! We discovered that the majority of the voyage crew were "old hands" who had all been on her before. I knew many of them from previous trips, and it was just great catching up with them. Captain Chris was pretty astonished to see Adelia, all the way from New Zealand. We were like a couple of kids on Christmas morning – you would have thought we hadn't seen her in years, and it was really only six months or so.

Many of the Fremantle guides had driven down to be there as well, so there was a wonderful reunion. The *Endeavour* family was back together again. Indeed, many of the voyage crew on this leg were lads who had built her but had not previously had the opportunity to sail on her. This included the chief shipwright, who seemed delighted with how she looked. "When she left, she was almost a bit *too* pretty", he said. "Now she looks like a working ship."

We were not to join her for a couple of days, which allowed us to have a look around the town and the surrounding country. We visited the replica of the *Amity*, the brig that brought the first convicts to Western Australia from the UK in 1826, and the war memorial at the top of Mt Clarence. We got to the memorial just as the sun was going down, and I found the experience very moving. Albany was the port from which many World War I diggers sailed for Gallipoli, and would have been the last sight of Australia for many of them.

We had hardly stowed our gear and got allocated into watches when the work started again. There was the usual replenishment of victuals and loading of other supplies plus a lot of maintenance on the "to do" list. The captain wanted her looking her best when she sailed back into Fremantle, so we set to with a vengeance on the sanding and painting and chipping and polishing. Within a couple of days it hardly felt like we had ever left her in Auckland some six months or so before. We had a nice send-off from the townspeople of Albany, and then we were off – heading "home".

Of course Adelia had heard about the storm we ran into just prior to Cape Leeuwin during the maiden voyage in 1994. And of course she understood that we had to round Cape Leeuwin again, in the opposite direction. Given that so many of us on board had been on that first voyage, poor Adelia became the main target of the tales of high winds, huge seas, rocking and rolling and seasickness, all in fairly graphic detail. As some time had passed since then, the winds and the seas had become bigger in the telling of the story and the *mal de mer* had got much more colourful and disgusting. We could see that she was getting a little nervous, which just made the storytelling by us wretches all the more gleeful.

The Southern Ocean lived up to its reputation for a couple of days, as it was cold, wet, windy and bleak, and we rolled around quite a bit. That was the downside; the upside was that there were some whales about, which are always wonderful to see, and albatrosses were giving us their fantastic flying displays again. It also meant that it was a bit too rough to attempt any meaningful maintenance, so we concentrated on sail handling and getting to know the new people on board. These included another television film crew, this time from Channel 9 in Perth, one of the ship's sponsors.

We went round Cape Leeuwin on the morning of 22 May, and it was a complete non-event. Adelia could hardly believe it after all of our stories. The wind had died away to very light airs, and we even had the t'gallants up. In fact we had the engines on, as there was barely enough wind to get us round the cape without them: as always, we had a schedule to keep. It was an interesting experience, however: our captain reminded us that Captain Cook himself had gone around Cape Horn with his t'gallants up, as the weather had been so clement. There was that sense of *déjà vu* again.

A notable incident on the way home from Albany was a "rendezvous" with Space Shuttle *Endeavour*. The crew on the shuttle would not have known we were at sea below them, but we knew when its orbit would coincide with our journey and were watching out for it. It was only a tiny moving light in the sky from our vantage point, but we knew it was the shuttle. It was all the more meaningful because in the stem post in the Great Cabin there is a trunnel that had been taken into space by a previous *Endeavour* shuttle crew in 1992. When it was brought back, the shuttle's captain was invited to hammer it into place during the course of the ship's construction. So there we were, a few years later, watching the *Endeavour* in space from the *Endeavour* at sea.

About 7 o'clock one morning, we were adjacent to Busselton with its long, long jetty. Though we had all the sails up, and must have looked pretty good, no-one had come out in their small boats to see us. The captain decided we'd better wake the town up, so the cannons got fired in quick succession. That stirred the pot a bit. We weren't calling in at Busselton, but we thought we'd give the townsfolk a treat anyway.

The Channel 9 news team was due to be taken off at Bunbury and transferred to a helicopter so that they could take some aerial shots, and the pilot boat was coming out to get them. The sixty-four thousand dollar question was whether Clyde would be the pilot. And he was! Those of us who had been on the New Zealand trip all greeted him like a long-lost buddy, and he came on board for a quick visit and to catch up with the captain. He also dropped off a *Sunday Times* crew who would stay with us for the last couple of days to get material for an article in the following week's paper. The ship's homecoming certainly seemed to be generating a lot of interest and publicity.

Just after we left Bunbury a pod of dolphins joined us, and stayed with us for a couple of hours, playing in our bow wave and generally having a great time. They surfed down the face of waves, and every now and again would perform huge leaps into the air. The adults appeared to be teaching the young ones how to handle all of this. It was just wonderful to watch and such a privilege to observe nature at her best. Eventually they turned away and headed back towards Bunbury. I found out later that there is a resident pod in Koombana Bay, and felt sure it must have been them.

With our arrival back in Perth imminent, the captain wanted to put on a good show for the Perth people so we got all the studding sails (or stunsails) out and rigged up, mostly as a practice. We didn't have them when the ship left Fremantle in 1994, so this would be something new for the sightseers provided the weather obliged on the day of our arrival. The plan was that we would anchor for the night off either Port or Scarborough beach, depending on the wind, and then do the grand entrance into Fremantle the following morning. Hopefully the publicity machine would have been at work and there would be a lot of people to welcome us home.

I was on bow watch as we neared Scarborough Beach and went back to the poop deck to report "a large hotel dead ahead sir", which caused a bit of a laugh. Indeed Observation City, and the beach, loomed about five hundred metres away. At the last minute we turned to starboard and continued sailing on down past the metropolitan beaches. What a showman the captain is! His timing had been impeccable, and we must have looked absolutely spectacular from the shore. Nearly all the sails were up, the sky was blue, and it was a bright clear day – a photographer's dream in fact. We couldn't have asked for better.

As we headed towards Cottesloe Beach, however, the wind suddenly picked up and one of the stunsail booms snapped. We could hardly believe it. She had sailed almost fifteen thousand nautical miles and we snapped a boom about five hundred metres offshore when we were nearly home – that's sailing ships for you. We had to pull in the stunsails. To make up for that disappointment, the captain decided to fire the cannons just as we passed Swanbourne Beach. By way of explanation to those who don't know the Perth area, Swanbourne is our recognised "nudie" beach, albeit not officially so. There were a considerable number of sunbathers lying and dozing on the sand, blissfully unaware they were about to get a rude awakening. Some of us watched through binoculars as the cannons were fired. It was great fun seeing the nudists leap up in alarm, with various parts of their anatomies wobbling and dangling. To add icing to the cake, all the car alarms in the nearby car park went off too. Hello Perth! *Endeavour*'s back in town!

We anchored off Cottesloe Beach for the night and strung up all the lights in the rigging so that we would look grand from the shore. There was a "last supper" being held in the 18th-century deck, which meant that we could all eat together rather than in the usual two sittings. The bosun got sent ashore in the safety boat to get some booze from the pub: only a skeleton crew was required for watch-keeping duties that night, so the rest of us could party in true *Endeavour* style. This would probably be the last such bash on board for a long while, so we had to make sure it was a good one. There always seemed to be some amazingly talented people who blossomed at these impromptu evenings – singers and shanty-men, guitarists and poets who had been hiding their lights under bushels. It was great fun, and yet another memorable evening.

Next morning dawned bright and clear, and we all turned to very early, as there was a lot to be done before we sailed into Fremantle Harbour. Most of us were a little fragile from the night before, but time and tide wait for no man. There were decks to be scrubbed and other jobs to be done before we weighed anchor and started setting sails again. By the time we got under way a small flotilla of boats had gathered to escort us in, and as we got closer to the harbour entrance the flotilla continued to grow. Looking ahead we could see that there were hundreds of people lining the harbour and foreshore areas. Not surprisingly, the people of Fremantle and Perth had turned out in their droves to welcome back "their" ship. The cheer that went up when the "Made in Western Australia" banner was rolled down the shrouds would have warmed the cockles of anyone's heart. We were home!

We tied up at Fishing Boat Harbour this time, rather than Victoria Quay. Among the crowd were most of the Fremantle Division Guides, a shanty group, a band, television crews from several different channels, quite a number of VIPs who were coming on board for lunch, a contingent of tall-ship fanatics from the *Leeuwin* and, of course, members of the public. It was all rather splendid. After some formal speeches by the Mayor of Fremantle and the captain, among others, the crew were allowed off for a couple of hours while the lunch was being held, so we set off looking for our loved ones among the crowd.

We had to be back on board at 2 pm to destore the ship, do some more polishing and tidying and get her into museum mode again, as she would be going on exhibition to the public once more the next day. We had to pack up our own gear, too, as we would all be getting off. That done, we adjourned to a tent on the jetty to watch a special programme being broadcast on Channel 9 called *Endeavour Returns*. It was amusing to see ourselves working the ship, and we all had a good laugh at various bits that had been "Hollywoodised", if I could call it that. At one point I had been interviewed by the TV crew, and had been happy to oblige. I didn't know the voice-over would refer to me as "a self-confessed *Endeavour* groupie" however! Oh dear, I'd have trouble living that down at the office.

Many of the permanent crew were leaving the ship here and, in true naval tradition, it was decided that they should be flung into the harbour. Much to the delight of the watching crowd this actually turned into a bit of a free-for-all, with nearly all of us getting thrown in. By this time it was dark, and so you couldn't see how much muck was floating around in the water, but the locals among us knew what it was usually like and weren't too keen to end up among it.

I took off up the dock chased by a couple of the lads who were just as determined to get me in the water as I was to stay out of it. To no avail. They were faster, bigger and stronger, and in due course I got heaved in. I did manage to take one of them with me, though, and got a great cheer from the watchers on the dock and the ship for my efforts. The locals passed the word around the showers to use some disinfectant while getting cleaned up, "just in case" … You really didn't know what was in that water.

The net result was that we went to the pub smelling of a mixture of perfume, aftershave (depending on your gender) and disinfectant. The Sail and Anchor smelled us coming before we ever arrived. Most of the people in the bar had been down at the dock to see us come in and were aware of the dunkings, so the aroma was tolerated with good humour. As had been the case when we arrived in Albany in 1994, we could hardly buy a drink: everyone was "shouting" us. It never ceases to amaze me the effect this ship seems to have on people – wherever we go. The sense of camaraderie is almost tangible. People just want to be part of the *Endeavour* experience in some small way, even if it is only by buying one of the crew a drink.

Most of us slept on board that night – it would be our last together for who knew how long – and the next day the farewells would have to be said again. They were perhaps not quite as dramatic as I'd experienced before, partly because many of us were local and could catch up at the reunions that would certainly be held. And the ship, after all, was home for a few months' exhibition, so I would still be involved with her as I resumed my guiding duties. Adelia, however, had only another day or two left of her holiday before she would have to fly back to Auckland, and that really was a gut-wrenching parting. We had become so close during both this trip and the Sydney – New Zealand voyage that it was very hard to say goodbye. But we both knew deep inside that we would see one another again, although it might be a long time later.

Life returned to "normal" again, but it was very hard to settle down. I was back at work, running a house and doing all the mundane things that seem to consume our lives at times, as well as ship-keeping and guiding on *Endeavour* once a week. In addition to being on exhibition, the ship was having some maintenance work done in preparation for her first trip to the United Kingdom. She was scheduled to leave in October with no firm return date. Much would depend on her reception in the various places she would call at in Britain. While this was very exciting for the ship, my family and work commitments were such that there was no way I could go with her. As the time drew nearer for her departure, I became quieter and sadder.

Following the maintenance and refit work, one last little voyage was scheduled – just down the coast to Bunbury and return. This would put the ship through her seagoing paces again and double-check that everything was in order before she left to cross the Indian Ocean. I managed to get myself on to the Bunbury-back-to-Fremantle leg – it would be only two or three days, but it was a last little taste of my beloved *Endeavour* before she left Fremantle for a long absence, so I wasn't going to say no to the opportunity. Being such a short trip, it was a low-profile episode, but it was nice to catch up again with Clyde, from the Sydney – New Zealand trip, and quite a few others whom I knew from previous voyages. We arrived back in Fremantle on 3 October, one day more than the second anniversary of her maiden voyage.

Far too quickly 16 October 1996 came around. That was the date my beloved ship was leaving for the UK and beyond, and this time I wouldn't be on board. The day dawned bright, sunny and clear, and a big farewell had been organised again. As usual there were hundreds of people to see her off and bands and speeches, with everyone, it seemed,

115

in a very happy frame of mind: everyone except me. I appreciated that this was a big occasion – our "little ship", locally made, was off to spread her wings in the big wide oceans of the world – but I just couldn't share in the celebratory mood.

A charter boat had been organised for us *Endeavour* guides to escort her out, and we were joined by the inevitable flotilla of private boats. Balloons and streamers abounded, and it was all very jolly. An ABC television crew was on board the charter vessel with the guides, and the cameraman seemed quite intrigued by how upset I was and kept trying to get me on film, teary-eyed and snivelling. I ducked and dived around the boat trying to stay out of his lens, all the while getting more and more distraught. One of our elderly guides commented to me that at least I could be sure of seeing the ship again some day, somewhere. He cheerfully pointed out that, as he was in his eighties, he might be dead before she got back. That stopped me in my tracks. It needed that sobering thought for me to pull myself together and stop wallowing in self-pity.

The seas were very calm that day, so we were able to escort her out of the harbour and follow her up the coast a little way. In due course we had to turn and make our way back into the harbour, and my last sight of the *Endeavour* was of her turning west from Scarborough Beach and heading off into the setting sun with all kinds of adventures ahead of her. I wouldn't see her again for three years, when I rejoined her in Vancouver to do the trip to New Zealand. But I didn't know that then.

10

NO-ONE TOLD ME

The remainder of 1996 passed uneventfully. I was busy at work but getting very twitchy to be off and doing something again. The gods must have heard me: early in 1997 I was contacted by an old boss and head-hunted onto a job with Western Mining Corporation, which proved to be very challenging and even busier than the one I resigned from.

The job involved preparing contracts for the expansion of the Roxby Downs uranium mine in South Australia, and I would be based in Adelaide for the best part of a year. From time to time I flew up to the mine site for a day or two as well, but in the main I was in Adelaide. It was necessary that I join the project team on a single-status basis, but as part of my contract deal it was agreed that I would be flown home to Perth for a long weekend once a month. Naturally enough I had concerns about leaving both my partner and my elderly mother for that length of time.

As is the case with most of these projects, we worked minimum ten-hour days and, although it was officially a Monday-to-Friday job, as often as not we were in the office on Saturdays too. That meant there was one day a week to relax, shop, clean house, take care of laundry and the rest of it, leaving very little spare time. Once cheaper airfares became available my one weekend per month in Perth became every second weekend, which was lovely on the one hand but a bit hectic on the other. Thoughts of tall-ship sailing were completely overtaken by the job, and there wasn't much time for brooding about anything.

Adelaide also has a tall ship, the *One and All*. She is similar to the *Leeuwin*, inasmuch as she is basically a sail-training ship, but is of a different style and rig. She's a wooden-hulled two-masted topsail schooner, around thirty-five metres long, and rather pretty. Her permanent berth is located close to the South Australian Maritime Museum, at Port Adelaide. One weekend I managed to get some time to visit the museum, see the ship and make myself known to some of their people. One of them was a former *Leeuwin* captain with whom I'd sailed many times, so I was greeted very warmly and invited to go sailing with them. Unfortunately the demands of the job were such that it wasn't possible, but it was nice to know that I could if ever I did manage to get some time off work. It planted the seed again.

The rest of the year passed in a whirlwind of work activities and flights back and forth between the mine site and Adelaide and Perth. Before I knew it my contract was almost at an end. Ken and I had decided to go to Tasmania to spend Christmas with his family, so I began to look forward to that as well as to having some time off again. It was arranged that he would fly over to Launceston directly from Perth and I would fly in from Adelaide a couple of days later. So I was on my own when I got off the plane in Tasmania and saw before me at the airport a very large poster on which were emblazoned the words "The Tall Ships Are Coming". Are they indeed? No-one had told me.

Of course I stopped to read it and find out what this was all about. Because I'd been so busy at work and out of the tall-ships scenario for the best part of a year, I didn't have a clue what this poster could be referring to. Meanwhile Ken was waiting at the other side of the arrivals area wondering what had happened to me.

According to the small print on the poster, there was going to be a tall ships race from Sydney to Hobart in January 1998 to celebrate the anniversary of George Bass and Matthew Flinders's discovery of Bass Strait and their circumnavigation of Tasmania. It would commence on Australia Day, 26 January, so I figured that I had time to find out more about it – and to try to get onto one of the ships. I'd always had some kind of hankering to be involved in the annual Sydney-to-Hobart race, even though yachts are not my cup of tea. Here was an opportunity, perhaps, to do it in a tall ship. Oh-ho!

My brain started ticking away. I had finished my contract, and had no work commitments to lock me into a date that dictated my return to

Perth. Ken was here; mum was fine. The plot was starting to take shape. I noted down a few phone numbers from the poster and eventually appeared at the other side of the arrivals door, very excited. Poor Ken thought it was because he was there! Well, it was partly. Thankfully, he'd become used to my occasional disappearances off to sea and didn't get too upset about the idea. He also thought I didn't have much chance of getting onto anything at that late stage.

The next day I started making phone calls to find out more about the race. Because it was so close to Christmas I didn't have a lot of success, many offices being closed already. I did manage to learn from the tourism office in Launceston that a great many ships would be involved and that huge celebrations were being planned for their arrival in Hobart. It was getting more and more interesting, but there was little that could be done until after Boxing Day. I would just have to bide my time for a few days.

We had a lovely Christmas in the meantime, with me meeting many of Ken's family for the first time and enjoying relaxing in the small community with no work pressures or deadlines to meet. There was a Christmas pantomime in the village hall and a Christmas parade with Santa Claus ensconced on the back of the village fire engine. Everyone seemed to know everyone else, and I was made very welcome. Christmas Day at Ken's sister's house began early, with the little ones shrieking with glee in the wee small hours when they discovered that Santa had been. Within about ten minutes you'd have thought a tornado had hit the house.

Three generations were present for dinner, and we all ate too much and drank too much and generally overindulged. It was quite a memorable occasion for the family as it was the first time in about twenty years that Ken's mother and father, and all five of their adult children plus spouses and kids, had all been in the one place at the one time. Cameras were clicking madly to capture this rare get-together.

As soon as Christmas was over I hit the phone again. First I rang the *Leeuwin* office in Western Australia. No, she wouldn't be taking part. I tried the *Young Endeavour* office in Sydney. Yes, she would be taking part, and in fact would be one of the escorting safety and radio vessels; but no, I couldn't get on. Everyone except for the professional crew needed to be less than twenty-five years old and, besides, they were full. I rang another couple of contacts for ships in Sydney, but they also had no vacancies. Then I remembered the *One and All* in Adelaide. My call happened to be answered by the former *Leeuwin* captain who knew me. Given that they only had a skeleton crew manning the office because of the Christmas break, that was a real stroke of luck. Yes, they would be taking part, and as a matter of fact there had just been a cancellation and a berth was available. Did I want it? Yee-ha! I was on. Thank heavens for credit cards. I got it all pretty well organised in the one phone call. Details of where and when to join the ship would follow.

Ken and his sister were having breakfast on the patio when I emerged doing a little war dance! "I'm on, I'm on!" Pauline thought I was slightly insane and Ken reminded me that all my sailing gear was back in Perth. Also that I would need to change all my travel arrangements. "They're only little problems that can be fixed", I responded. Indeed they were, but not quite as easily as I'd imagined.

An appropriate shop was raided to kit me out with the minimum of what I needed, and Ken could take home with him the stuff I didn't need. It might mean excess baggage, but that wasn't a real problem. Getting the flights changed was, however, another matter. There are only a certain number of flights in and out of Launceston and, because it was school holidays, they were full. I looked at flying from Launceston to Melbourne and then on to Sydney – full. I looked at driving down to Hobart and flying from there to either Melbourne or Sydney – full! This was proving to be a bit harder than I thought. Tasmania of course, is an island, so you have to either fly there or sail there.

Then I had a brainwave. I'd *sail* to Melbourne and then fly up to Sydney: there are heaps of flights available between those two cities. I knew there was a regular car-ferry/passenger service between Devonport and Melbourne, so I made enquiries about that. A passage was available, but in the process of getting that clarified I also discovered that there was a new fast catamaran service being tried out between Georgetown and Melbourne, which was much cheaper than the regular car ferry. I had already seen the cat on the Tamar River, and it looked absolutely spectacular. She is capable of forty knots, and could do the crossing from

Georgetown to Melbourne in six hours … Never mind the "normal" ferry, I'm going on *that*.

A local Tasmanian company called Incat, which has subsequently sold catamarans all over the world, built the *Devil Cat* in Hobart. At ninety metres long and capable of carrying 900 passengers, 240 cars and up to four coaches, it was pretty impressive, but it was the paint job that really knocked me out. Her very sleek bow was painted to look like a Tasmanian devil's nose, complete with whiskers, and each of her twin hulls was a front paw, complete with claws. The rest of her was basically black, as is the animal she was painted to look like. After crossing Bass Strait on her, I would catch one of the shuttle flights up to Sydney from Melbourne. I also managed to get my booking to Perth changed – as I would be flying out from Hobart after the end of the school holidays, that wasn't a drama. It just meant a bit more money had to change hands …

With arrangements basically all in hand, we still had about three weeks in Tasmania, so we set off to do some touring and organised things so that we would be in Hobart for New Year's Eve. Constitution Dock is a bit of a yachtie's holy grail at that time of the year, as most of the boats that had left Sydney on Boxing Day in the traditional Sydney-to-Hobart race have arrived by then. Sure enough there were many of them in dock, and we were lucky enough to bump into one of Ken's nephews, who had sailed in the race, and we were invited to join in the general New Year's revelry on board his yacht. Another little item on my "things to do before you die" list could be ticked off – Constitution Dock on New Year's Eve.

We spent a couple of days looking around Hobart, which was good background for me given that I'd be back again in about a month. Not only did I get my bearings, I checked out a couple of cheap hotels in case I was unable to stay on the ship until it was time to fly out. It's always good to have Plan B as back-up in case Plan A goes awry, especially when ships are involved.

Then we headed off down the Tasman Peninsula to visit the famous Port Arthur Penal Settlement and its marvellous ruins. It was in this area that the explorer Abel Tasman landed in 1642, and named Tasmania "Van Diemen's Land" in honour of the then Governor of the Dutch

121

East Indies. At last – somewhere Captain Cook hadn't been and didn't name! It was also at Port Arthur that perhaps the most infamous mass murder in Australian history had occurred, but in very recent times. It had nothing whatsoever to do with the fact that it's a penal settlement, and had no connections to the pioneering history of the place. It was an event that stunned Australia at the time – thirty-five people were shot dead by a young man named Martin Bryant in 1996 for no apparent reason. Ken and I paid our respects at the memorial that has been erected there, before continuing our touring.

We visited the massive Gordon River Dam and Power Development, which was quite controversial in the late 1970s and early 1980s as its construction flooded some sensitive areas. The end result is spectacular, with many absolutely beautiful lakes set in lovely countryside. We also visited several national parks, marvelled at the huge Huon pine trees and massive tree ferns that abound there and enjoyed seeing many waterfalls. Tasmania truly is a very lovely place, particularly the rugged south-western corner, which is all either national park or World Heritage listed, so it will be protected for future generations forever.

Somewhere along the way I had an accident. We'd climbed up an embankment to view the scenery at a particular lake, and I lost my footing on the way back down and ended up at the bottom of the embankment moaning. Ken said he knew I was hurt because I was lying on my back, arms and legs in the air, looking like a dead cockroach. Furthermore I wasn't muttering or cursing, just moaning! I'd done my ankle in badly by the feel of it. Oh no, maybe the *One and All* would be getting another cancellation. Ken helped me hobble back to the car, where I collapsed into the seat and got my leg up on the dashboard. Foolishly, we had no first-aid kit with us, but at least I had my hiking boots on. I kept the boot on, as I just knew the minute I took it off my foot was going to blow up like a balloon.

We were only about an hour from the next town, so headed there as quickly as we could, checked into a motel and got a bucket of ice from reception. It certainly wasn't to chill champagne! I got my foot into that while Ken found a chemist and got hold of some strapping and anti-inflammatory medication. As I'd suspected, my ankle swelled up, but the ice stopped it getting too bad. I strapped it up, took some of the anti-inflammatory medicine and stayed off it for a couple of days.

Ken wanted me to go for X-rays, but I refused. I knew, deep down, that it was more serious than a sprain but was making light of it – I was going on that ship come hell or high water. I found out about six weeks later that I'd actually cracked a bone as well as torn the ligaments, but it wasn't a weight-bearing bone, so with care – and strapping – I had managed to cope with it.

We headed off again, although the bush walking was drastically curtailed. Still, we managed to visit a number of places before heading back to Lilydale, where we were staying, via Cradle Mountain and Dove Lake. There are apparently only about five sunny days a year at Cradle Mountain and Dove Lake, and we happened to be there on one of them. I took this to be a good omen, and anyway my foot was now feeling much better, although I secretly had doubts about being able to climb aloft. "Wait and see, Fran", I thought. "It's amazing what adrenaline can do." I had about another ten days before joining the ship in Sydney at any rate, so presumably it would be a bit better by then. I didn't know about the broken bone at that stage.

In due course it was time for me to head off to Melbourne and beyond. The family all came to see me off at Georgetown, about an hour's drive from where we'd been staying. The *Devil Cat* looked even more impressive close up. The distance between Georgetown and Melbourne is about 420 kilometres across Bass Strait, which has a pretty notorious reputation weather-wise. I discovered when I boarded that it's the world's longest open-sea ferry route and that this trial of the cat had started only a month previously. I felt very lucky to be in the right place at the right time.

We cast off, turned around and headed down the Tamar River to the open sea. A few of the passengers were looking a little nervous, I thought. I was exploring the vessel and loving it. As soon as we were out of the river mouth the throttle was turned up and we were doing forty knots in no time at all. The wake was an awesome thing to see, and we fairly flew along. It was a daylight crossing, so you could watch the wake, and the ocean, but there wasn't much else to see. We had to slow down a little at one point as we hit a bit of a swell, but we still made it across to Port Melbourne in around seven hours. It would subsequently take me seven *days* to sail back again, the other way. (OK, Sydney to Hobart isn't exactly the equivalent of Georgetown to Melbourne, but I still saw some irony in the contrast.)

I got my gear, grabbed a taxi and raced out to Tullamarine airport. Because it took us a little longer than scheduled to cross Bass Strait, I'd just missed the last flight to Sydney for the day. Damn! Both Melbourne and Sydney airports have night-time curfews, which preclude planes taking off and landing between midnight and 6 am, so the airport doesn't stay open all night. I couldn't sleep there. Or could I? The lass at the check-in counter turned out to be a tall-ship sailor as well, so she got me bedded down at the back of her counter, and tipped off the security guards to leave me alone but keep an eye on me. The worldwide "tall-ship family" connections had struck again. I flew out first thing next morning and arrived at my friend's house in time for breakfast. We had a couple of enjoyable days together before I had to join the ship.

One thing we managed to do was have a sail on Sydney Harbour one afternoon on another friend's boat; we also checked out Darling Harbour, where the tall ships were starting to gather for the race. There were far more than I had imagined, and I started getting really excited. The *One and All* was already there, having sailed over from Adelaide, so I knew which berth she was at. She was dwarfed by some of the bigger ones – ships I'd never seen before and in some cases didn't even know existed. There were tall ships from Japan and Mexico and Russia and Indonesia and England – I was so glad that I'd made an impulse decision to take part in this. The foot, by this time, was feeling reasonably good, but I still had doubts about being able to climb. "I'll deal with that once I've signed on and I'm aboard", I thought.

Joining day came, and I was halfway down the dock at Darling harbour when I heard someone shouting my name. Neither the *Endeavour* nor the *Leeuwin* was taking part in this event, so who could it possibly be? I looked around but couldn't see anyone. Then I heard the voice again. "Up here Fran." I looked up, and there, high on the rigging of another ship, was one of the lads who had been on the construction crew of the *Endeavour*. "What the hell are you doing here?" he shouted.

"Going sailing", I replied, laughing. So was he, on another wooden ship he'd been helping to build in Melbourne, the *Enterprize*. She is a replica (and a very pretty one too) of the ship in which John Batman sailed from Tasmania to Melbourne in the early 1800s to start another colony on the mainland.

I reported to the duty officer at my ship, signed on, and was shown where to stow my gear. It would be a couple of days before we sailed out in a Parade of Sail down Sydney Harbour. Inevitably, there was a lot to do before then. This ship was smaller, and had a different rig to either *Leeuwin* or *Endeavour*, but the routine was similar. There was about thirty-five of us aboard, and we got allocated into watches, had safety briefings and training, and were generally made familiar with the running of the ship. There was another woman about my age, a Tasmanian named Sally. Almost inevitably we chummed up, and it was fortunate that we were in the same watch.

There were food and other stores to be brought on and stowed away, which was all pretty familiar to me from voyages on other ships. But, because this was an international event and there were about thirty ships from various countries taking part, there were inter-ship sports and games too. We vied with each other in tugs of war, knot-tying and other competitions. The fun and games and inter-ship activities would culminate in a crew parade through the city. Some 1400 of us would take part in this – another memorable occasion to be involved in.

The naval training ships' crews could all march properly, so the mate took us in hand for a couple of hours the day before the parade to try and get us marching at least reasonably. He ranked us by height, with the shortest in the front, which looked very unmilitary! We were a bunch of civilian amateurs, and it seemed many of us had two left feet. We all thought it was very funny, but he was starting to despair. Many of the large ships also had their own bands, and there would be other bands taking part in the parade from such organisations as the Australian Navy and the Salvation Army. It was going to be huge.

After a while we decided to adopt a different tactic. Rather than try to be serious about it all and march properly, every now and then we would stop at the mate's pre-arranged signal and boogie! We also raided the galley for pots and pans and wooden spoons with which to bang them, we put rice and chickpeas in containers to make maracas and took whistles out of the life jackets – armed with these items we would be our own band. The result wasn't the slightest bit harmonious, but what we lacked in talent we certainly made up for in enthusiasm.

The ships' captains were seated at a specially erected podium outside the Town Hall together with the Mayor of Sydney, diplomats from each of the countries represented and many other civilian VIPs. Meanwhile the crews, bands and other participants in the parade all gathered in Hyde Park. The route would meander down through several main streets of the city, past the Town Hall and finish at Darling Harbour Park, where there were marquees full of food and drink ready for an enormous post-parade, pre-race party.

The traffic lights were all stopped, point policemen were on duty, and there were thousands and thousands of people lining the streets ready to cheer us on and wave little flags. It gave me a huge thrill to think that all the city traffic in Sydney was stopped for *me* (and all my shipmates too of course). We assembled into the order in which we were to march, and off we set, led by the Australian Navy band. Everyone was in uniform, and one person led each vessel's crew with a banner declaring which ship they were from.

We were immediately behind the crew of a very large Russian navy training/cadet ship. They marched beautifully, were immaculately turned out and looked very serious. You got the feeling that if one of them got out of step they would have ended up in a Siberian salt mine. They had their own band, too, and it was all very formal. There was no way we could compete with them. We marched along as best we could for a little while, banging our pots and pans and shaking our "maracas" in time to the Russian band, and then the mate turned and shouted, "Two, six, *boogie*". We stopped where we were and started dancing and bopping about in the street. The crowd absolutely loved it, and some of them broke ranks and joined us. The Russians were not amused, but we were having a wonderful time.

This continued on for the whole length of the parade, and it seemed to us we were getting bigger cheers and more applause than all the other groups. That, of course, just made us stop and boogie more often, much to the chagrin of the Russians. Then we got to the corner where we had to turn into George Street and pass the Town Hall where all the captains and VIPs were viewing the parade. Each ship's captain would have been looking for his own crew and noting how smart (or otherwise) it was. The Russians went by, and we could see that their captain approved of their turnout by the look on his face, and the collective nodding of heads that was going on across the podium. He saluted them as the officers marched past.

And then we rocked up. Of course the mate made the call for us to boogie. Who were we to disobey the ship's mate! We started boogieing and dancing around with great gusto, much to the crowd's delight and our captain's horror. The more embarrassed he looked, the more wildly we danced and the more zealously we created our cacophony of noise. Again, the crowd broke ranks, ran into the street and joined us. Everyone laughed and cheered and waved, and wished us fair winds and a good race. The bonhomie was almost tangible. Many, many people came up to us later at the party to tell us we were the most fun group in the whole parade – everyone else had been a bit too solemn. The captain, however, didn't forgive us for days, which we thought was wonderful.

We partied fairly hard that night, dancing and singing and making friends with sailors from other ships, and we all promised to catch up with one another "at the other end", i.e. in Hobart. While we would be racing against each other, it was all pretty friendly and not terribly serious – just a wonderful gathering of international peoples who loved the sea. It was serious enough, though, for the ships to be categorised into groups according to their different rigs, sail capacities and sizes and for appropriate handicaps to be allocated.

Australia Day, 26 January, duly arrived, and we all turned to very early to get organised for the Parade of Sail down Sydney Harbour. This would have to be one of the most spectacular harbours in the world. There are many vantage points all along the way right out to the Heads for spectators to gather and view events such as this one. Plus, there is Sydney's famous Harbour Bridge which can be accessed by pedestrians and which we would all sail under: a terrific vantage point. Sydneysiders are also great sailors, and there were hundreds and hundreds of small boats getting into position to escort us out. Harbour police and maritime authorities cleared a path for our progress, and one by one we all left our berths and got into line.

Because of the limited manoeuvrability of most of these square-rig ships, and for safety reasons, we were allowed to use our engines during the Parade of Sail. This would permit a slow and spectacular progress down the harbour. Most of the ships, ours included, had people aloft dressing the yards, with crews standing on the yards and other sections of the rigging as the ships slowly passed by. For spectators this looks fantastic, but it can be fairly hard on your feet if you're standing on a footrope and scarcely moving for quite a time.

It didn't take long before the ship's doctor noticed me limping: after a couple of hours aloft my ankle had swelled up again. The disguised injury had been sprung! From my perspective, though, it didn't matter: we were off and on our way. He told me to keep it strapped up and to try and avoid going aloft as much as I could, and he would keep an eye on it. As the trip progressed it did curtail my climbing a bit, but I could still be a useful crew member and pull my weight at pretty well everything else. It wasn't until after I got home to Perth and had it X-rayed that I discovered the broken bone. I wasn't entirely surprised.

We all made our way down Sydney's spectacular harbour, and it was a most glorious sight. It was amazing to be there just to see everything, and even more amazing to be a part of it all. I'd been unable to get to Sydney for Australian Bicentenary celebrations in 1988, when the First Fleet Re-enactment armada of ships had come to Sydney, but felt that this more than made up for it.

I discovered some weeks later that my Hong Kong cousin, Wendy, and her husband were in Sydney watching this spectacle, having no idea that I was on one of the ships. This was before we all had mobile phones and instant email. She'd been ringing me in Perth and getting no answer as of course we were in Tasmania. Knowing of my interest in things maritime, she wrote me a long letter afterwards telling me how wonderful it had been to see all these ships in the harbour, and enclosed a couple of photographs. We did have a laugh together later when I told her that I was *on* one of them!

Anyway, back to the parade. The big Mexican Navy training ship *Cuauhtemoc* was just ahead of us, with a Sydney Harbour pilot on board as required by the local regulations. She looked very impressive, with her crew all dressing the yards and looking very smart. Then she came to an abrupt stop ... Oh no, what had happened? I don't know how, but she'd run into the jetty on Goat Island. They were stuck. We manoeuvred around them and kept going in the parade, and could only hope that they would get themselves sorted out. As things transpired she joined the race again fairly quickly, so there couldn't have been any damage done. It was rather ignominious at the time, however.

The actual starting line for the race was outside Sydney Heads in the open ocean, so there was a bit of tacking and wearing going on while we all jockeyed into position. The starter's gun fired and we were off. Next stop Hobart, hopefully. From this point on, no vessels were allowed to use their engines, so the voyage proved to be quite different to any I had been on previously. Normally, if the winds are unfavourable and you have a schedule to maintain, the iron topsail gets put to good use. Not this time.

There was much more emphasis on sail handling and having everything trimmed just right to get the maximum speed on this voyage, while still taking weather conditions and forecasts into account. We started off in very calm seas and light airs without realising that we were heading into one of Sydney's famous "southerly busters". Very soon the fleet had split up and we were all losing sight of one another. Each navigator would have plotted a course for their particular ship to make what they hoped would be the fastest route to Hobart. The weather had other ideas about this, however, and we were soon all doing battle with high winds, heavy seas and the inevitable *mal de mer*.

We had to take some sail in and change course somewhat to make conditions on board more tolerable. We were still following the coastline of New South Wales at this stage, while some of the bigger vessels had headed off into the open sea almost as soon as they were out of the harbour. As our ship was much smaller, and had a fairly inexperienced crew, our officers decided that being close to the shore was a more prudent option for *One and All*, though it might cost us some time.

Over the radio the next day we heard that a number of vessels had already withdrawn from the race and pulled into Eden, down the coast from Sydney. One of the big Indonesian ships, the *Arung Samudera*, had

129

snapped one of her masts and retired. We were grateful for the decision to hug the coastline. Although we'd blown out a couple of sails, we were still in one piece, the seasickness was passing, and we were still headed in the right direction and still in the race.

That one storm was the only really inclement weather that we encountered, and the rest of the journey varied between pleasant to exhilarating sailing. Apart from mending the blown-out sails and keeping a vigilant eye on lines that could suffer from chafe, there wasn't a lot of maintenance being done on this trip. That was something else that was different to the regime on any voyage I'd done before. It was rather a treat not to have to get covered in tar regularly and spend hours chipping and scraping rust.

Something that was exactly the same, though, was the competitiveness that developed between the watches, the camaraderie that developed among the crew and the general fun and games, nonsense and practical jokes that emerged. Not the least of these was a "Crossing the Pond" ceremony. Bass Strait is known locally as "the Pond". We weren't Crossing the Line on this trip, but we were still trespassing into Neptune's domain, according to the captain, so we had a Crossing the Pond initiation instead. It made no difference that I was a qualified shellback and had paid my dues to Neptune many years earlier. I'd not crossed the Pond before, they said.

"But I have", I protested, loudly. "I crossed it last week on board the *Devil Cat*."

"That didn't count", I was told. "That's a stinkboat! You have to *sail* across the Pond."

For my insubordination I had to wear, for twenty-four hours, a necklace of string that had been soaking in a sardine tin for about three days. As you can imagine, it stank. I raided the galley, pinched some aluminium foil and wrapped the string in it. That helped contain the smell a bit.

For my "thieving of ship's stores", however, I had to clean the heads, twice. You can't win! It's all done in good fun, though, and at least you don't get flogged these days. Though we have had some mock floggings on board both the *Endeavour* and the *Leeuwin*. One in particular was aboard the *Leeuwin* during a day-sail for school children. They absolutely loved it, particularly when we ripped off the victim's shirt and they discovered his back was covered in welts. What they didn't know was that they had been painted on before the flogging by a face-painter. They looked so effective, though, that when I showed some friends photos of the "victim" they were appalled. I had to hurriedly explain it was "pretend".

Each ship radioed in their position daily to the escort vessel, and we could all listen to one another's locations and then plot them out on our respective charts. We weren't doing very well, it seemed, though no-one seemed very perturbed about it. We were all enjoying the sailing, the sunsets and sunrises, the dolphins and seabirds and everything else about being at sea. I hadn't realised just how much I had missed it.

We were sailing down the east coast of Tasmania by this time, past the Eddystone Point Lighthouse, which I'd visited just a couple of weeks before with Ken. On we went down past the Freycinet Peninsula and Wineglass Bay, past Cape Pillar on the rugged south-east corner of the island. This had been one of the few places that Ken had not been able to take me to, as it's inaccessible by land. By then we realised that we would not be able to finish the race within the timeframe allocated, so we radioed in our formal withdrawal. It was decided to anchor at Port Arthur for the night.

This gave us the opportunity to catch up on some much-needed sleep – we'd been sailing non-stop since leaving Sydney – and also to have the traditional Sods Opera. While that's usually held on the last night on board, it seemed sensible that we did it here, in a sheltered anchorage. It was also a good idea to hold it earlier than the last night, as some people were going to have to rush off to catch planes as soon as we got into Hobart. It turned out to be one of the better Sods Operas that I've been involved in.

There was a host of hidden talent among the crew: great singers and musicians and storytellers. The doctor, who was in our watch and very active in amateur dramatics and musical comedy in his home community, had written a skit for us to perform. There was a role for each watch member, all of whom he'd been observing since coming on board so that he could devise a part that would suit each personality. There were criminals and crooks, police, pirates, prostitutes and a couple of heroines. It was very inventive considering the short timeframe he'd had to devise it and put it together. He narrated the story from the sidelines, *à la* the *Rocky Horror Show*.

The gist of the story was the supposed kidnapping and abduction of identical twin girls from England at a very young age. They were separated, and found one another again years later as adults on board a ship on the way to Tasmania. One of them had stowed away and the other was on board legitimately. One had become a famous actress in the meantime, and the other was a whorehouse madam. The hold was full of gold, which had been obtained by a heist on the Australian Mint and with which the captain had been bribed. I won't tell you which character I was; suffice to say the whole thing was absolutely hilarious and much enjoyed by everyone. The captain declared he would forgive us for our performance during the crew parade in Sydney in exchange for one of the imaginary ingots.

A lot of the Sods Opera was filmed by an ABC television camera crew that was on board to get some footage for a documentary about the race. They had cameramen on three or four different ships. Somewhat tongue-in-cheek, we all threatened to sue if our skit turned up on national television at some point in the future. Acting out those roles had required some very strange behaviour, as you can imagine, and we all had careers, families and so forth to consider. Although it had been a lot of fun on the night, we really didn't want to see ourselves on national TV.

Next day we weighed anchor and headed off for the last part of our run towards Hobart. We had the engines on by now. Having formally withdrawn from the race, we were no longer bound by any such restriction. It was just as well: most of the fleet was becalmed. The weather gods had really given us a taste of everything, from the storm off the New South Wales coast to the Derwent River being like a mirror. When you're dealing with the sea you can never tell what you are going to encounter. Later that same year the traditional December Sydney-to-Hobart yacht race was the really bad one. It was estimated that the waves were as big as twenty-five metres at the height of the storm. The fleet was decimated, many boats were sunk and six people lost their lives. I'm sure those of us who'd sailed in the tall-ships fleet all got the shivers when we heard about that tragedy. There but for the grace of God …

We made our way into Constitution Dock to discover that the majority of the other vessels that had not pulled out of the race had arrived before us. One or two of the big ones, Russia's *Pallada* and even Mexico's *Cuauhtemoc* – the one that had run into the jetty on Goat Island – had been there for two days already. Oh dear! At least we weren't the last: there were about five still to come in, one of them being Hobart's own tall ship, *Lady Nelson*. She is another replica, but a very small one, normally carrying only a dozen or so crew. Apart from the captain and one other officer, on this occasion she was being crewed by teenagers, all from Tasmania. She sailed in last, but what a welcome she got from the locals. Unlike us, she hadn't given up and turned on the engines, but sailed the whole way from Sydney. The kids on board were bursting with pride at their achievement, and so they should have been.

Lots of celebratory functions were held for all the race crews for about the next week, and we joined in several of these, caught up with some of the sailors from other vessels with whom we'd made friends in Sydney and generally got into "party mode". Then it was time for me to catch my flight home to Perth, so the goodbyes had to be dealt with again. The party was still in full swing when I flew out, with my sailor's heart full and happy, and my need to be at sea sated again, for a little while anyway.

11

HALIFAX TO AMSTERDAM

When I got home from the *Endeavour* trip in early 2000 I discovered that Ken had bought a computer while I was away. Among other things I now had easy and instant access to the Internet. I set about exploring it, and discovered some wonderful websites about tall ships. One of them I got onto very early in the piece was about a special event that was coming up to celebrate the new millennium. There was going to be a race, to be run in stages, from England to the US and Canada via Spain and Bermuda and all sorts of other interesting places. The race would officially finish back in England, and the whole event would culminate with a huge gathering of ships at Sail Amsterdam 2000. My antennae pricked up – and then started to vibrate like crazy!

In 1992 the five-hundredth anniversary of Columbus's discovery of America had been celebrated with a huge tall-ships event, which, as I've mentioned, I didn't hear about until it was far too late to do anything about trying to participate. Prior to the Internet, even contacting half of the ships involved would have been nigh on impossible from Australia. I have a video of the event, and there is a particular section where the mass of tall ships stretches right across the horizon. It looked amazing. I have never watched the video without thinking to myself, "I should have been there". With this event coming up, it was almost as if I was now being given the chance to have a bite at the cherry.

I had known a little about this Millennium race prior to going off to join *Endeavour* in Vancouver, and had half promised Ken that, if I were successful in getting on board *Endeavour* again, I wouldn't pursue this other race idea. I fibbed! The more I trawled the website the more interested I became – but perhaps I'd left it a little too late? There was a company in England acting as agents for many of the tall ships, and it seemed they were still recruiting crews for the later legs of the race. The first stage would commence at Southampton between 12 and 16 April, which was only a couple of months away. But that was OK. I was interested in the Halifax-to-Amsterdam leg, and that didn't start until late July.

The event was billed as "the tall ships race of the century". Some seventy or so ships from twenty-five countries would take part. It would cover fifteen thousand kilometres and involve several thousand young people between fifteen and twenty-five years of age. It was being organised by the International Sail Training Association (ISTA), and the usual race rules required that at least fifty per cent of the crew be in this age group. By default, that would limit the number of places available for anyone older than that. I couldn't resist trying, however, and fired off an email enquiry to the recruiters in England. Their response was encouraging. There were still places available on five square-riggers. One of these was the *Europa*, a lovely Dutch barque that I'd seen during my previous visit to Holland at Sail Amsterdam in 1995. She had rather caught my eye then. The other available places were on three of the Russian ships and another one not known to me at all. I decided to try for the *Europa*.

I completed the paperwork and sent it off with the registration fees. Then I settled down to wait, rather impatiently I must admit. Within two weeks I had an email response back from the recruiters to say they had forwarded my documentation to the captain of the *Europa* for his comment. It seemed he had the last word. As I continued waiting I became more and more impatient, very conscious of the fact that I was well and truly beyond the fifteen-to-twenty-five age range. In the meantime I checked that my passport and inoculations were in order and kept trawling relevant websites, which were getting more exciting by the week. Then it came! – another email advising me that I'd been accepted and would I please forward a bank draft for the required full amount, about $3000 as I recall. These voyages all cost money. Never mind, it was fantastic news.

That all attended to, off I went to the travel agent to make flight bookings. Sometimes this can work out to be rather expensive, as you need to buy a one-way ticket to where you're joining a vessel and then another one-way ticket back to your home from where you get off. In this case that would have meant a flight from Perth to Halifax in Canada and then a flight from Amsterdam back to Perth. I decided to buy a round-the-world ticket: not only was it cheaper, it would allow me a few stopovers. Of course you have to keep travelling in the one direction on these tickets and are not allowed to backtrack. Not a problem: I'd go the long way around to Canada.

Then I got onto making arrangements with people I could visit on the way. After a couple of days in Sydney with friends and relatives I'd fly on to Auckland, where I could visit with Adelia and her family again. In Honolulu I could spend a few days with Laura and Chuck from the *Endeavour* Hawaiian voyage before flying on to Vancouver, where I could visit my cousin Helen and her family again and also catch up with some of the Canadians I'd met during the Hawaiian voyage. Then finally it would be on to Halifax with enough time to spend a few days looking round the area before joining the *Europa*. After getting off the ship at the end of the leg, my plan was to fly from Amsterdam to Hong Kong, where I could spend a few days with my other cousin Wendy and her family before returning to Perth. This would be absolutely perfect, all done on the one air ticket. I had little trouble in ignoring the fact that the bank account had another huge hole in it.

All my joining instructions and other documentation arrived in due course, but I never did get a receipt for the bank draft. I thought nothing of it at the time. Ken commented that he would have felt more comfortable if one had been forthcoming. All of these arrangements had been made either over the Internet or by mail, and I hadn't actually dealt with any real people, so to speak. I told him he was a "worry wart" and that everything would be fine. Bags packed and all set for another seagoing adventure, I flew out of Perth on 8 July heading for Sydney.

Sydney was all about catching up with old friends and flatmates from the 1960s. Having lived there for seven years when I first came to Australia and visited often enough since, I leave the sightseeing for tourists now. It was a great couple of days of camaraderie before my friends saw me off to Auckland, where Adelia was waiting to meet me. It's really quite amazing how many of my friends around the world are people I've met on tall-ship adventures.

Two or three lovely days were spent much as they had been in Sydney – chatting, drinking, eating and laughing, but in this case with a little bit of sightseeing fitted in also – before it was time for me to head off to Hawaii. I phoned Laura and Chuck to confirm that everything was in order at their end and, yes, all was well and they would meet me at the airport. The plan was that I would stay with them on their boat (they are live-aboards) at the marina in Honolulu for a couple of days.

That was where the first little hiccup occurred. When I arrived at Honolulu, very late at night, I got well and truly grilled by the customs and immigration officials. Most visitors to Hawaii would, I imagine, have hotel bookings rather than arrangements to stay with friends at a private address. The only private address that I was able to put on the immigration declaration form was a PO box number. "What is this address?" asked the immigration officer. That's my friends' address, I replied. "So your friends live in a post office box do they?" Oh dear, I had a wise guy. I explained that they lived on a boat. "What's the name of the boat?" Oops, I'd forgotten. "Where's this boat moored?" At a marina somewhere, I said. "What's the name of the marina?" I didn't know that either. "Just a minute", said the official, and off he went, looking very stern and sceptical, to get his supervisor. It wasn't looking very healthy at all.

The supervisor arrived, and I went through the whole thing again. It occurred to me to mention that I'd met these friends on the *Endeavour* voyage the previous year – I was pretty sure the customs people would remember *Endeavour* being there. It's not every day an 18th-century ship with her history turns up in port, and they had given us a huge grilling then. Thankfully he did remember, and was also able to verify what I said because my American visa was still in my passport and it clearly stated, "Crew joining *Endeavour*". I also had an ongoing plane ticket *out* of Honolulu, so it should have been apparent that I wasn't some illegal trying to get in.

Just at that moment the door to the customs area opened as someone else from my flight left, and Laura and Chuck spotted me and began calling out. Saved! "It all seems OK", the supervisor drawled, and my passport got stamped. Laura, Chuck and I had a good laugh together when I told them what had happened. Off we went to their boat, whose name I've still forgotten, and we got settled down for the night after the inevitable chatting and reminiscing.

It's quite an amazing place to live: the marina is right in the middle of Waikiki but pretty quiet at night. They are within walking distance of virtually everything, on top of which rent at the marina is much cheaper than it would be for an apartment. They both work full-time, eat out most nights, get their laundry done at the marina's laundrette, have a circle of friends who are mostly "yachties" and often take their house sailing at weekends. It's an enviable lifestyle in many ways. We had a couple of days together, but then they had to go back to work.

Left to my own devices for a day or so, I did a bit of sightseeing, went to the Maritime Museum and headed for Waikiki Beach, where I had a couple of rides in one of the huge outrigger canoes. As on my previous visit, I thought this was fantastic fun. I'd watched them for a little while, picked out the "beach boy" who seemed to always manage to catch waves and joined his boat. Each outrigger takes about a dozen people at a time, at $US10 per person for three waves, which I thought was worth every penny. The beach boy I picked must have been pushing sixty years old and was as brown as a nut. He'd obviously been there for a while and, at those prices, probably had a very nice apartment overlooking the beach somewhere. It's interesting seeing how other people live.

We met up with some other ex-Endeavourites on my last night in Hawaii, and all of us went out for a meal at a restaurant called Bubba Gump's in the Ala Moana shopping centre. What a fun night it was. The place is named for a character in the film *Forrest Gump*, and all the background music was from the movie. The theme of the place was late 1960s, the waitresses wore roller skates, and memorabilia and art deco artefacts from that period were everywhere. One that got us talking was a sign from Queensland advertising "Baptist Women's Boxing" at a fairground. My mind boggled at that. There were three classes: lightweight, middleweight and "husky", the latter being for "ladies who weighed more than 280 lbs". We did have a laugh at it. I've never seen such a sign anywhere in Australia, so it was intriguing to ponder where they might have got it. We'll probably never know. As the evening drew to a close, farewells had to be said. It was on to Vancouver.

After a very long but uneventful flight, I was relieved to find that the customs and immigration procedures in Vancouver were much more relaxed than in Hawaii, and the formalities seemed to be dealt with in a flash. It might have become much stricter since what the Americans call 9/11. My cousin Helen was at the airport to meet me again. Our reunion was a bit less emotional this time around, though, as it had been only a few months since my last visit. It's an odd thing that it had taken me all of my life to get to North America, and here I was back again inside twelve months. All because of my passion for tall ships.

I had about a week in Vancouver so we did a bit of tripping around. After Vancouver Island, which I thought was fantastic, we went up the mountains to the ski resort at Whistler. We looked for brown bears from the chairlift, but unfortunately didn't see any. I didn't see any real Canadian Mounties either, just as I hadn't the last time I was in the country. Helen explained that they are actually based in the capital, Ottawa, and that British Columbia has its own state police. In any case the famous red-coated Mounties are generally only seen at ceremonial functions now. For the obligatory photo we had to make do with a life-size wooden one that we found in a tourist shop somewhere. I'd promised my mum that I would get a photo taken with a Mountie, and I figured that her eyesight was now so poor that maybe she wouldn't notice the difference.

While in Vancouver I also managed to catch up with Jack and some of the other Vancouverites who had been on the *Endeavour* trip. A dinner at his house was arranged and, when Helen and Tommy dropped me off at the designated address, Jack appeared at the top of the steps and shouted back into the house, "All hands on deck". Half a dozen of my old shipmates rushed out to stand at attention while I got piped up the steps by the bosun's whistle. It was brilliant. *Far* too much drinking and merrymaking went on that night, but from what I can remember it was very enjoyable. Photos and videos of the trip got dragged out and viewed, and we all commiserated with one another that we weren't still on board. I discovered then that there were a couple of other people from the *Endeavour* voyage who were also going to Halifax to join ships taking part in the Millennium race. Maybe our paths would cross again? I'd find out soon enough.

Getting to Halifax, on the other side of Canada, would involve flying over the famous Rocky Mountains. I hadn't realised that Canada is actually wider than Australia – when the airline pilots were threatening to strike, and I suggested that perhaps I could go across by train if necessary, this caused great hilarity in the house. That would take five or six days. Goodness. The threatened strike didn't eventuate, and I duly flew out, but just managed to land in Halifax before the whole place got fogged in for a day or so – quite a common occurrence, I was told. My schedule was now pretty tight, so I was grateful that there'd been no need for my plane to be diverted off somewhere else.

I'd used the Internet to book into a hostel for a few days prior to joining the *Europa*, so got the airport shuttle bus to drop me off there. It looked OK from the outside, and I felt sure it would be fine. It would be my last land-based bed (or bunk perhaps) for quite a while, so I intended to make the most of it. When I checked in I discovered the place was absolutely full, as was the whole town, because of the tall-ships event. Indeed, almost everyone at the hostel was about to join a ship taking part in the race. None of them was joining my ship, but that didn't matter: instant friendships were made as we all had the same thing in common. As always seems to be the case with these big events, the town was in party mode, and there were lots of fun activities to join in – crew parties, concerts and dancing, not to mention a bit of sightseeing before signing on with the *Europa*.

Some of the ships had arrived already, and a couple of my new friends and I wandered down to the docks area to have a look at them. What a picturesque set-up it was too. The boardwalk is nearly a kilometre long and there were vessels tied up alongside two and three deep the whole way along it. They were illuminated at night, and the whole scene had a fairytale ambience about it. Thousands of people were promenading up and down taking in the sights, listening to shanty groups that were busking, stopping to dance at different spots where bands were playing and generally having a good time. The atmosphere was absolutely fantastic, and our excitement levels starting building again. When we went into a pub for a drink I ran into Ian, a Canadian chap who had been on the *Endeavour*. We greeted one another like long-lost friends and quickly established that we were both joining the *Europa*. This was just getting better and better. It would be two or three days before she came in, though, so I determined to see as much of the town and surrounding countryside as I could before heading off to sea again.

A couple of the girls from the hostel and I booked a bus tour for a day, and I discovered to my delight that the bus driver, who looked like he could have been the original Santa Claus, was wearing the kilt. Nova Scotia of course means New Scotland, and they certainly took the connection seriously. In the town itself most of the hotel concierges, bank tellers and people working in the tourism industry wear the kilt or at least something in tartan. Hoots mon, they were more Scots than me!

We ended up at a picturesque spot called Peggy's Cove, whose village dates from 1811. There is a lighthouse there, no longer used as such, which I understand is the only lighthouse in the world to be an official post office with its own special postmark. It was also selling special "Millennium Race Tall Ship" stamps, so some of those had to be bought as souvenirs. While walking around the rocks at the lighthouse and general shore area, we came across a monument to a plane crash that had happened not that long before. I vaguely remembered hearing about it on the news at home. A Swissair flight had crashed into the sea in September 1998, with the loss of all on board, 229 people. The location hadn't meant a great deal to me at the time, as I'd had no idea that one day I'd be standing just there, virtually where it happened.

The next day I visited Halifax's famous Citadel, which sits on the top of the hill with spectacular views all around. It's a national historic site full of interesting displays and information, but also still a barracks for a regiment of soldiers. Much to my surprise I discovered that they were "kilties". I'm not sure now which regiment it was, but they were rather resplendent in their uniforms at midday when they went through the changing of the guard ceremony in the quadrangle. I got chatting to the ones who had just come off duty, and they assured me that they were "true kilties" as well, i.e. they didn't wear underpants! I had a good laugh and said I'd take their word for it. On second thoughts I told them I'd come back on a windy day to check them out.

Part of the display within the building dealt with how Halifax had become a strategic port for British warships during the Seven Years War. The nearest naval dockyard had been in Bermuda, almost 1300 kilometres south, and the Royal Navy needed facilities for its ships closer to the action. Halifax quickly became important to the maintenance of the North Atlantic Squadron. And who was it that was sent to supervise construction of the dockyard and complete the task of surveying and mapping Halifax Harbour in 1760? None other than Lieutenant James Cook – this was long before he became a captain. Here I was, halfway around the world, coming to join another ship, but I was still crossing paths with Captain Cook. It seemed to me to be some kind of sign.

Something else that I seem to have crossed paths with several times now is the tragedy that was the *Titanic* disaster. It started the day that I emigrated to Australia, as my sailing date was the anniversary of the sinking. It continued when I did "the tall ships pilgrimage" to England in 1995 at the exhibition in Portsmouth, and now here it was again. The Maritime Museum of the Atlantic in Halifax has a fantastic exhibit about it, including what's believed to be the only remaining original deckchair. They even have a poster advertising the return voyage, which had been scheduled to commence on Saturday 20 April 1912.

Halifax is also where many of the bodies recovered from the sea were taken for burial, and the story about their retrieval is quite harrowing. I went to the cemetery to pay my respects and came across a very sad headstone that read, "Erected to the Memory of an Unknown Child whose remains were recovered after the disaster to the Titanic – April 15th, 1912". I understand that the local fishermen who were involved in the recovery were so moved by the whole business, and in particular by the fate of this wee mite, that they raised the funds for the headstone. Later, in 2004, I saw a documentary on television that claimed this child had been identified using DNA technology. He was Finnish, his relatives have been traced, and they have been to visit the gravesite. Rest in peace little Eon.

I was in need of some cheer after all this solemnity, so headed back to the docks again the next day. The *Europa* should have been there by this time, and I was anxious to check out my home for the next thirty-five or so days. I was a little alarmed to discover an empty berth where she should have been, as most of the ships had arrived. I suddenly felt an awfully long way from home, and Ken's comment about not having been sent a receipt for the trip payment began to niggle at me. Oh no! Surely this hadn't been some kind of Internet scam.

'Where's the *Europa*?' I called out to anyone within earshot on the deck of the *Oosterschelde* as she came alongside her berth at the quay. I was standing at the large empty space at the dock where the placard told me the *Europa* was supposed to be, next to the *Oosterschelde*. Things can, and do, go wrong with ships' schedules. I'd already heard that *Gloria*, a Columbian square-rigger, had been held up in Boston. It transpired, however, that the *Europa* was across the harbour at the oil depot taking on fuel, and would be berthing soon. Relief flooded over me. Sure enough, shortly afterwards I saw her heading for her berth, and what a sight for sore eyes she was.

The *Europa* was bigger than anything I had sailed on previously, and even had skysails. Skysails are carried above both t'gallants and royals – I'd never been aloft quite *that* high before, and looked at them with more than a little trepidation. As she drew closer to her berth, I was delighted to spot an English girl called Chris on the deck: we had met some years previously on the *Soren Larsen* in Auckland. Another familiar face was Seth, a gentle giant of a Dutch deckhand, whom I also knew from the *Soren Larsen*. My anxiety instantly disappeared, and I was consumed with excitement at the prospect of the voyage across the Atlantic.

When I actually joined the ship, I discovered that she was much better appointed than most of the vessels that I had been on before. Apart from there being more living space generally, it had a library and a deckhouse complete with bar, but what I thought was positively decadent was that every cabin had its own *en suite* shower and toilet. The irony turned out to be that, because we were on a long voyage and there were fifty-nine of us on board, fresh water was rationed, and we were only allowed to shower once a week! My shipmates back home on the *Leeuwin* roared with laughter when I told them about this on my return – laughter with a little "serves you right" tinge to it. Those on board ranged in age from fifteen to seventy-two, and represented 11 different nationalities. This was certainly going to be an interesting trip.

There was also a ship's dog, called "Gander", which I discovered when I asked what a "Den Gander Scrubber" was when I found it in a cleaning cupboard in the fo'c'sle. He belonged to the captain, Klaas, and turned out to be a real personality, complete with sea legs, all four of them! It was the permanent crew's job to wield the Den Gander Scrubber during the voyage when Gander left a little deposit on the weather deck.

The cabins were mostly four-berth, and I was bunked in with two Dutch ladies and a Kiwi girl called Mitch. Not surprisingly, perhaps, and mostly because of the language differences, the two Dutch ladies became good friends while Mitch and I gravitated toward each other, although all four of us were pals. Another two shipmates who would become good friends were Roger, a Canadian, and Ellie, an English girl. Roger, Ellie and I were all in the same watch, while Mitch was in a different one. Ian, from the earlier *Endeavour* voyage, was also in a different watch. This turned out to be quite a good arrangement, as we all got to mix with everyone aboard.

Introductions done, cabins and watches allocated and gear stowed, it was time for safety briefings and a practice climb up the mast. It wasn't actually intended that we go all the way up at this stage, but I decided I wanted to tackle the skysail while we were still safely tied up alongside. Memories of the episode on the *Endeavour* when I'd got stuck on the way to the t'gallant loomed large in my head. I figured that once I'd done this it would be less daunting to deal with while at sea – perhaps at night when the ship was pitching and rolling. After being instructed in the proper donning and use of the safety harness, which was quite different to the ones I'd used before, I was given permission to go up to the skysail yard.

As I slowly and steadily made my way upward, I was concentrating so hard that I didn't realise I had an audience on the quay watching my progress with interest. There were thousands of visitors from all over North America and beyond in town for this event, and it seemed that all of them, as well as the many interested locals, were promenading up and down the boardwalk at the harbour enjoying the spectacle of the tall ships berthed there, most of which were open to the public during the day.

All went well until I got to the spreader bars you need to go through to get to the t'gallant and beyond. These were not designed for solidly built middle-aged ladies. On the way up, my bottom got well and truly stuck, and it was only by turning sideways a bit and doing a lot of jiggling and heaving and muttering under my breath that I finally managed to get through. As I didn't have the benefit of a running jackstay – or some other kind of safety line at that point that I could have clipped my safety harness onto – I was really glad I'd decided to attempt this while alongside the berth. I only became aware of the shoreside audience when I finally reached the skysail yard and a huge cheer went up from the dock. How embarrassing.

On the way back down I turned sideways a bit before tackling the spreader bars again, with the intention of making it easier to get my hips through the space. I won't get stuck this time, I thought to myself. Wrong. Now my bosoms got wedged in the space, much to the delight of the watching crowd. They proceeded to yell up all sorts of advice about how to extricate myself. I was very red-faced by the time I got back to the deck, and am not sure to this day whether I was flushed with achievement, effort or embarrassment. Perhaps it was a combination of all three. Nevertheless, the skysail had been beaten, and I felt more confident about whatever I might encounter during the voyage. I subsequently discovered that the skysail wasn't actually as high as the top of the *Endeavour*'s main mast, which I'd been up many times, but it's interesting what tricks and mind games the brain can play. *Skysail! … Ooooooh!!* Fear had set in without being invited.

Before the race itself commenced there was going to be a crew parade through the town and up to the Citadel. Prizes for place-getters from the last leg of the race would be awarded, followed inevitably by yet another party. The oncoming voyage crew was invited to take part along with the offgoing crew, so we needed to be briefed on proceedings.

It was decided that we would build a float for the parade, which would take the form of a raft, complete with small mast and sails made from some of the spare equipment on board. A mermaid, in the form of Boogie, one of the (male) deckhands, would adorn the

145

raft in bikini, long blonde locks and tail. The rest of us would each carry a flag indicating what country we were from and walk alongside, holding the lines that held up the sails and generally assisting the progress of the raft. It sounded like a fun idea, so we all got to work preparing the props.

A large flat hatch cover appeared out of the fo'c'sle, and this would form the raft. Four shopping trolleys were "borrowed" from the local supermarket and the hatch cover was lashed to them. A short spar was used as a mast with a couple of broomsticks as the yards. It was all coming together nicely. Ropes got shredded to create Boogie's long blonde hair – in fact enough was made for all of us – and one of the girls made a tail for him from some old green canvas. Costumes and other props were created to depict Neptune and other denizens of the deep.

We'd run out of time by this stage, and the ship didn't have a small Australian flag that I could use, so I fastened my silky Aussie-flag boxer shorts to a boat hook and used that instead, much to everyone's amusement. We are perhaps a little less respectful in Australia about our flag (and lots of other things!) than they are in North America, and a pair of boxer shorts bearing the design of a national flag was something they hadn't seen before. As I waved them around on the end of my boat hook, it was fairly obvious what they were, I must admit. The crowd loved them!

We got dressed up in our various outfits, complete with our "Boogie's braids", put a couple of oranges into Boogie's bikini top and lined up to take our place in the parade. In front of this motley crew was a huge banner with the globe painted on it and the words "Europa Unites the World". It was obvious which ship we were from. As had been the case during the crew parade in Sydney in 1998, there were bands from the navy and lots of very smart crews marching along in splendid uniforms. There was even a contingent of Royal Canadian Mounted Police on their beautiful horses. Aha, I thought to myself, proper Mounties. Maybe I can finally get that elusive photograph. We would all end up at the Citadel, so I might get the opportunity then.

Off we set, trundling the trolley/raft along the road with the mermaid sitting atop it, holding the mast that held up the spars and sails, and waving to the crowd in regal fashion. As planned, we were marching alongside, helping to steer the trolley/raft, holding the lines that connected to the sails to make them look as though they were actually set, and waving our respective flags. There were tramlines in the street, so we had to be careful not to fall foul of them with the trolley wheels, or our mermaid would have got tipped off the raft very unceremoniously. The only problem was that we were so busy paying attention to the tramlines below that we didn't notice the telephone wires above. Oops … the mast got tangled up in some of them and we pulled a couple of lines down, to the cheers of the crowd. At about that point the captain decided to disown us. Amidst all of our laughter I had a sudden sense of *déjà vu*: the Sydney crew parade of 1998 was definitely being revisited here.

In due course we arrived, relatively unscathed, up at the Citadel, where a huge crowd had gathered to cheer all the crews as they came into the quadrangle and assembled. I spotted some Mounties, by now off their horses and just hanging about with the crowd, waiting for the formal presentations to start. I shot over, camera in hand, Boogie braids hanging down out of my hat and boxer shorts fluttering in the breeze off the boathook, and asked if I could have my picture taken with them. "Looking like *that*?" was their response. In hindsight I can't say that I blame them, but they good-naturedly obliged. I finally had my picture with a real Canadian Mountie: two of them in fact. My mum would be pleased.

The rest of the day passed uneventfully, and we all meandered back down to our ships to get changed out of our parade clothes and adjourn to the various pubs along the dock. This would be our last chance to let our hair down for a while, as the seagoing preparations would be starting in earnest the next day. And we certainly let our hair down: we danced so hard in one of the marquees that we broke the dance-floor.

After a couple of days of hectic preparations, trying to learn the ropes and rigging (in Dutch!), the day of the big Parade of Sail around Halifax Harbour dawned sunny, bright and clear – great for the thousands of spectators and auguring well for the trip. Led out by the famous Canadian schooner *Blue Nose II*, the parade was an incredible sight, much bigger than the Parade of Sail out of Sydney in 1998.

In addition to the wonderful, majestic square-riggers, hundreds of other vessels of all shapes and sizes, full of people, were either moored to watch us leave or accompanying the fleet. It was a truly memorable occasion. The start line for the race was about a kilometre outside of Halifax harbour, and we all jockeyed for a good position, given our various rigs and sail configurations. The really big ships, with much more sail than we carried, seemed to shoot away and leave us behind very quickly. By nightfall most of them were over the horizon and the fleet had spread out quite considerably. I really didn't expect to see any of them again during the North Atlantic crossing, but this proved to be wrong.

The weather at this stage was mild, with fairly light winds and a slight sea, but the forecast told us we were in for a blow in the next couple of days, and sure enough blow it did. The lee-rail club already had one or two members, and many more were to join as the wind got up to force seven or eight and the seas rose accordingly. Our course initially took us quite a distance south-east to get beyond the limit of icebergs, as indicated on the chart, before we turned at the waypoint and started heading east.

The notation of icebergs rather startled me: they had not been a consideration in any of my previous sailing escapades. Indeed, we sailed very close to the *Titanic*'s last reported position of 41.46'N, 50.14'W. Having visited the *Titanic* exhibition at the Halifax Maritime Museum and gone to Fairview Lawn Cemetery to pay my respects to the 121 victims from the disaster buried there, I found myself a quiet corner on the deck to reflect a bit about the night of 14 April 1912. I like to think that their deaths were not in vain: so many maritime regulations were tightened up after the inquiry that perhaps many more souls have been saved in later years. Not the least of these was the requirement for ships to carry sufficient lifeboats for all on board.

As the voyage progressed, we settled into the normal shipboard routine of four-hour watches interspersed with lectures about sail handling, weather systems, navigation and other nautical topics. We looked forward to mealtimes and off-duty fun and games like the sports day and a flea market, where the most amazing things got bartered and bought or sold. I swapped my Aussie-flag boxer shorts for the captain's cap from the US Coastguard vessel *Eagle*, on the understanding that I would never divulge from whom I'd got it! When multiple tall ships are in port at the one time, good-natured raids on one another are commonplace, but a captain's cap was a definite coup. I'm not entitled to wear it, of course, so when I got back to Perth I gave it to one of my favourite captains from the *Leeuwin*. He was mightily chuffed, but understandably curious as to how I'd come by it.

Those who had had the foresight to bring a large stash of cigarettes and chocolate with them did particularly well at the flea market. It's funny how humans develop cravings for things they can't have (no shops at sea!) but which they normally would hardly eat. We had about fifteen youngsters on board from Bermuda, who promptly got nicknamed 'the Bermudian mafia' as they seemed to be particularly well stocked with goodies. They had no qualms about selling them at exorbitant prices – we suspected that someone had tipped them off about the potential for profitable trade before they joined. Their prices for smokes and chocolate got higher by the day.

The sports day was good fun, although we ended up with some casualties. Mitch sprained both her ankles when she landed heavily on the deck after coming down a rope too fast and someone else ended up with an arm in a sling, not to mention a variety of bumps and bruises. Roger had already taken a tumble on the foredeck and had his ankle strapped up with a suspected sprain, all of which meant that the ship's doctor was very busy. One day when he wasn't available I re-strapped Roger's ankle for him – after my own ankle calamity in Tasmania I'd become quite competent at this – and he said it felt better than the doctor's bandaging. We didn't want to upset the doctor, so every day after Roger and Mitch had had their strapping done we would find a quiet corner somewhere and I would re-do them, trying to make them look the same as the doctor's job so that he wouldn't notice. The doctor, by the way, didn't speak much English. We found out in Amsterdam that he had actually been a gynaecologist, which perhaps explained why my ankle-strapping was better than his.

One day we had a meteorological class, complete with diagrams on a whiteboard, conducted by one of the Dutch crew. Her English was excellent, but occasionally she used the word "uplift" in an inappropriate way. In Australia there would be very few advertisements on TV for brassieres that didn't refer to "uplift", and my sense of humour kicked in. The next time she had her back to us while drawing on the whiteboard and said it again I couldn't resist it: I took hold of both bra straps and jiggled my boobs. Mitch, Roger and Ellie were sitting with me, and they cracked up. We tried to giggle quietly as I responded to the word again, but the lecturer knew something was going on. Then she used the word "turbulence". Well, the boobs went mad then, didn't they, and we couldn't keep our laughter quiet any more. Quite rightly, she threw us out of the class for being disruptive.

Whenever any other ships, whales or dolphins (or perhaps they are porpoises in that part of the world) were spotted, there was great excitement and everyone rushed to get their cameras. One day, when quite a large pod of dolphins came up from our stern and was cavorting alongside, Gander ran down the companionway and raced excitedly along the deck to keep abreast of it. Up till then we had thought he could get up the companionway but not down: he would sit at the top looking completely pathetic and turn his big brown eyes on us until someone took pity on him and carried him down. As he was quite a solidly built dog – he weighed too much for me to lift – this was quite an undertaking. He totally blew his cover the day these dolphins came by, much to the captain's amusement. Apparently Gander sucks a new voyage crew into the lifting-and-carrying business on every voyage.

Another entertaining diversion from the routine of shipboard life was a "blind date" competition that we engaged in via the ship's radio with the crew of a Danish vessel also in the race. Some monumental whoppers got told over the air, about who looked like Brad Pitt and who had a body like Elle McPherson. Everyone had lots of fun, and we figured it was unlikely that we would meet up among the throngs expected in Amsterdam anyway, so it was pretty harmless. Another assumption that ultimately proved to be wrong …

Writers far more eloquent than I have already written much about the infamous North Atlantic Ocean, so I won't make any attempt here to surpass them. Suffice to say that during our voyage we experienced all kinds of weather from fog to very rough seas to a surprising dead-flat calm, when we took the opportunity to go over the side and have a swim and shampoo our hair in spite of the water temperature being only seventeen degrees Celsius. Invigorating, I think it's called. Then again, only one shower a week on board was a great motivator. Given my Scots accent, other people thought I shouldn't have screamed with the shock of the cold. I should be used to it. So I had to explain – again! – about having lived in Australia for years and years.

There were occasions when we were on fairly long reaches on the one tack, so sail handling wasn't quite as demanding as on other trips I'd done previously. Because we were racing we kept as much sail up as possible, which inevitably meant that we blew some sails out too. Several of us became quite adept at using a sail-maker's palm, and learned to stitch them up again the old-fashioned way. I already knew how to do this, courtesy of the *Endeavour*'s sail-maker, so became a regular in the library area stitching "blow-outs", which was quite pleasant work. It was rewarding to be able to pass on my knowledge to some of the young ones too.

In spite of the blown-out sails, we must have done a reasonable job of navigating and racing across the Atlantic Ocean as we eventually came third in our class, only being beaten by two huge Russian ships, *Kruzhenstern* and *Mir*. We crossed the finishing line opposite St Catherine's light on the Isle of Wight at 11.35 pm GMT on Tuesday 15 August, the voyage having taken some twenty-two days, six hours and thirty-two minutes, sailing the whole way. Klaas had the ship lit up like a Christmas tree, blew the *very* considerable foghorn a few times and broke out the champagne, after which there was much celebration on deck. For a change no-one minded the graveyard watch of midnight till 4 am that night, as we were all up anyway. We couldn't quite believe the race was over, although there were still a few more days of the adventure left to go.

None of the ships were due in Amsterdam until 24 August, for the big Parade of Sail up the North Sea Canal to herald the beginning of Sail Amsterdam 2000. Those that had already completed the race headed off to various ports for a few days until it was time to gather at Ijmeiden, at the mouth of the North Sea Canal, where we would all have to enter via a lock system. We put into Ramsgate in the south of England for a day, basically to paint the hull and get the ship looking good for her return to her homeport of Amsterdam. This was mostly taken care of by the permanent crew. The majority of the Anglophiles on board headed off looking for an English fish-and-chips shop, an English pub and an English sweet shop (for chocolate), not necessarily in that order.

We "borrowed" a shopping trolley from a supermarket nearby and put Mitch and her injured ankles in it so that she wouldn't miss out on the shore visit. As we pushed her through the town, several different groups of women thought we were a bunch of university students doing some sort of charity stunt, and kept thrusting money at us. "No, no," we said, "it's nothing like that: we're from that big ship down there." They insisted we keep the money anyway, so we raided the chocolate shop a second time and got enough to share around. Thanks heaps, Ramsgate community!

The food on board had been pretty good and pretty healthy, with a distinctly European flavour, but a little repetitive. Breakfast every morning had been a selection of thinly sliced ham and other cold meats, cheeses, bread baked by the midnight-to-4 watch and cereal. There was nothing at all wrong with that. It was just that the ham and cheese re-appeared, with soup, at lunchtime. One morning we could smell *bacon* getting cooked. Joy oh joy! When it appeared, it had been chopped into minute pieces and floated into the white of the fried egg. It was also distributed fairly thinly. We felt cheated. It only happened the once too. After twenty-two days of ham, bread and cheese, we were ready to kill for some chips or other English-style food.

We also wanted a long, unrationed, hot shower at the yacht club and marina, where we were made very welcome. There was a big yachting regatta on at the time, and the *Europa*'s crew was invited to join a party in the marquee that night. This we did with a vengeance, upholding the ship's honour when one of our lads won the limbo competition and one of our girls won the wet tee-shirt competition. The ship's foghorn beckoned us out of the marquee just before midnight, and we all ran pell-mell down the dock to get back on board before Klaas left without us (which he'd threatened to do, if we weren't back in time).

Off we sailed again, into the night, to cross the English Channel and spend a few days at Schreveningen in the company of some of the rest of the fleet before heading for Ijmeiden. Incredibly, while in Schreveningen

152

I bumped into a lad I'd previously sailed with on the *Leeuwin*. I had never even heard of the place (it's kind of the port for The Hague), and yet I met someone I knew there. His family was actually Dutch, and he was in Holland visiting cousins and on a working holiday for a year. He knew Sail Amsterdam was about to happen, and had heard on the radio about some of the tall ships berthing in Schreveningen, so thought he'd come down and have a look. I think he got an even bigger surprise to see me than I got to see him. The tentacles of the "tall-ships family" extend all over the world and catch up with you in the most unexpected of places. It was great, though, as I could invite him on board as my guest, show him around and share some "shippy" gossip.

We also met up with our "blind dates" from the Danish ship, as they had also pulled in to Schreveningen. Not surprisingly, we discovered that no-one *really* looked like Brad Pitt or had a body like Elle McPherson. We ended up lighting a huge bonfire on the beach that night, and had a fantastic singalong with sailors from all of the ships that were in. What an amazing sense of camaraderie there was: dozens of people all singing sea shanties like "What shall we do with a drunken sailor" in some half a dozen languages. Interestingly, while we couldn't understand the Polish or Russian words to that song, the tune was exactly the same. No doubt it had been spread around the world many, many years ago by some of our forefathers in these same kinds of ships. I also bumped into a Dutch girl called Charlotte who had been on the *One and All* when we did the Sydney to Hobart tall ships race back in 1998. We renewed our friendship and have stayed in touch ever since.

The Parade of Sail into Amsterdam was an even more incredible sight than had been the case coming out of Halifax. Many more tall ships took part in this parade, as the Tall Ships 2000 fleet merged with the Cutty Sark races fleet in Amsterdam. These were supplemented by many other vessels, including traditional Dutch side-keelers, gaff-rigged boats and almost anything that could float, or so it seemed. The new Dutch clipper, the *Staad Amsterdam*, led the parade, and she's quite possibly the most beautiful ship I've ever seen. Once we'd berthed we tried to get aboard her for a look around; but, as they were having a cocktail party for their sponsors, VIPs and the Crown Prince, we had no hope.

The spectator craft and steam-driven traditional Dutch tugs accompanied us for much of the way up the canal, an estimated four million people watched and greeted us with samba bands, other music, flag-dipping and a general carnival atmosphere. The whole thing was completely overwhelming – far beyond my wildest expectations. This atmosphere prevailed for the whole time that Sail Amsterdam was on, the only dampener being that soon it would be time for most of us to disembark from our respective ships and go our separate ways.

But before the parting of the ways came, we had another crew parade to contend with, similar to what had happened in Halifax. We decided to do more or less the same thing again, but in a more sophisticated manner. As we were in *Europa*'s homeport, the captain had lots of contacts. A trailer was borrowed, and, instead of a hatch-cover raft, we used the ship's boat. This worked out to be much better, if a tad more unwieldy to manoeuvre along the street.

It also would allow the "walking wounded" among us to not be left out too. Roger and Mitch could be *in* the boat, and indeed we put Mitch up at the bow – as the figurehead with the long blonde "braids" again. We were still in the process of rigging everything up on the dock, getting ready for the parade, when I heard someone call out my name. It was Martin and Ruth from the *Endeavour*. They had flown across from England for the day to come and see Ian and me. It was wonderful to see them again, and so unexpected. They enjoyed the spectacle of the tall ships in port, of course, but they had primarily come over to see us. More friendships got renewed again, with promises to keep in touch. The crew parade here was much less eventful than the one in Halifax but just as much fun.

Back at the ship again, people were starting to pack up their gear and drift off in separate directions – to stay in hotels for a day or two, catch planes and go home, and generally return to normal life. Before we left, however, some of us attended a memorial church service for the sailors who had died when the Russian submarine *Kursk* had sunk in the Barents Sea on 12 August. We had heard about it over the short-wave radio while we were in the Atlantic, although we didn't have much detail. Several of the ships in the race were Russian, and this service was arranged primarily for their benefit, although we were all welcome to attend. Like the singing around the bonfire at the beach not long before, it didn't matter that we couldn't understand the language – we could empathise with them and share their grief. After all, we were all sailors.

I flew home to Australia the day after the fleet sailed back out of Amsterdam. Many of the ships were going on to Bremerhaven for its sail festival, and others were heading for their respective homeports all over the world. As I would probably never see many of my new friends – because that's what we had all become – or the *Europa* again, I couldn't bring myself to go down to the harbour and see her off. It would have been far too upsetting.

Another adventure of a lifetime had come to an end. There certainly won't be another new millennium in my lifetime, but who knows what sailor's soul I may have inherited from the past, so just *maybe* I would get to do it again somewhere. I had no idea that the biggest trip of all was still to come.

12

THE PRODIGAL DAUGHTER RETURNS

The next eighteen months or so passed by with life pretty much back to "normal", inasmuch as I went back to work and didn't do much in the way of sailing. There were a couple of short trips on the *Leeuwin*, just up and down part of the West Australian coastline, but that was all. Perhaps it was just as well, as my financial status needed to recover.

When the *Endeavour* set sail from New Zealand, where I had left her in January 2000, she headed back to the Australian mainland and toured up the eastern seaboard again. The Fremantle *Endeavour* guides continued to have meetings from time to time, and if anyone had been in any of the ports when she visited they would bring photos and newspaper clippings to the meeting and share them around. Some of us could also keep track of what the ship was doing through the Internet and keep the others informed. All of us were waiting for her to come home to Fremantle, but we had no idea when that might happen, or even if we were clutching at straws in imagining she *would* return. She was actually registered in Sydney, and so Sydney is officially her homeport, but those of us who lived in Perth and who had helped build her saw things otherwise.

The ship was in fact pretty busy and had a full-on programme all the way up to Cairns and Cooktown in North Queensland. One of the BBC television services had chartered her to make a special documentary called simply *The Ship*. This would be a very different voyage indeed, as the producer of the programme selected all the voyage crew and the ship would be sailing very much in true 18th-century mode. The replica stove on the 18th-century deck was modified so it could be used for all the cooking, and the food would be more in keeping with 18th-century sailors' diets. It even included salt beef and hard tack! I spoke with the captain about it and he said I'd never have survived under this regime – there would be no coffee for a start. The documentary was shown on television in Australia some months later and, watching it as it unfolded over some six weeks, I think the captain was probably right: it looked much tougher than normal voyages.

After that charter work was finished we heard the news we'd all been waiting for: she was coming home. She would be in Fremantle for only a short time, however. After disembarking the special crew from the charter work in Bali, she started to work her way back around to Western Australia, going over the top of the country via Darwin and other ports in the north-west of the continent. The plan was that she would be open for exhibition in Fremantle for a few weeks, undergo a big refit, and then head off for England and Europe again on an extended voyage of two to four years. This time she would take a different route – via Cape Horn. That's every sailor's "holy grail". Everyone who was remotely interested in sailing on the *Endeavour* began to get excited again, busily looking at their schedules to see whether the trip could be fitted in. Needless to say I was among them.

Meanwhile the existing *Endeavour* guides would have to be re-activated, and there would probably be a need to recruit some new ones. With no ship to guide people over for some time now, some had lost interest and fallen by the wayside. The old stalwarts were still around, though, and were a good base from which to start re-energising things. Neither the gentleman who had formed the guides in the first place, way back in the late 1980s, nor the Chief Guide latterly, felt they wanted to take on the role this time around. My name got put forward to the captain.

One day I got a phone call asking me if I'd like to take on the role of Guide Coordinator for Western Australia and get the wheels in motion again. Would I? Wild horses wouldn't have stopped me. I told the captain I was almost finished the contract I was working on and would be available shortly. This was around April or May 2001, and the ship wouldn't be arriving in Fremantle until December, so I thought I had plenty of time to get things up and running. This would be a paid position, too, a very different arrangement from my previous involvements with the ship, when I had been either a volunteer or a paying crew member. Little did I know how much work would be involved.

I started working from home. That seemed a perfectly good arrangement, as I had a computer on which I could set up databases and so forth, and I could keep a running log of phone calls and other expenses and get reimbursed somewhere down the track. Calls went out to all of the existing *Endeavour* guides, not just to find out if they wanted to guide again but to see whether they might have any friends, family members or neighbours who might be interested in becoming involved. It's interesting to note that we have never had to advertise for guides in Perth: word of mouth has sourced enough suitable applicants. New application forms were devised and sent out, and the word began to get round. Before long the whole thing had built up such momentum, and my home was getting so swamped with paperwork and phone calls, that it became very obvious I needed an office to cope with it all.

The Fremantle Chamber of Commerce came to the rescue. John Longley, who had previously been the Endeavour Project Manager and CEO, and who remained on the *Endeavour*'s Board, was now the Executive Director of the Chamber, and he was more than willing to assist. A small office in their building was made available along with the necessary equipment, including a computer. The Foundation just had to pay for the phone and any usage of fax and photocopier. This was brilliant. Soon I had 115 guides lined up for the Fremantle port visit. Many of them were from the "old guard", but we had lots of new recruits as well. There were even some experienced guides from England, who were coming out to be with us for what we saw as "the homecoming".

There would also be visits to Dampier and Geraldton, and guides had to be organised for those ports too. Local people in each place were appointed as coordinators, and they carried out similar recruiting drives. Training would need to be organised and new guide handbooks printed, new uniforms and hats and their ribbons (called tally bands) organised and issued. The Foundation's head office was still in Sydney, and the staff there was an enormous help to me in getting things printed or made, preparing press releases and keeping me on track with arrangements generally.

As word spread about the *Endeavour*'s homecoming, I got calls from more and more people wanting to help. Many of them had been involved with her before and they simply came out of the woodwork, often dragging a few friends along with them. It was a wonderful thing to experience, and it reinforced for me, yet again, that this ship has a fascination and magnetism about her that people find hard to ignore.

At the same time as I was knee-deep in guides, another two Endeavourites were organising ship-keepers and volunteer crew for the day sails that would take place while she was in Fremantle. I was also on the committee that had been set up to organise the welcome-home reception. This was going to be quite a big event, and preparations involved liaising with the Fremantle Port Authority, the Fremantle Council, the Water Police and local police, and the State Emergency Service, among other bodies. We also had to contact the elders of the Traditional Owners of the area and get their blessing and, hopefully, their participation in the reception. Also to be organised were the Muzzle Loaders Club, the Royal Australian Navy Band, the Naval Reserve Cadets, the Fremantle Sailing Club Pipe Band and various other notable groups that might agree to take part in the event. Phew! It had begun to get bigger than Ben Hur, to borrow one of Chris's favourite expressions.

In the middle of all of this I got another phone call. The local coordinator who had been appointed in Darwin was no longer able to take on the position. Did I think I could handle, or at least oversee, what was happening up in Darwin as well? Of course I said yes, but really didn't know how I was going to cope. It was easier being an 18th-century sailor on the deck, pulling lines when I was told to, eating and sleeping when I was told to and not having any responsibility. This was a whole new ball game, but a wonderful challenge. Could I rise to meet it?

Sydney office sent me all the details they had about people in Darwin who had applied to become guides, ship-keepers and so forth, and gave me many useful contacts, so I picked it up from there and ran with it. The Darwin Port Authority and the Museum and Art Gallery of the Northern Territory, particularly, were just fantastic – they couldn't do enough to help. Everyone at "the Top End" seemed to be very excited about the *Endeavour* coming to visit. She had never been there before, and the local schools were very keen for the children to see over her. As we started organising school visits, I found myself talking to teachers and headmasters from as far afield as Katherine, Maningrida and other outback Indigenous settlements. They would make a full day's school outing of the visit, bussing the kids to Darwin and return. I was amazed, especially considering how far away from the sea many of these places were.

Things had begun to fall into place. I liaised with the captain at sea, the Sydney office and the shore manager regularly. The shore manager was an amazingly capable young woman called Donna, who had been with the Foundation for many years. She drove the Foundation's big truck, with its information stands and other gear that were set up at every port. All of the merchandise, literature, guide handbooks, uniforms and other relevant paraphernalia usually went ahead of the ship.

Donna also liaised with harbour masters to ensure berths were confirmed and suitable gangways available, whether a pilot was needed and the myriad details necessary to smooth the way for the ship's arrival. I knew Donna from my earlier days as a volunteer, and was confident that I could depend on her advice and experience unreservedly. She had been with the Endeavour Foundation for a long time, and had even gone to the United Kingdom, America and New Zealand with the ship, so she'd had lots of practice at this.

She had already driven the truck and all the gear up to Darwin, and was now having a few days' leave in Perth. It was decided that both she and I should be there when the ship arrived from Bali. We would fly up a few days earlier, which would allow Donna to check that all the port arrangements were in hand and allow me to meet up with the new guides and get a bit of training done. Their familiarisation tour of the ship would, of necessity, have to wait until the *Endeavour* had docked and been cleared through customs and immigration. There'd been a few minor hiccups, but arrangements for the *Endeavour*'s visit to Darwin were looking pretty good.

Early in October Ken took me to the airport to catch my flight to Darwin. Donna was booked on the same flight, but I couldn't see her anywhere when I checked in, so I called her on my mobile. Apart from wanting her to confirm that she was on her way, I was looking for reassurance that the last of the uniform bits and pieces had arrived from Sydney safely. Yes, she was on her way to the airport, just running a bit late. "Have the tally bands turned up yet?" I asked her. We had been waiting on them to arrive from the manufacturer. "What? I can't hear you. It's not a good connection." I asked again, louder this time: "Have the tally bands turned up?"

I suddenly got a vicious prod in the ribs, and a dirty look from Ken. "Keep your voice down", he said, urgently. Then I became aware that some of the people nearby were looking at me rather strangely. The penny dropped. This was only a couple of weeks after the terrorist attacks on the Twin Towers in New York, and I was at an airport asking someone on the phone about "tally bands". With my accent, Ken said it sounded like "Taliban". We had a laugh about it afterwards, but I can imagine how jumpy I must have made some of my fellow passengers, albeit innocently.

We arrived in Darwin unscathed, and settled down to our separate tasks. Guide handbooks and uniforms would be issued at a meeting/training session for the new guides that was to take place at the Museum's lecture theatre. Any changes to rosters and so on would be dealt with then, and any questions answered. That was when I first met Peter, one of the most enthusiastic of the Darwin recruits. They were all enthusiastic, to be fair, but Peter turned out to be what I'd call "one of my mob" – an *Endeavour* junkie. He had already read everything he could get his hands on about the ship before I got there; then he devoured the Guides' Handbook, which became his bible, and by the time he stood his first duty you'd have thought he had come to Australia on the original *Endeavour* with Captain Cook. He was amazing – and rock-solid reliable too. If he said he'd fix something you knew you could leave him to deal with it. We became good friends and have kept in touch ever since.

As a consequence of Peter's passion for the *Endeavour* and his involvement with it, he has added a new member to his family. The new addition has been christened "Horatio" (after Nelson and/or Hornblower) and sits proudly at the front door of his home. It's a smaller version of one of the ship's carrick heads, which he has cleverly carved out of a solid block of wood using only photographs, memory and a scale drawing that he'd drafted. As I said, he is an *Endeavour* junkie. Horatio looks absolutely splendid. I'm sure our original ship's carver will be impressed with it if she ever gets the opportunity to see it.

Arrival day dawned, and we headed down to the port early. I'd forgotten how humid and sticky it could get in Darwin just before the wet season starts, and it was good to get the breeze off the water. Then we spotted the *Endeavour*, slowly making her way into port. The tides in this part of the world are absolutely huge, and great care needs to be taken over the time when ships go into and out of ports. It's quite easy to get stuck in the mud.

The deck was quieter than usual, as there were only about sixteen delivery crew on board bringing her back from Bali after she had disgorged the BBC documentary crew. Captain Chris wasn't on board either: he had also disembarked at Bali. The ship had a relief captain, a man I hadn't met before called Gil, and a sailing master, one of the former *Leeuwin* captains who I knew really well. He was in fact the man to whom I'd given the stolen captain's cap from the USCG *Eagle* when I came home from the *Europa* trip. This was going to be fun. I knew that he was on board the ship, but he had no idea that I was going to be in Darwin to meet it.

There were quite a number of people waiting to meet the *Endeavour*, including a battery of customs, quarantine and immigration personnel. I was dying to get back on board, of course, as I hadn't seen her since New Zealand, but I was told I'd have to wait until they'd been through the ship and cleared everyone and everything to their satisfaction. No amount of pleading on my part appeared to make any difference. Bother!

As she drew closer, everyone on the ship and everyone on the dock was waving, and then Captain Dai spotted me. He couldn't believe his eyes … "What on earth are you doing here lassie?" he shouted over the diminishing space between the ship and the pier head. He's Welsh and I'm Scots, and for years we've had great fun taking the mickey out of each other over our respective accents.

"I came up to see you", I replied, jokingly.

"That's wonderful", he said. "I'll be right there". Before the ship was even tied up properly, he'd jumped onto the wharf and was giving me and everyone else he knew a big hug.

So much for the customs, quarantine and immigration people. Gil was shouting "Unhand that bloody woman and get back here, you mad Welsh bastard" (or words to that effect) and the officials were looking decidedly nonplussed. Donna and I thought it was hilarious. I mean you could get arrested for doing something like that in other countries. I thought about the hard time the customs people gave me on my second visit to Hawaii. But Darwin's a pretty laid back place, and once all the formalities had been taken care of we managed to smooth ruffled feathers by giving the officials a tour of the ship.

The crew and shore party met up for dinner later, and I explained I was the new guide coordinator/manager-cum-girl-Friday-cum-whatever-else for WA and was in Darwin for only a few days to get the new guides settled in. The local replacement guide coordinator would keep everything ticking over after I'd flown back to Perth, where I still had lots to do. Donna would be staying on in Darwin and then driving the truck ahead of the ship as she sailed down the coast. Gil would still be on board when they came into Fremantle, so I'd catch up with him again there. Little did we know I'd catch up with him a few more times as the years went by. We got on famously right from the word go, so it's been good to keep in touch.

I stayed on in Darwin for another couple of days, getting the guides settled in and seeing that the school visits were happening successfully. Apart from the fact that the crew had to deal with the daily ten-metre tides, things were going well. The huge tides meant a lot of adjusting of mooring lines, and occasionally some of the smaller children had to be carried onto the ship, as the angle of the gangway was just too steep for them. With everything under control, I flew back to Perth and left Darwin looking after itself. The ship was actually making two visits to Darwin, with a couple of short sails to the Coburg Peninsula and other outlying spots in between. Some of the guides ended up signing on as voyage crew for those trips. The *Endeavour*'s magic had got to some more people ...

Back in Perth, momentum was picking up with all the preparations for her arrival, although it was still a couple of months away. Letters went out to all the yacht clubs inviting them to make up a welcoming flotilla; invitations to attend the formal welcome were sent to VIPs; rosters for guiding duties were drawn up and changed half a dozen times. The new uniforms were being made. Everything seemed to be going according to plan.

The *Leeuwin* port wardens in both Dampier and Geraldton, the two West Australian ports to be visited by the *Endeavour* on her way down the coast, had been happy to volunteer their services to assist with the visits, and had some locals lined up to help as required. As these visits would be for only a few hours each, and there would be a full crew on board, it had been decided that guides would not really be necessary in either place. I could concentrate on finalising arrangements for the Fremantle homecoming and the three weeks that she would be open to the public.

Following her two very successful visits, the ship left Darwin and started her homeward voyage. That was when things started to go awry: she ran into a bout of very heavy weather and sustained some damage to her bowsprit area. It was quite serious, and could have affected the integrity of the rigging as a whole. There was nothing else for it but to call in somewhere and get emergency repairs done, and she pulled in at Onslow, which had suitable facilities. This development threw the rest of the schedule out quite badly – because of the delay for repairs and the heavy weather that was still affecting the West Australian coastline, both the Dampier and Geraldton visits had to be cancelled.

It also threatened the timing, and indeed possibly the date, of the arrival at Fremantle. Oh no! We had everything pretty well organised and were expecting thousands of people to turn up. Captain Chris was back on board by now, and he and I were in almost daily phone contact. "Don't you dare be late", I said to him. "If you can't make it in time for all the pomp and ceremony at 10 o'clock on the Saturday, don't come in at 4.30. There'll be nobody there! Go and anchor at the back of Rottnest Island and come in at 10 o'clock on the Sunday." That became Plan B, so we had to put everyone on standby for the next day "just in case". The Governor had accepted our invitation to attend, but we hesitated about asking him to go on standby and just hoped for the best.

The day before she was due in I was still ringing Chris and asking, "Where the hell are you? Are you going to make it?"

"No problems", said Chris. "It's a bit tight, but if we motor-sail all night we'll be there in time. Don't fret!"

I was getting more panicky by the hour. Then, at 6 am on Saturday 15 December, a friend of mine phoned me from the beach, where she was walking her dog. Normally I wouldn't have been too pleased to get a call so early, but I was *very* glad to get this one. "I can see a square-rig ship on the horizon", she said. "I'm pretty sure it's the *Endeavour*. I thought you'd like to know ..." She was chuckling as she conveyed the news: she knew how anxious I'd been. What a relief.

About an hour later Chris rang me, thinking he'd get me out of bed, no doubt. "We're here", he said, laughing. "Where's the party?"

I shot down to Fremantle to make sure everything was in place and deal with any last-minute problems that might have cropped up. The navy cadets and the bands and all the other participants turned up as arranged. The guides arrived, resplendent in their new uniforms. The traffic barriers and portable toilets and other amenities were in place. All seemed well – much to everyone's relief, not just mine. Next, the VIPs and members of the platform party were greeted and seated as they arrived. Then someone spotted the masts of the ship over warehouse roofs just before she pulled into view: "She's coming, she's coming!" What excitement – it was infectious. Having come into full view with her accompanying flotilla of boats, she sailed up the harbour, crew aloft, cannons blazing and pennants flying, did a triumphant loop of the harbour and finally drew alongside the berth. It was exactly 10 o'clock. What a consummate showman Captain Chris is.

There was a lot of waving and yelling, and then, once all the pomp and ceremony had been completed, much hugging and laughing and crying between the landlubbers and crew. Many of us had known one another for a long time, and some of the Fremantle guides in particular had not seen the ship for years. It was a very happy and emotional occasion, but we had to get down to business fairly quickly. The ship would be open to the public on exhibition from the next day, and she had to be spruced up before then. The voyage crew all packed up and left, and the permanent crew got the museum set up and generally readied her for visitors.

Some of the first visitors to come aboard were a class of schoolchildren, all decked out in 18th-century gear and looking absolutely wonderful.

One of our Fremantle guides, Debbie, is a schoolteacher, and she had been teaching her kids about Captain Cook and the *Endeavour*. When she had asked them if they would like to visit the ship, the answer had been an enthusiastic yes. The mums all set to and helped make appropriate costumes, Debbie taught the children a little 18th-century dance, and on the day they delighted us all. We had known about the visit in time to contact local newspapers, so Debbie's school, and the ship, got a nice little bit of positive publicity out of it – and all the children had a wonderful time.

We were busy. Apart from Christmas Day, the ship was open to the public every day from 16 December 2001 until 2 January 2002. School holidays were upon us, so we had lots of families come through. One family I spoke to were actually on holiday from Whitby, in Yorkshire, which is regarded as the *Endeavour*'s "spiritual home". They told us that, when the ship had gone there in 1997, the queues to get on board had been so long that they had given up in the end. They couldn't believe their luck: here they were twenty thousand kilometres away and finally had managed to get on board. They were going to submit a story and photographs of their visit to their local paper when they got home – everyone in Whitby, they said, would want to know the latest news.

In addition to her being open to the public for inspection in museum mode, a few daysails and twilight sails were being organised to give members of the public the opportunity to have a short sail on her. The *Leeuwin* was also in Fremantle at the time, so it was decided that the two ships would go out together on the twilight sails and have a mock battle at sea, firing cannons at one another. Advertisements to this effect were placed in local papers, and the phone went absolutely crazy. We had organised only the one phone for my little office, thinking that would be plenty, but every morning I found the message box was at its limit of forty messages from people wanting to buy twilight sail tickets. Could I please phone them back? By the time I did that, the box would be full again. I recruited some extra volunteer help to deal with the demand, and we borrowed an additional phone from the Chamber of Commerce.

A gentleman called George phoned about a dozen times and left as many messages. I rang him back, of course, but every time I did so he would be out, and it would be my turn to leave a message. Eventually

The *Leeuwin* under sail off Fremantle, 1990.
Photo: author

Furling the *Leeuwin's* staysails.
Photo: author

Dressing the yards *Leeuwin*-style: we do the "can-can".
Photo: author

Musket salute on departure of the *Endeavour's* maiden voyage, 1994.
Photo: author

Swamped by streamers.
Photo: author

"Made in WA" brought a huge cheer.
Photo: K. Turner

Our girl's grown up – she's
leaving home.
Photo: K. Turner

The *Devil Cat* at Georgetown, Tasmania.
Photo: author

On my way down the Tamar River to Melbourne.
Photo: K. Turner

The *One and All*, my ship during the Sydney–Hobart Tall Ships Race in 1998.
Photo: Kodak Express Imagepoint (Hobart)

Start of the race.
Photo: Kodak Express Imagepoint (Hobart)

Up *Endeavour's* rigging to wave to the public at Honolulu.
Photo: author

Blowing a welcome on conch shells.
Photo: author

Hula girls galore.
Photo: author

Crowds of well-wishers.
Photo: author

What a welcome!
Photo: author

Leaving Hawaii at sunset.
Photo: author

The *Europa*, my ship for the Millennium Race, 2000.
Photo: MAX / Tall Ships Originals

Mending a sail in situ.
Photo: E. Perrin

On board at the start of the race, Halifax, Canada.
Photo: E. Perrin

Tug o' war at games day.
Photo: author

"Shopping" at Ramsgate, England.
Photo: author

Aloft in the North Sea Canal, Amsterdam, at race end.
Photo: E. Perrin

Santa found us in Antigua, 2004.
Photo: author

Our on-board Xmas tree, thanks
to the chippie.
Photo: author

And in New Zealand in 1999.
Photo: author

One of *Endeavour's* carrick heads,
with "snow" and "earmuffs."
Photo: author

Peter Drescher's scale model,
not quite finished.
Photo: courtesy P. Drescher

Laying aloft and furling on the *Endeavour*, 2004.
Photo: author

Furling the topsail.
Photo: J. Warburton

On the helm: a favourite place.
Photo: M. Morant

Negotiating the main mast futtocks.
Photo: M. Morant

Repeat offenders re-united in 2005: we all sailed together in 1999.
Photo: M. Gardener

Deck showers.
Photo: J. Warburton

Fire in the hole.
Photo: M. Morant

Hairdressing salon open.
Photo: M. Gardener

The captain is rowed ashore at Tahiti.
Photo: M. Morant

Captain Chris (Blake) in formal attire.
Photo: M. Morant

Happiness is a fizzy drink and a cigarette
after 26 days at sea without them.
Photo: M. Morant

The formal welcome at Point Venus, Matavai Bay, Papeete.
Photo: M. Morant

Crew getting in on the act.
Photo: M. Morant

Our beautiful hotel in Moorea.
Photo: author

Taking the ensign down – perhaps for the last time.
Photo: A. Hallett

Riding at anchor in Botany Bay;
almost home.
Photo: D. Gibson

Home – on display at the National Maritime Museum, Sydney.
Photo: D. Gibson

we managed to talk to one another, and he got a ticket organised for the twilight sail on the Friday evening. First thing on the following Monday morning I had a visitor at the office. It was George, who turned out to be a charming Hungarian man in his seventies. He'd had so much fun on the Friday night that he now wanted to go sailing on her properly. Would this be possible?

The ship was actually going to undertake a short sail down to Bunbury, about two hundred kilometres down the coast, following her exhibition in Fremantle and before she went into refit. Would he be interested in going on as a supernumerary? "Definitely", was George's immediate response. I made arrangements with the crew manager in Sydney, and all was in order subject to George providing a medical certificate. This was forthcoming, with the proviso that he mustn't climb aloft or undertake anything too strenuous.

"It shouldn't be a problem," I said, "as you'll be a supernumerary rather than voyage crew." I told him this meant he could do as much as he felt capable of, but didn't have to do anything really. He was delighted.

It had been decided that we wouldn't need to organise and train guides for the Bunbury visit, as the voyage crew that was taking her down would be staying on to bring her back to Fremantle, and they could act as guides if necessary. That meant I would get to have another little sail, as I would go with the ship and teach the voyage crew about the guiding aspects. Whoopee … I was going to sea again, even if it would be for only a few days. It was better than nothing.

I had already come to the conclusion that I couldn't possibly undertake the voyage round Cape Horn and beyond. By this time my mum was pretty frail and in a nursing home. I just couldn't leave her and head off across the ocean, particularly on a voyage that would be taking the ship into such an extreme place as Cape Horn. I'd discussed it with Captain Chris, and of course there was no way he could guarantee to get me home in a hurry in the event of some emergency. It was disappointing, but I felt it was the right decision. I would have to make do with a couple of days down to Bunbury and back – and they turned out to be great fun.

We left Fremantle with slightly less hoo-ha than usual, as we would be back a few days later. One or two of the Fremantle Division Guides had signed on as well, and there were lots of familiar faces among the voyage crew. The "repeat offenders" were to the fore in fact – George was beside himself with excitement. On the way down we hove to somewhere to allow us to go over the side and have a quick swim. George thought this was marvellous, and was one of the first in. He might have been in his seventies, but he was game for just about anything, had a great sense of humour and very quickly became one of the more popular members of the ship's company.

After we'd had our dip, we started making our way back on board. As always, we had a schedule to keep. George had quite a bit of trouble climbing back up the side of the hull using the steps and manrope, and a couple of the lads had to give him a hand. When he finally managed to get over the rail, he looked a lot like a beached seal as he slithered down the wet deck, reminding me instantly of the exhibition I'd made of myself getting back on board at Geraldton all those years ago. I resolved to tell George about that incident to alleviate any self-consciousness he might be feeling, but I needn't have worried: he was enjoying it all far too much. He looked up at me from his prone position on the deck with a mischievous twinkle in his eye and said, in his Hungarian accent, "You vill not tell my doctor, no?" It's remained one of my fondest memories from that trip.

The trip might have been short, but it was certainly sweet. George is another one with whom I've remained friends, and he has become yet another *Endeavour* repeat offender, sailing with her much further afield than Bunbury. He has also done several voyages on the *Leeuwin*, and turns up regularly to help with her daysails, refits and fund-raising events. As he said, it might have come a little later in life than he would have wished, but he'd found a new passion – tall ships.

It was a successful visit to Bunbury, and we seemed to manage OK without a whole battery of guides. Many of the voyage crew helped out as we had intended, and a number of the Fremantle guides had driven down to be there while the ship was open for exhibition. We even had the Melbourne guides coordinator there, which was particularly fortunate when I was temporarily incapacitated and he could take over from me. What happened was that I had a whack on the head from one of the blocks just as we were coming alongside at Bunbury and was knocked out. There was a lump on my forehead the size of an egg and I was a bit concussed, so it was reassuring to have someone competent and experienced to hand over to until I came good again.

The sail back up to Fremantle was fairly uneventful, except for a couple of hours when the resident pod of dolphins from Bunbury's Koombana Bay arrived to accompany us. They played and dived in and out of our bow wave, and it was just lovely watching them. There were some young ones in the pod, and you could see the mums teaching them how to catch and surf down the face of the waves. What a treat. In due course we sighted the lighthouse at Bathurst Point on Rottnest Island, and were soon back alongside Victoria Quay in Fremantle.

This time around the ship would not be opened for exhibition, though, as she was going up on the slips to have her bottom scraped as part of a major refit being undertaken at the shipyard in preparation for her next big voyage. This would take her across the Great Australian Bight to Tasmania and then to New Zealand, following which she would go around Cape Horn and beyond to Britain and Europe. She would be away from Australian shores for several years, it seemed. George had already applied to rejoin her for the leg from Rio de Janeiro to the Azores.

The refit was carried out over a period of about three weeks, after which everything was shipshape and ready to go. I was in the throes of finalising accounts, packing up the office and generally helping out. There were quite a few changes in the permanent crew, and the voyage crew started arriving in Perth a few days before the ship would sail. Among them were many more repeat offenders, not the least of whom were the English couple Martin and Ruth. It was lovely to see them – and I was very envious of the journey they were about to embark upon.

Flying back the other way to England was Gil, who was going to take up the position of Shore Manager in the UK and get everything set up for the ship's arrival and subsequent tour of British and European ports. He asked me to go along as Guide Coordinator, which was very flattering, but of course I couldn't because of my family commitments. Captain Gary and Sailing Master Dai would take the ship to Hobart, and Captain Chris would rejoin her there.

Towards the end of February 2002 the fateful day dawned. The guides assembled once more on the dock to form a guard of honour, hundreds of well-wishers from the general public came along and lots of small boats got ready to escort her out. I was happy and excited for the ship and everyone on board, as this would truly be a *huge* adventure, and needless to say sad at the same time because I wasn't going with them. There would be very few people in the world who could claim to have rounded Cape Horn in a sailing ship these days, especially an 18th-century one, and I desperately wanted to be one of them. It wasn't to be, though.

With her mooring lines cast off, the *Endeavour* pulled away from the dock and headed off down the harbour. We all stood and watched until we couldn't see her any more, by which time I was in tears again. If all went to plan she would be away overseas for between two and four years. I had no idea when I would see her again, but I felt in my bones that I would. She had become such a huge and important part of my life that I simply couldn't imagine things otherwise.

13

THE WINDS OF CHANGE

It would be almost three years before I next saw the *Endeavour*. As had happened the last time she was away for a lengthy period, the Fremantle guides continued to meet occasionally, but the frequency of the meetings diminished as the years went by. We followed the ship's activities on the website, and there were many hair-raising and interesting captain's and crew reports to read. Topics included training with survival suits in Hobart harbour, being delayed by storms, rounding the Horn and having on board a National Geographic film team, some of whose footage would ultimately be used in the movie *Master and Commander: The Far Side of the World*. There were problems with officials and supplies in Rio de Janeiro, which, interestingly enough, was a port where Captain Cook had encountered similar problems all those years ago. Finally there was their triumphant arrival in London, with Tower Bridge being raised to let her pass underneath – stopping all the traffic, no doubt to the captain's great delight.

She spent some considerable time on exhibition and calling in at a variety of ports around the United Kingdom. One of these was Greenock, in Scotland, from where I had left on my school voyage on the *Dunera* in 1961. Oh, how I wished I could have been there. I wondered who would have found the note that I'd stuck on the relevant chart of the area when they came to use it. One of the tasks I'd undertaken during my stint in the Fremantle office was sorting out and cataloguing all the ship's charts before she left. In doing so, I'd come across one of the Greenock area, which was sufficiently detailed to show the location of my old house in Helensburgh. I couldn't resist, and drew a Smiley

Face on a Post-it note with the words "Fran's old house" and an arrow pointing at the spot. Perhaps it was found by some new officer who didn't know me and who wondered who the hell Fran was.

After touring the United Kingdom, she headed across to Europe, and visited many new ports, taking part in maritime festivals in many places along the way and visiting such areas as the Azores and the Canary Islands. Time went by, and life went on. Sadly, my mother passed away eventually in September 2002 at the ripe old age of eighty-nine. I have never found out who told him, and I don't know to this day where he telephoned me from, but Captain Chris rang me to convey his condolences from somewhere on the other side of the world when he heard the news. That's the kind of man he is, and I shouldn't have been surprised really. He knew that I was close to my mum, and also knew that she was one of the main reasons that I'd decided against doing the Cape Horn voyage. It meant a lot to me at the time, though, that phone call.

There were another couple of trips on the *Leeuwin*, one of which was a splendid eco-adventure voyage around the Kimberley region of Western Australia. I joined in Broome and ended up in Darwin, calling in at some spectacular spots along the way. My *Endeavour* friend Peter and his family were kind enough to host me in Darwin for a few days after I disembarked. Naturally enough, we spent many pleasant hours talking about the *Endeavour* and looking at photographs and videos and catching up with some of the other Darwin guides. The end result was that by the time I flew home to Perth again I was itching to get back on my ship. But she was still away in Europe somewhere and it didn't look very hopeful at all: it was possible that she wouldn't be back in this part of the world until 2006. And then the rumours started flying.

One day I received an email from someone. Had I heard that the *Endeavour* was coming home? No, I hadn't heard. Oh joy, oh joy! This was late October 2004. I made a few phone calls to other guides to find out if they had heard anything. No-one had any formal news about it. I sent off an email to the captain to find out what was happening so that I could tell the guides at the next meeting. His reply confirmed that, indeed, the ship was coming home. But she wouldn't be coming to Fremantle. Big changes were in the wind, and he had been *told* to bring her back to Sydney. Something was up! I checked the ship's website after a few days.

Sure enough, part of the latest report read as follows: "The Australian Government, with the support of the NSW Government, wish Endeavour to return to Australian waters and go on exhibition at the Australian National Maritime Museum in Sydney. Directors of the HM Bark Endeavour Foundation have accepted this decision as, by the time that Endeavour returns to Australia it will be more than three years since Endeavour left Fremantle heading for Cape Horn and Whitby." Then followed a list of the ports to be visited on the homeward-bound voyage. Hmmm, perhaps this wasn't so good after all ... I sensed that things were going to be very different after she got back, as she would be under the custodianship of the ANMM, and it sounded as though she would be more or less on permanent exhibition at the museum, not sailing.

I emailed the captain again. "What's happening after you get back?"

"Don't know yet", was his reply. Another email went back to him.

"You'd better put me on from Gisborne to Sydney then."

"Done", came the response. And then I started thinking about it a bit more. The scheduled stop prior to Gisborne was Tahiti, which our *Endeavour* had never visited. Going to Tahiti to observe the transit of Venus was, of course, the purpose of Captain Cook's first voyage on the original *Endeavour*. Maybe I should join at Tahiti? The stop before Tahiti was the Galapagos Islands. Now *there's* a place I've always wanted to visit. I looked up the cost of one-way airfares from Perth to Tahiti and to the Galapagos. They were *very* expensive.

My brain was in overdrive by this time. Another email went to the captain. "Are you taking voyage crew the whole way? Is there a discount if you do the whole trip? Could you put up with me for that length of time?"

The answer came back almost immediately: "Yes; yes and 20%, good question – decline to comment! You're mad. Good on you! Joining date is 6th November in Whitehaven." He obviously knew what I was contemplating.

It took me all of thirty-six hours to make my decision and convince Ken that I just *had* to go. It meant I would be away for Christmas, New

Year, and his birthday – indeed he would have to look after himself for nearly six months. Everything in my being was telling me that this might be my last shot at a really big trip on the *Endeavour*. It had to be done. Mum was gone now, there were no job commitments to consider and, provided I could get Ken's blessing, there was nothing to stop me. He agreed, if somewhat reluctantly. I emailed the captain back immediately: "I'm on my way. See you in Whitehaven." Where on earth is Whitehaven? I'd never even heard of it. This was on the Tuesday.

The timing was really, really tight, and I flew around like a mad thing for the next couple of days. I cashed a term deposit and sent the money off to the Whitby office of the Endeavour Foundation to confirm my booking. It was much better value doing the whole trip than joining somewhere like Tahiti or the Galapagos. Next stop was the travel agent to get me booked on a flight to Manchester, which I'd found was the closest airport to Whitehaven. By going there I would also eliminate the hassle of Heathrow. Done. Fortunately both my passports were up to date, and because of my dual nationality I didn't need any visas – one or other passport would be acceptable everywhere the ship was scheduled to call.

Needles were all up to date except for yellow fever, so I shot into a clinic to get that attended to. It's supposed to be done fourteen days before you leave the country. Sorry, haven't got time. If I react to the vaccination and get a bit sick, someone on the ship will look after me. The clinic wasn't too happy about it, but under the circumstances they obliged. I also collected some malaria tablets, as we would be visiting Panama, where malaria is endemic. A visit to the dentist and a haircut, and I thought I'd covered pretty well everything. All I had to do was organise things so that I could use ATMs overseas, send an email to everyone I could think of ("Sorry, you won't get a Christmas card from me this year – I'll be on the high seas") and pack. I flew out of Perth on the Thursday. Ken was stunned: he doesn't do things as quickly as I do at the best of times, but this had been exceptional.

I must admit that, even for me, it had all been very quick, but there hadn't been even a little bit of time for procrastination. My route was Perth to Dubai, where I had a couple of hours between flights, and then Dubai direct to Manchester. It wasn't until I was hanging around Dubai airport that everything really hit me, and I began to think to myself,

"My God, what am I doing here?" Doubts and guilt began to creep in about leaving Ken for so long, being at sea for so long and lots of other things that one can allow to take over one's mind if one lets them. I very nearly changed flights, turned around and came home. Fortunately I got chatting with an English chap who was going home after a visit to Australia and who had seen the *Endeavour* in the UK somewhere. He was so envious of what I was about to do that he fired my enthusiasm up again, and dispelled all my doubts.

Some old friends of mine who live in Manchester had been on the phone to me in response to my email about no Christmas cards, and they insisted on meeting me at Manchester Airport and driving me to Whitehaven. We would all stay overnight in the same bed-and-breakfast place and catch up on one another's news before I joined the ship. This was the most wonderfully generous offer, and turned out to be a real godsend. Without them I would have been trailing around on two or three different trains, with gear, between Manchester and Whitehaven, and I'd forgotten that it gets dark so early in the UK in winter. I'd also forgotten how cold it can get too! It took about four hours to get to our B&B, and I think Dolly and I drove poor Clive mad as we nattered non-stop from Manchester. We *did* have about ten years of one another's news to catch up on after all.

After getting ourselves settled for the night we went into the town to see the ship and get something to eat. It was Guy Fawkes Night, which we don't celebrate in Australia, and there was a huge bonfire with lots of fireworks. It was all quite festive, although very cold. We saw the ship, but there wasn't anyone around whom I knew, so we adjourned to the pub to continue catching up on our news. We didn't have a lot of time to spend together.

The next day dawned bleak, grey, wet and cold, and when I looked out my window and saw a very brooding and malevolent sea the "What have I dones?" hit me again. The three of us went down to the dock for me to dump my gear and report to the ship. We met up with the captain and some of the crew, most of whom were new to me, although I knew Chris and Allan, the chef. I'd previously sailed with Allan many times on the *Leeuwin*, as he had been the chef on there for a few years. I also knew Malcolm, one of the watch-leaders, and Ally, the bosun – they were fellow West Aussies and we had sailed together a few times. Those who knew me greeted me very warmly – and then I spotted Ruth and Martin, from the Hawaiian voyage. Wonderful! Were they coming on this trip too? The fears and doubts were totally dispelled, and when I went on board I felt like I had come home ... again! Dolly, Clive and I said our cheerio's and they left me to "my shippy people".

It turned out that Ruth and Martin had come through from Durham, on the East Coast, to see the ship and see us off. They *were* joining the voyage, but not just yet. It had all come about too quickly for them to be able to sail from Whitehaven. I looked forward to them coming aboard soon. Also from the East Coast to see us off were the Whitby guides – a whole busload of them. They were very disappointed that the ship hadn't had time to revisit Whitby before returning to Australia, so they had thought, "If she can't come to us, we'll go to her". We all had a very jolly time in the local pub that night, and met up with some of the local guides and more of the crew. By the time the next day came, I was feeling like I'd never been away.

Actually only six voyage-crew members joined at Whitehaven, and no supernumeraries. I think this was partly because it had all come about so quickly and partly because it was getting fairly close to Christmas. At that point I was the only paying voyage-crew member who had booked to go all the way to Sydney. I was certainly the only one who had flown in from Australia to join her. No doubt that was why Chris made the comment in his email about me being mad. One of the six new voyage crew was Margaret, or Mags, as she became known, an English woman about the same age as me. We zoned in on one another and chummed up immediately. She had booked to sail only to Madeira, our first stop, but was thinking about going further if she enjoyed the experience and wasn't too seasick. The *Endeavour* got to her pretty quickly, and she ended up going all the way to Australia. We became great buddies.

We spent a couple of days doing the usual pre-voyage training, going through the safety routines and getting allocated into watches, which were a bit sparsely populated this time around as we had so few voyage crew. Normally, there are around ten to twelve people in each watch, but this time we had only about six, and half of them were either permanent crew or volunteers, the latter being a new category in my experience.

The volunteer crew were people who had done some of the shorter sails around the United Kingdom or had been involved with the ship during a refit or in some other way. They were virtually working their passage to Australia, and might even have had to get off somewhere along the way if there were enough applications from prospective voyage crew – in other words *paying* crew – so their tenure was a little shaky.

Introductions and training done, all the stores had to be loaded and the ship made ready for sea. We had a little time off between work sessions, so managed to make phone calls home and do some last-minute shopping before we actually left Whitehaven on 8 November. Once again we had a huge send-off, with hundreds of people gathered, fireworks going off (leftovers from Guy Fawkes Night no doubt), a jazz band playing and lots of TV crews and other media people there. All of the local guides, the Whitby guides, guides from other parts of the country and previous crew members had travelled there to farewell us. I knew quite a few of them, as we had sailed together before or they had already been in Australia. Others would be joining us as voyage crew along the way. It was all very exciting, and any qualms I had about doing the voyage were long gone by now.

With Madeira about ten days away we headed out into the night, first having to negotiate a very tight dogleg-shaped breakwater before getting out into the Irish Sea. As we were going through the breakwater, we had only about fifteen centimetres of clearance on either side of the hull. We had to run back and forth madly, adjusting fenders and bracing and re-bracing the spritsail yards to avoid hitting anything. It must have looked quite perilous from the shore to the huge gathering and the TV audience. Not a good time to have an accident. Of course we didn't: the captain in his inimitable manner got us safely through the tight spots. As he said, "I got her in – I can get her out!" What a seaman!

It wasn't long before we were charging down the Irish Sea and the Bristol Channel doing around eight to ten knots, as we had some great winds. The ship was rolling quite a lot, and some of the new hands got a bit green round the gills, but the sailing was superb. Add to that some of nature's delights – great flocks of gannets and terns dive-bombing shoals of fish in the water and a huge pod of dolphins that frolicked alongside us for ages – and it was just wonderful to be back at sea. We

177

could still see land at this stage, though, and it wasn't until we passed the Scilly Isles that we got into the situation that I really enjoy – no land in sight anywhere.

We settled into the ship's routine and began maintenance work. This voyage would turn out to be very different to any that I'd done before for several reasons. One of those was that we had volunteers on board; another was that there were no supernumeraries (at this stage anyway) and very few voyage crew. Many of the permanent crew had been on board for a couple of years, so they had laptops and DVD players and other modern gadgets that had not previously been allowed, as this was virtually their home. This created a different ambience during off-duty time, and the cards and board games that we used to play took a back seat to watching movies and using computers. But the main differences would be the length of time that I would be on board, and the amount of maintenance that would be undertaken before we got to Australia. We were virtually going to refit at sea. I could see that I would have to pace myself or exhaustion would take over pretty quickly.

One of the main jobs being done between leaving the UK and arriving in Madeira was the complete refurbishment of the men's heads and change-room area. This was a huge task, during which the showers and loos couldn't be used, so we ended up sharing the girls' heads and change-rooms with them for a while. The lads were all pretty good about knocking before they came in, and had a variety of comments that accompanied the knock, like "Boy coming in", "Bloke coming in", "Are you all decent?" One chap, who was a very manly "alpha-male" fellow, and who worked for the Outward Bound organisation taking young people trekking in the wilds of the Scottish Highlands, had a different comment. He would knock and then simply call out "Male" in his deep, foghorn voice before coming in. He would have cringed with embarrassment if he'd known that half a dozen of us were quietly giggling like a bunch of schoolgirls and saying to one another, "Oh yes, very definitely: you're male all right." It became the girls' private joke for quite some time.

Over and above taking part in group maintenance activities like scraping paint and chipping rust, most of us had some special project that we took on as our own particular responsibility, depending upon individual talents. Along with an American lady called Elaine, Mags and I somehow became the "sewing team". We would be under Rachel's supervision. As the ship's steward / museum curator, Rachel was responsible for the care and maintenance of all the museum exhibits among other things. There was heaps of sewing to do: all the 18th-century uniforms needed mending. In addition to being on display as part of the museum exhibit, these are sometimes worn during filming or at special events. Lots of the flags and pennants also needed repairing and, as we settled into our task, an amazing number of private jobs started coming from the permanent crew. We didn't mind, as it was quite pleasant work, and I could certainly handle a needle and thread more efficiently than an angle grinder.

Mags, Elaine and I got to know one another pretty well during our "stitch and bitch" sessions. Elaine was a real character, and had led a pretty interesting life by the sound of it. She introduced herself as being "from the United States and Portugal". As well as being part-owner of a vineyard in Portugal, where she spent a lot of time, she ran a boutique B&B in the States. She swore Mags and me to secrecy regarding her age, so let's just say that Mags and I were both in our late fifties and Elaine had quite a few years on us. She was on as voyage crew too, rather than a supernumerary, and she climbed aloft and pitched in with everything else the rest of us did. It was admirable. She was only going as far as Madeira, however, like the rest of the voyage crew on this leg.

The winds were very favourable, and we charged along at a great rate. At this pace, we would arrive in Madeira well ahead of schedule. We crossed the Bay of Biscay in a couple of days in very mild seas and fair winds. I was extremely disappointed and said to the captain, "I was hoping to be bouncing off the bulkheads" given the experience I'd had on the *Dunera* during my school voyage. He laughed. He was familiar with the *Dunera* and had spent some time as an officer on one of her sister ships, the *Uganda*, early in his career. He assured me I was probably the only one on board who was hoping for rough weather going through the bay, and that a lot of my ideas about it were most likely fanciful notions anyway, tempered by the passage of time. The *Dunera* was a steel-hulled ship of some ten thousand tonnes, and she would have handled big seas much better than the *Endeavour*. I'm sure he was right, and there was still

179

plenty of time to encounter rough weather. Plus there was the fact that I wasn't a teenager any more. What might have seemed a big adventure at fourteen could perhaps frighten the living daylights out of me now.

Being so far ahead of schedule, we had time to fit in an unscheduled stop at Porto Santo. The captain called these unscheduled stops "flat tyres". We would have quite a few before we got back to Sydney as things turned out. Porto Santo is one of the two principal islands of the Madeira archipelago, the other being Madeira itself. A number of smaller uninhabited islands complete the group, which now has its own parliament, or Regional Legislative Assembly. Porto Santo was the first land discovered by the Portuguese during the Voyages of Discovery and overseas colonisation, which began in the 15th century. I was blissfully ignorant of all this, I'm afraid, until we got there. Apart from having a rough idea of where it was located, all I knew about Madeira was that it produced the wine of that name and that it was basically Portuguese. I didn't even know that there was more than one island.

Calling in here was an additional treat. The island is volcanic in nature and hilly, with interesting vegetation and a couple of nice beaches. Once we got into port and were safely moored, some of the crew went for a swim, but it was still a bit too cold for me. After so many years in Australia, I like the water to be a bit warmer than what was on offer here.

Mags and I went exploring instead. We discovered a vista of houses that had whitewashed or cream walls with shutters at the windows and red-tiled roofs sporting individual family gargoyles on their corners. "Quaint" was a word that sprang to mind. The township was pretty small, but charming. Tourism was just getting started, and it was much quieter than Funchal, the capital on the main island of Madeira, would prove to be. There were a bank and post office and a few shops, and some nice al fresco cafes where we could indulge in leisurely coffees and have a smoke. This was positively decadent, given the smoking ban on the ship. It was actually good to be ashore for a while, and to be able to dine slowly without having to rush back on deck to take over the watch. We still slept on board at night, though, as it was just a very short stopover. We were hoping for a few days off at Funchal.

The next day most of us went on a bus tour around the island, which is only about fifteen kilometres long by seven kilometres wide.

We therefore managed to see virtually all of the sights, and visited a very pleasant private garden estate. On the way back to the ship I made my most amazing discovery about Porto Santo. Christopher Columbus had had a house here, and it still existed! Now basically a museum, it's the house where he lived around 1480 during his brief marriage to the daughter of the governor of the island. I was astonished, and really excited to be there. It seemed I was following in the footsteps of Columbus as well as Captain Cook. I wanted to share my discovery with Ken, so I borrowed someone's mobile phone and rang home. He wasn't expecting a phone call until we arrived at Funchal. "Ah, the albatross has landed", he said when he answered the phone.

"You're never in a million years going to guess where I am", I said, excitedly. "I'm standing in Christopher Columbus's *house!*"

"Is he in?" replied Ken, with his dry sense of humour. Honestly, some people have no sense of reverence.

From the top of the hill on Porto Santo we could see the island of Madeira itself, about seventy kilometres away, so it wouldn't take us long to get there. There is a ferry that runs between the two islands on a daily basis, and many locals and holidaymakers come over to Porto Santo from Madeira for day trips, primarily because of the golden beaches, I understand. Madeira itself doesn't really have any beaches. We motor-sailed overnight between Porto Santo and Madeira, and had another new experience on the way.

During the evening before we got into Funchal, the voyage crew was invited into the Great Cabin for drinks with the captain and officers. This was something new, I told Mags. Normally drinks in the Great Cabin were exclusively the prerogative of the supernumeraries, and us scurvy dog sailors didn't get invited. All that I'd ever done in the Great Cabin on previous voyages was clean it, polish it or paint it. It would turn out to be the first of many invitations into the Great Cabin. As the captain said to me, "You and Margaret are the only two paying voyage crew who are going the whole way. You are going to be wined and dined like you've never been wined and dined before." I wasn't going to object to that at all. As I said earlier, this voyage would turn out to be different to any of the others that I'd been on.

181

14

MADEIRA AND THE ATLANTIC

Funchal proved to be absolutely delightful. With its population of around 120,000, the capital of Madeira is much bigger than the little township on Porto Santo. The entrance to the harbour is dominated by a 16th-century fortress, still in very good condition. (I find historic buildings really interesting – there is absolutely nothing in Australia more than a couple of hundred years old.) There's a huge tidal surge into the harbour here, which proved to be quite challenging. It took us about three hours to moor properly and we cracked two timberheads in the process. More maintenance to be done … Eventually we tucked ourselves in between two large cruise ships, which helped protect us from the surge.

We were going to be here for a few days, so some time off was organised for those of us going on further than Madeira. That was basically Mags and I, as the rest of the voyage crew got off here, along with one or two of the volunteers. Elaine had enjoyed herself so much that she said she'd be back to do another leg of the voyage. "We'll see", we thought, given that she was going back to the United States.

Mags and I booked off the ship and found a little *pensione* room right in the middle of the town for three nights. It was great having a permanent buddy: apart from having one another's companionship, we could share expenses. This would allow us to have a few days off in many ports during the whole voyage. We did have a laugh, though, about costs. We thought we'd done really well with respect to the hotel room, which was cheap and cheerful and clean. Ironically, we ended up spending almost as much getting our laundry done, as there didn't appear to be such a thing as a laundromat in Madeira. We had to pay someone else to do it.

Funchal is full of quaint old-fashioned cobble-stoned streets, wonderful buildings and elegant shops, and the people were very friendly. We visited the fruit and flower market, which was ablaze with colour, and took a cable car to the top of the hill to visit the Monte Palace Tropical Gardens, which is an amazing place. It covers some seven hectares, is full of exotic plants, contains several lakes and has at its centre a grandiose building that was originally a palace but is now a museum. There is so much to see that we spent most of the day there. We could see the ship down in the harbour from the scenic lookouts – this can be quite comforting when you are a long way from home. The *Endeavour* had virtually *become* our home for a while.

When we left the gardens, we discovered the *carreiro*s, or basket carriages. I'd seen pictures of these before and said to Mags, "We absolutely have to have a go on them". She wasn't too sure, but I talked her into it. They are like wicker-basket toboggans, with upholstered seats and back, and take two or three passengers at a time. Underneath there are two greased wooden runners, like skis, which enable them to slide down the pathways – only they don't run on the pathways, they run on the road! They are controlled by two men, also called *carreiro*s, who stand on a wooden platform behind the seat during the descent.

We hurtled down the hill with the whole of Funchal Bay spread out before us. It was absolutely exhilarating, and took me back to my childhood tobogganing days, zooming down the hills in Scotland. Somewhere on the way down there is a professional photographer waiting to take a picture as you fly past, and by the time you get to the bottom the photo has already been developed and is presented to you in a nice framed format – for a cost of course. It's one of my more memorable pictures of the trip. Mags looked a bit wary in it, but I've got pure unadulterated glee written across my face, like some ten-year-old up to all kinds of mischief.

Back downtown, we met up with some of the others from the ship and we all went out for a meal and a few drinks. The town was even more charming at night, as the whole place was beautifully decorated with Christmas lights. We had almost forgotten: it was only about a month till Christmas. You're inclined to lose all track of time when you are at sea, as the daily routine is dictated by the weather rather than the calendar. Later still, when we retired to our little room, our beds felt positively decadent after hammocks, and it was delightful to be able to sleep in a bit. The cathedral bells woke us up the next day, and we went off for more exploring and shopping. We wanted to make the most of our time in Funchal, as the next leg would be quite a long one – across the Atlantic to Antigua, in the Caribbean.

When we rejoined the ship we discovered that no new voyage crew were getting on, although another couple of permanent crew joined us. Cian, the UK shore manager who had taken over from Gil, and Sarah, coming on board as guest navigator, would be with us from here to Australia. I knew both of them, as Cian was another West Australian and I'd sailed with Sarah before. The next batch of voyage crew would embark in Antigua, which is where Martin and Ruth were getting on. We would be pretty light on in terms of manpower on the way across the Atlantic – there were only twenty-seven of us instead of the usual fifty-odd when the ship is full. This had its good points and its bad. There was more room in the sleeping area to spread the hammocks around and the change rooms were less crowded, but there would be fewer hands on deck for sail handling. I was sure we would manage, however.

We left Funchal on 26 November, making a noisy exit as usual. A couple of days before, another large square-rigged ship had dropped anchor nearby. It was the beautiful Dutch clipper *Staad Amsterdam*, which I'd seen in Holland in 2000 when I'd been on the *Europa*. Our second mate on this trip was a Dutch girl called Eefje, so she was given the honour of lighting the cannon that we fired at them as we did a lap of honour around the ship. It was a pity we hadn't had the opportunity to see her under full sail – I'm sure she would have looked magnificent. The sky was blue, the weather was warming up, the winds were fair and the open seas of the Atlantic Ocean beckoned. I was champing at the bit. We were off. Next stop Antigua, due in on Christmas Eve.

We had several different nationalities on board: English, Scottish, Irish, Welsh, Dutch, Canadian, Kiwi and Aussie come to mind. I don't think there were any Americans at that stage. This would be quite a long haul, so we just settled down into the ship's routine. The watches were run with minimum personnel: one person on the helm – unless the weather got rough, when sometimes two were needed – two people on the bow and one on the stern. We always have a stern watch when in open oceans: commercial vessels travel much faster than we do, and we need to be on the lookout for them coming up behind us as well as for anything in front of us. The radar had broken down, and we were unable to get the part needed until we got to Panama, which added another level of vigilance to the lookouts' duties.

When we were not the duty watch we got stuck into the maintenance with a vengeance. The next two big projects were refurbishing the girls' heads and locker room and the 18th-century deck, where we slept. The girls now had to share the boys' ablutions area, so we reverted to the knocking and calling out "Are you decent" and "Girl coming in" routine. Maybe the boys had some private jokes about us this time, but we never found out. It was another big job, though, and would take a few weeks.

All the paintwork had to be scraped down first, both in the heads and in the 18th-century deck. At least the heads could be isolated, but the 18th-century deck was where we slept. We decided to do it a half at a time, and rigged up tarpaulins lengthwise down the middle of the deck. The hammocks were slung on one side while we scraped and sanded on the other. It was fairly arduous work and seemed endless. Some of the deck head (ceiling) was too high for me to reach, so I pinched a big block of wood out of the carpenter's store to stand on. Whenever the ship rolled, though, I'd fall off. Hmm, there had to be another way. I rigged up something to hang on to using my safety harness, so that when the ship rolled I just swayed rather than fell off my block of wood. I looked as if I was "strap-hanging" on the London tube. The captain came by. "Inventive", he said. "Necessary", I replied. He laughed.

Gradually the paint all came off, sometimes in great lengths of several feet at a time, at other times in minuscule flakes. We had competitions to see who could get the longest length off without it cracking – it helped relieve the tedium of the work. The tiny flakes were, however, a law unto themselves. They got into everything. It didn't seem to matter how carefully we did the job or how meticulously we cleaned up at the end of the day's work, for weeks afterwards we were all finding flakes of paint in our hammocks and in jocks and socks and bras.

When we finished the scraping and sanding on one side, we shifted to the other side and began again. It felt a bit like the Sydney Harbour Bridge – would we ever get to the end of it? I remember reading somewhere that the pope of the time was supposed to have called up to Michelangelo when he was painting the Sistine Chapel, "When will you make an end?" In our case the captain had begun to take on a pope-like aura as he tried to gee us up. Once all the scraping and sanding were done, we still had to wash everything down with sugar soap and paint it all. It made repainting the household kitchen seem like child's play – there was just so much of it. Inevitably we got it finished, and it certainly looked much better when it was done. Thank heavens for that. What's the next item on the agenda?

The sailing had improved considerably after the first few days. At the morning meeting on 29 November the captain advised us that we had sailed some 360 nautical miles since we'd left Madeira three days previously, but only 58 of them had been in the right direction. Oh dear. Of course sailing ships can't sail in a straight line, and must use the wind as best they can, irrespective of where it's coming from. Things had even got to the point where the engines had been used for a little while to keep us going in the general direction of the Caribbean. But then the wind had changed and picked up a bit, and we were now sailing along on a reach beautifully, and in the right direction.

The sail across the Atlantic turned out to be one of the best I've ever been involved in, on the *Endeavour* or any other ship. For a lot of the time the wind blew at a nice steady pace in the right direction, almost all of the sails were up, the seas were slight and the sun shone. It was fantastic. Being on the helm is one of my favourite places, and it was an absolute delight to be steering in these conditions, particularly when the "full and by" order had been given. That means keeping the sails full, and sailing by the wind, which is much more satisfying than steering a rigid compass course, as you really get the feel of the ship. You get the wind in your wings, so to speak. Glorious stuff.

We didn't see much in the way of other shipping on our way across the Atlantic, but we saw lots of dolphins, great squadrons of flying fish and a few whales as well as spectacular sunrises and sunsets – and shooting stars. It's quite common to see shooting stars from the deck

186

of a ship, but there are usually only a few per night. One night we had the most awesome display; it was overwhelming to the point where you began to wonder if something was actually wrong. Was the end of the world happening or what?

I was on watch from 8 pm till midnight that night and saw dozens and dozens of shooting stars. I said to the guys who were coming on duty at midnight, "You missed a fantastic exhibition of shooting stars tonight". Wrong! It transpired that they saw even more than we had. And the 4 am watch reported that they'd seen one in particular that was bright green, very big and so close that it lit up the deck of the ship as it flew past. What on earth had we just seen? It certainly wasn't your average shooting-star display, if there is such a thing. And there had been so many of them that no-one had the remotest chance of counting them.

We found out much later in the voyage that we had actually experienced "the Geminids". This is a meteor shower that happens most years now, having first appeared in the mid-1800s. The phenomenon is active between 6 and 19 December, usually peaking on 13 December. Indeed, that was the night in question. To see them to their best advantage you need to have a dark, moonless night and be away from the light pollution of cities, and that had been exactly our situation. A NASA web page on the topic states that in 1996 observers saw as many as 110 per hour. As it is contended that the showers are intensifying every year, it's quite possible we saw even more in 2004. However that may be, it was absolutely awesome. What a privilege to have been a spectator. And how humble it makes you feel: you realise that, in the overall scheme of the cosmos, you are barely a speck of dust (or flake of paint even).

The days went by as we engaged in the simple routine of shipboard life and the weather got warmer and warmer. The sailing continued to be great – and the maintenance seemed endless. We were all so dirty and sweaty by the end of the day that we had reverted to having deck showers in our bathers, courtesy of the chippie and the fire hose. After the first gasp of shock at the temperature and intensity of the water, these are actually quite refreshing and a lot of fun. It's even better, though, if you can manage a very quick fresh-water rinse afterwards. Deck showers certainly helped keep globs of paint, tar and who knew what else out of our newly refurbished heads and change room areas.

Instead of having a deck shower, we sometimes got the chance to go over the side and have a swim. This was absolutely wonderful, and we often took our salt-water soap and shampoo with us and did our ablutions in one of the biggest baths in the world. The safety boat usually got put in the water "just in case", and there would be a couple of people aloft as shark spotters, but we were never bothered by anything untoward. Occasionally we had to be very careful of the current, which could sometimes be deceptive, but we would all swim on one side of the ship and keep an eye out for one another, lending a helping hand whenever necessary.

That was the drill for six days a week, with Sunday a lay day. Lay days were looked forward to, as no maintenance work was carried out and only minimum watch duties were attended to, so they afforded a chance to rest and recharge batteries. On normal days, in addition to watch duties and maintenance work we had sail-handling lectures, rules-of-the-road lectures, knot classes and various other activities, not forgetting morning meetings and daily exercises afterwards. There isn't time to get bored on the *Endeavour*. I recall that the very first time I went to sea on a sailing ship – for a weekend on the *Leeuwin* – a wise old sailor said to me, "If you get the chance to eat, sleep or pee, take it. Because you never know when your next chance will be." This proved to be very sound advice over the years.

15

STAND ASIDE, BOYS

The morning exercises were sometimes serious and sometimes a lot of funny nonsense, depending upon who had volunteered to lead them. We all had to take turns to lead the classes and, if someone didn't volunteer for the next day, the mate volunteered you anyway. By sheer weight of numbers the guys dominated these sessions: there were more push-ups than I cared to count and "blokey" sorts of exercises. One day we, "the girls", decided we were sick of this and volunteered as a group to take the class in a couple of days' time. Our plan was to do some "girly" stuff for a change, and it turned into a complete hoot.

We commandeered someone's CD player and found some Jane Fonda-type exercise music. We got ourselves decked up in sports bras, bike pants, striped toe socks and bandanas and put a routine together in a tongue-in-cheek attempt to look like a team in one of the professional exercise videos. There was much muted laughter and giggling in the change room while we tried to practise it without revealing what we were up to. We deliberately concentrated on dancing and stretching, and did lots of unblokey exercises, knowing full well that most of the guys wouldn't be able to do what we could do. It's called revenge I think.

Catcalls and hoots came from all directions after the morning meeting when we peeled off our outer layer of clothes to reveal our "fitness gear". We were all shapes, sizes and ages, and certainly didn't look like a bunch of professionals in an exercise class, but the captain loved it. We got ourselves into position on the quarterdeck, started the music and got bumping and grinding away. As we planned, many of the moves and stretches were just too difficult anatomically for a lot of the

189

blokes, and groans of pain emanated from various spots on the deck, much to our satisfaction. The captain declared us a roaring success and maintained that we had "raised the bar" on the standard of the morning exercises. Everyone else would have to lift their game from that point on. Talk about issuing a challenge to the boys! The gauntlet had been thrown down.

All joking aside, there was an amazing bunch of really competent girls on this trip. Eefje, the twenty-something Dutch girl I've mentioned already, was our second mate. She had a considerable number of years' seagoing experience and the necessary formal qualifications behind her already, and had sailed as first mate on other ships prior to joining the *Endeavour*. You have to put in a certain amount of sea time before going to maritime college to study for your Master Class V ticket. Then you go back to sea, gain more sea time and experience, return to college and study for the next level up, and so on, progressing through the ranks until you get to Master Class I, the highest level. It takes many years to achieve this normally, but Eefje already had her Master Class III and no doubt would continue onwards and upwards.

Then there was Canadian Laura, another girl in her twenties. She was the bosun's mate, with very competent hands-on skills. Her knot classes were absolutely brilliant – she explained things very clearly – and she's the only person who has managed to teach me how to tie a sheet bend. The last I heard of her she had been at maritime college studying for her Master V ticket, which she gained, and is now sailing as bosun on the *Soren Larsen*, based in New Zealand.

Another Canadian girl on board was Tiffany, who on this leg was my captain o' tops, and a very good one at that. An assistant director in the movie/TV industry when she's in "the real world", she had signed on as paying voyage crew on the Round the Horn trip, and proved herself to be so good that the captain offered her this paid position.

Ros, the captain's clerk, a highly educated woman who can speak several languages, dealt with all the paperwork involved with clearing all of us, plus the ship, through customs and immigration everywhere we went. This is a complex task that needed a lot of attention to detail, especially considering how many different nationalities were involved. She is a marine biologist by profession.

190

Rachel, the ship's steward/curator, is another highly educated and very competent lass. She has a master's degree in audiology, and at that time her professional life was concerned with industrial noise levels. Her duties on the ship included supervising the setting up and breaking down of all the historical artefacts, and making sure that they were all in tip-top condition. She also took care of the captain, which was no mean feat in itself. Once we had supernumeraries on board, she would also act as steward for them.

Katie had been the shop manager shoreside during the ship's time in the UK and Europe. She was a young Australian lass who had deferred her university studies to travel overseas and join the *Endeavour* for a spell. She was on board as a volunteer this trip, virtually working her passage back to Australia. With several voyages around the UK and Europe under her belt already, she was another very experienced and competent girl, and could turn her hand to just about anything.

Clare, Lucy and Keelin were all young volunteers from various backgrounds. Clare is from Sydney and was the youngest on board at nineteen. She had deferred going to the National Institute of Dramatic Art to come on the trip. Lucy and Keelin both turned twenty-one during the voyage. Lucy had also deferred her university studies (in marine biology I think) to come on the trip. The last I heard of her was that she had secured a cadetship with the P&O shipping line, and was going to make the sea her career. Keelin is already some way down that path, as she has several years' experience at sea, having started at sixteen on sail-training ships. She is now attending maritime college back in Ireland to gain the first of her tickets.

And then there was Sarah, an extraordinary young woman also in her twenties. I had first met her on the *Endeavour*'s Hawaiian voyage in 1999, when she was on board as the shipwright's apprentice. She had actually started her involvement with the ship shoreside in the United Kingdom as one of the assistants in the souvenir/merchandise shop (a "shoppie" to the *Endeavour* family). She had done a couple of short trips, loved it and managed to get herself on board as a crew member. Indeed, many of the *Endeavour* crew had been shoppies until they fell under the ship's spell.

Since I had last seen Sarah, she also had attended maritime college and gained the first – or was it the first two? – of her tickets. I knew that she had sailed as second mate on other *Endeavour* voyages that I wasn't a part of since 1999. Now here she was back on board as guest navigator, or "naviguesser" as she self-deprecatingly described herself. Apart from being very good at her job, she had a great sense of humour, lots of patience and a nice, non-technical down-to-earth manner of teaching. She taught most of us who were interested how to use a sextant, and even had some success with me, although I still got lost when it came to the calculations. Much more highly qualified and experienced seamen had tried to teach me before, but I never understood it. Sarah used to say to me, "Don't be frightened by trigonometry – it's just a fancy word for a lot of f…..g triangles." She took the mystery out of it for me, although she didn't quite manage to turn me into an actual navigator.

She was something of a captain's protégé, I think, and he issued her a challenge a bit later in the voyage. When we were leaving Panama he suggested that she try to navigate us to the Galapagos Islands the old-fashioned way, using 18th-century navigation techniques. This involved lots of sun-sights and star-sights and much number crunching using formulae and tables. The duty watch took part in this, too, as it involved putting the log line over the stern of the ship several times a day and taking readings. That was the ordinary sailors' job, as indeed it would have been in the old days.

The log line has a wooden triangular chip on the end. It would be put in the water over the stern for a defined period of time, usually one minute, and allowed to run free from its roll. It would be being pulled off its roll by the force of the water meeting the resistance of the chip. You would then count the number of knots on the line that had passed through your hands during that time. This gives an indication of the ship's speed. (Hence the measurement used at sea – knots per hour.) That's oversimplified, but it will give you some idea if you're not a sailor.

The speed we measured would then be reported to Sarah, and she would disappear into the charthouse for ages, assemble all of her data from the latest sun or star sights plus the speed as reported by us, consult charts and astronomical data and work everything out. She wasn't allowed to read the instruments on the ship's binnacle or check anything on the GPS system. The captain did that discreetly and kept the information to himself. Every day at the morning meeting she would produce the relevant chart, point to a spot and say, "We're about here according to my calculations" and add some detail. The captain would give us the thumbs up behind her head if she was in the right ballpark, or shake his head if she was *way* out. He didn't shake his head very often. She did such an amazing job of it, in fact, that she ended up navigating us the whole way back to Sydney from Panama the 18th-century way, which was quite an achievement.

Since leaving the *Endeavour* she has undertaken more studies to gain her next level of ticket and sailed on the *Leeuwin* as first mate for almost two years. I've crewed with her a few times. There were even one or two occasions when Sarah took the *Leeuwin* out in the capacity of captain. Captain Sarah – the *Leeuwin*'s first female captain! Though I'd had nothing whatsoever to do with her success, I was so excited for her that I felt like a proud mum. I emailed Captain Chris to tell him so. His reply was, "How do you think I feel?" Her latest position is as first mate on *Spirit of Bermuda*, another sail-training ship based in Bermuda and Captain Chris's newest command. No doubt he will continue to mentor her.

While Sarah was the first female to captain the *Leeuwin*, she's not the first female captain that the *Leeuwin* has produced. Several of the girls who started off as paying trainees or voyage crew have developed a taste for the sea. Quite a few of them have gone on to secure cadetships with big shipping companies and further their training, or have gone to maritime college privately, passed all the necessary exams, gained their sea time and progressed that way. At the last count the *Leeuwin* has had a hand in producing many first and second mates and at least three female captains, one of whom has her Master Class I and is now captain of one of those huge vessels involved in the oil industry – an FPSO (floating production and storage offtake) vessel.

Many more of us (including me) have continued to sail in an enthusiastic amateur capacity, undertaken some maritime studies and gone on to become watch-leaders, pursers, programme coordinators, bosuns, bosun's mates, cooks, cook's mates and so forth. Many of these positions are purely voluntary, but one still needs qualifications and experience to fill them. Times have certainly changed since the days when I wanted to try this career path and wasn't even allowed to board a sailing ship – much less enrol at a maritime college – simply because I was female. Go girls!

16

THE CARIBBEAN

The *Endeavour* made such good time crossing the Atlantic that we were well ahead of schedule again. We weren't supposed to be docking in Antigua's English Harbour until 24 December, whereas it was only the middle of the month. The captain made all kinds of enquiries on the radio about going in early, but in the end had to concede that it wouldn't be possible. It's a fairly small dock area in a very popular port, and with Christmas approaching it was even more popular. The simple fact was that English Harbour was full – we just couldn't get in until Christmas Eve. The captain decided that there was nothing else for it but to have another flat tyre, and so we headed for Guadeloupe, another island in the Caribbean about 130 kilometres from Antigua.

Just before we got there, two celebrations were held on board. One was the *Endeavour*'s birthday, she being eleven years old on 9 December. That was her launch date, as opposed to when she left on her maiden voyage. Allan, the chef, baked a monster chocolate cake, appropriately decorated, and some special homemade biscuits, one for each of us. To make sure that everyone took only one biscuit, the cook's mate had iced our names individually on each. It must have taken him hours. Afternoon tea was very handsome that day.

The other occasion for celebration had a different flavour about it altogether. Eefje told us of a Dutch custom according to which each of us had to leave our left shoe at a designated spot in the mess when we retired for the night so that "Klinky Klaas" could visit us. None of the rest of us had heard of this custom, but we thought it sounded quite charming – and fun – so we complied anyway. In the morning we discovered that indeed Klinky Klaas had found us in the night, and our shoes were all filled with sweets (wrapped, fortunately, as the shoes were pretty smelly by this time) and "yowies", which contain chocolate and some little toy that needs assembling. We were like a bunch of kids on Christmas morning, and it didn't take long before the mess tables were full of these little toys and we were playing with them. Remember, we're all adults on this voyage – I think!

These two occasions had us getting into the Christmas spirit, and a decorations committee was formed. We set about cutting old charts into strips and making paper chains, swiped heaps of Alfoil out of the galley and made lots of stars and shiny bauble things out of that and anything else we could lay our hands on.

"We haven't got a Christmas tree", we complained to the captain.

"Don't worry about that", he said. "I've put the word out on the radio, and at last count we've got thirty-six of the buggers lined up to be delivered to us in Antigua. We can *all* have a Christmas tree – each." He was exaggerating of course, but we had a good laugh and hoped that there might be at least one waiting for us on the dock. If all else failed, perhaps the chippie could knock up a wooden one, as had happened when I was on that other big voyage in 1999.

The night before we arrived at Guadeloupe there was another invitation to drinks in the Great Cabin with the captain and officers, but I had earned this one. Captain's rounds had been done that morning, and invitations were extended to the person who had polished the brightest piece of brightwork, the one who had scraped the longest unbroken piece of paint from the 18th-century deck and the cleaner of the men's heads for the best cleaning job on the ship. Other invitations were extended for more dubious achievements, all in fun. Guess which one I received – there was that "Queen of the Heads" title coming back to haunt me again.

After the drinkies we had pizza and nibblies on the deck and played the game "Twister", which is a lot of fun on a moving ship. You end up in some very compromising positions, I can tell you. The weather was warm, there was a gentle breeze, the skies were clear and starry and it was a great night all round. After twenty-six days at sea, though, we were looking forward to going ashore and quite excited about the chance to visit another place that wasn't on the original itinerary.

The chart for this area was very interesting, as there are islands everywhere belonging to various countries. Some are British, some are Dutch, some are Portuguese and some are French. There were even some marked as Venezuelan. I suppose they reflect the nationalities of their original discoverers, but it made me wonder how on earth agreements were reached as to who should own what. And when all's said and done, the indigenous peoples who lived in these places originally wouldn't have been any of those nationalities in the first place. Early explorers and smugglers have a lot to answer for.

We dropped anchor in a bay at a small fishing town called Port Louis, which is on the northern coast of Guadeloupe and not a touristy place. Because of its shape Guadeloupe is called the butterfly island, and the main tourist areas are on the other "wing" of the butterfly, not the one we were anchored at. The island is part of the French West Indies, so the main language spoken is French, albeit with a Caribbean reggae accent, man. There wasn't a dock here that was big enough for the *Endeavour* to use, so we went ashore in batches in the fizz boat, and landed either on the beach immediately in front of us or at the marina where the fishing boats came in, depending on the swell at the time. It didn't take long before the whole community was talking about *le grand bateau* – the big boat.

At it happened, we were anchored in front of the retired school principal's house, and he was most hospitable and generous with his time. Whatever the ship needed, whether it was to obtain fresh vegetables or to get rid of our rubbish, he smoothed the way and got things organised for us. The rest of the community was equally friendly, and quite fascinated with our arrival. Because it's not a tourist area, they don't get too many visitors – particularly visitors from an 18th-century ship! We had great fun trying out our schoolgirl French, but it was very hard trying to get one's ears to comprehend anything said in their singsong reggae accent.

We must have managed well enough, as a journalist from the local newspaper interviewed Mags and me while we were sitting at a café one day. Heaven alone knows what the article said; it might have made interesting reading and been completely wrong. I think we did manage to convey at least that "Madame Margaret" was from L'Angleterre, and that "Madame Françoise" was from L'Australie. Surely they would have got that bit right.

There wasn't really anywhere to stay, so we all slept back on board at night but enjoyed getting onto terra firma for a little while during the day. Mostly we explored the village and its outskirts. It wasn't quite how I had imagined the Caribbean to be – a bit more Third World than I'd expected. I got an interesting photograph of a letterbox that caught my eye during our wanderings. It's welded to the door of an abandoned car that had been dumped outside the relevant house. Since it isn't a tourist area, it's probably far more indicative of the *real* Caribbean than what is presented in travel brochures. And the people were overwhelmingly friendly.

Some of the ship's crew were invited to attend a Christmas party at the local fishermen's cooperative. It was really being held for the children, but it seemed to me that the adults had just as much fun as the kids, especially once several rums had been consumed. Well, we *were* in the Caribbean … what else would you drink here? The thing I most remember about it was the "Papa Noel" who came to the party. Yes, Santa Claus turned up here too, in his traditional red suit and hat and boots. This one was as skinny as a rail, though, and sported a fantastic head of long black dreadlocks spilling out from underneath his Santa hat. He would have to be one of the funniest Santas I've ever seen, coming from my western expectation of fat, jolly men with white hair and beards. The kids didn't care and he had a sack full of goodies for them, so the spirit was the same.

Most of us managed to find a nice beach complete with palm trees to provide a bit of shade, and spent at least one of the days we were there just relaxing, sunbaking and swimming. After the confinement of twenty-six days on a ship at sea, it was wonderful to be able to stretch out a bit, have a little personal space and snooze under the palm tree. Especially when you could have a fresh, chilled coconut milk drink on hand when you woke up, or a pina colada ice cream. As Margaret succinctly put it, "Blissy, blissy!" We had a date with Antigua, though, and this *was* an extra stop, so after a couple of days chilling out it was time to up anchor and head off again. We didn't have far to go to Antigua, so motor-sailed across.

The larger island of the nation of Antigua and Barbuda, Antigua was discovered and claimed by Christopher Columbus in 1493. Here we were again, still following in Columbus's footsteps. The British settled it some 140 years later, and it was part of the British Empire until it gained its independence in 1981. It lies roughly seventeen degrees north of the equator in the middle of the Leeward Islands in the Eastern Caribbean.

Antigua is about twenty-three kilometres long and eighteen kilometres wide, with a population of approximately seventy thousand. The majority would be people of African origin – they were originally brought here as slaves – but there are small numbers of Portuguese, British and Arabic people as well. Tourism is the main economic base nowadays. Its capital is St John's, but we were going to English Harbour, on the south of the island. This is a real "yachtie" spot, and reputed to be one of the best havens in the Caribbean during hurricanes, as it's tucked into a very sheltered bay, surrounded by limestone cliffs.

On top of the cliffs are a number of old fortresses left over from Admiral Nelson's time. Indeed, where we were going was called "Nelson's Dockyard", once an important port of the Royal Navy. Very slowly and carefully we made our way to the entrance of the harbour. As we rounded the bend, we announced our arrival in traditional fashion – by firing the cannons. They echoed off the cliffs brilliantly, so that it sounded as though we had twice as many as we actually had. We must have looked and sounded like something out of the movie *Pirates of the Caribbean*. It was the afternoon of Christmas Eve.

The berth we were allocated was in between another tall ship, the *Tenacious*, and a very flash, extremely expensive looking motor yacht called the *Anson Bell*. Operated by the Jubilee Trust in the UK, the *Tenacious* caters for disabled people. She can even carry wheelchair-bound folk, which is just wonderful. She is much bigger than the *Endeavour*. We had to berth stern-in due to limited space – reverse park the ship in landlubber terms. There was no room for error here. Having been on board when we came out of the very tight space at Whitehaven, though, we all knew the captain would manage it.

The deck crew on board the *Anson Bell* didn't know that, however. They were looking very anxious indeed. "Don't worry," we called over to them, "our captain can park this thing on a postage stamp." They didn't look reassured. They were scurrying up and down the deck hanging fenders out between their port side and our starboard side. Good god, their fenders were cream leather; ours were homemade canvas ones, stuffed with god knows what. We backed in: gently, gently – ever so gently. We had our fenders out too, and we were all fiddling about, re-positioning them on both vessels constantly to protect our respective hulls.

Suddenly we realised that if we didn't cock-bill the spritsail yards, we would wipe out some of their superstructure. The fenders were semi-abandoned as we rushed forward to quickly adjust the yards and cant them up on a high angle to avoid bumping anything. The *Anson Bell* crew was having apoplectic fits by this stage, which we thought was hilarious. Their boat was on the market for something like $US28 million, and they didn't want even a tiny piece of our tar to drip on them, thank you very much. Nothing untoward happened, thankfully. Hello English Harbour – we're here for Christmas.

Our huge blow-up Santa Claus was erected on the mizzenmast top, waving cheerily down to the crowd on the dock. The engineer had fairy lights rigged up in the shape of a Christmas tree, which would be clearly visible at night when he switched them on. There weren't thirty-six Christmas trees waiting for us on the dock, by the way. The captain had fibbed! We ended up not having one, but it didn't really matter. We just had to figure out a way for everyone to get ashore now, as the stern was too high for the gangway to be used.

The bosun came to the rescue. We lowered the fizz boat over the side, and a rope-and-pulley system was set up so that we could pull ourselves back and forth, about six or so at a time, from the bottom of our man steps to the shore. That would work admirably. It was late afternoon by the time we had all this sorted out and the 18th-century deck done up with the Christmas decorations. Then we were ready to go ashore.

The *Tenacious* was having a carol service that evening and we were invited to attend. It was wonderful: here we were, thousands of kilometres from home, whether home was England or Australia, and

199

we had a Christmas Eve carol service to go to where we could sing our lungs out. They had a very good choir organised, and had obviously been rehearsing. Mulled wine and mince pies followed, and tradition abounded. We also got the chance to have a look around the ship and meet some of their paying voyage crew as well as their permanent crew. It was just marvellous to think that these people, even those confined to wheelchairs, had the opportunity to go to sea and have a huge adventure in the Caribbean.

The old Royal Navy tradition of issuing tots of rum to sailors was abolished somewhere around the early 1970s, I believe, but in English Harbour there was a group of residents, mostly ex-Navy, who had formed the Tot Club, and they had their own version of keeping the tradition going. We met many of them at the carol service, and a lively bunch of people they were too. Most were expatriate English, although there were one or two Canadians and Kiwis. Some of them had even taken out Antiguan nationality and were intending to end their days in this idyllic spot.

After the service we all adjourned to the nearest bar onshore and continued yarning about our ship, our voyage and things nautical with the Tot Club people. That was a mistake. They were exceedingly hospitable, and the drinks were getting lined up in front of us far faster than we could get them down. They were used to drinking, as they had regular sessions where they would "up cups and down tots" in the old tradition. We'd been at sea for twenty-six days, more or less without any alcohol, and our systems just couldn't handle it. Mags, sensibly, left fairly early and went back to the ship. I was deep in conversation with someone who had lived in Australia for a while and kept going. I thought I was OK: a bit tiddly, but no more than that. We still had to "punt" ourselves a few metres back to the ship with the pulley system and climb up the man steps, so it would have been risky getting drunk. You could have ended up *in* the drink, rather than consuming it.

I made it back on board OK, but somewhere around three o'clock in the morning I had to rush to the heads to make some phone calls down the big white telephone. Oh dear, I was ill. One of the lads found me on my knees hanging over the toilet bowl, and reminded me to close the valve on the dunny when I'd finished or I was in danger of flooding the ship. I needed *that* piece of information like a hole in the head just then, even though he was right. When I finally stopped vomiting, I got myself a bucket and my water bottle and crawled off into one of the favourite snoozing holes – the hammock pile. There was no question of trying to climb back into my own hammock, which I'd slung before I went out for the evening in what now seemed an impossibly high place. I was still in my hole late morning when Santa Claus (in the form of Liam, the mate) and his elves came around ho-ho-ho-ing and being appallingly cheerful. I vaguely remember telling them all to bugger off and leave me alone. Fancy telling Santa Claus to bugger off on Christmas Day – how disgraceful! They thought it was funny. Could there be anything worse than a self-inflicted hangover on Christmas morning I wonder? I don't think so.

Christmas Day was in full swing ashore with a huge all-day party going on in the quadrangle of the dockyard. Among the half-dozen bands playing there was a Jamaican-type steel-drum band that was very, very good, but sounded like it was inside my head. There were people everywhere and the whole place was jumping. A few private parties seemed to be in progress on board some of the privately moored vessels, but most folk were ashore dancing up a storm, getting stuck into the rum and having a lively, if now very *non*-traditional, Christmas. Another Santa Claus with dreadlocks was milling among the crowds and it was all very jolly. I wasn't my usual self, I'm afraid, and didn't really manage to do the party justice. What a missed opportunity! It served me right.

On board, the galley was a hive of activity as Allan and his helpers went about producing a full-scale Christmas dinner for the whole ship's company. The girls were putting the finishing touches to the decorations and the lads were setting up the bar. We were having Christmas dinner at 4 pm, so it was a late lunch/early dinner sort of affair. There were a few guests, as the Canadian girls' families had come down to meet them. Martin and Ruth had arrived to join for the rest of the voyage, and the girlfriend of one of the captains o' tops had also arrived from England to join for the rest of the voyage. Thankfully, by the time our meal was being served up (by the officers – another old naval tradition) I was feeling better and could join in, although I didn't really do justice to Allan's feast. And then what did we all do later on? Why, go ashore to

201

the bar of course! I took it *much* more gingerly, though, and left several drinks on the bar. I didn't care if they thought it was a bit lame of me not to be keeping up.

We were only in this amazing place for a couple of days, which was a bit of a shame as there was lots more to see in Antigua generally, and Nelson's dockyard was riddled with history. Most of the buildings are 18th-century Georgian and were part of the original naval base established by Admiral Lord Nelson to service and repair the English fleet in the West Indies. They have since been completely restored and converted into small hotels, restaurants, bars and shops. The place is quite charming, if very expensive. The local currency is the Eastern Caribbean dollar, and at the time there were about five of them to an English pound. They were useless anywhere else, and we were told that most banks in other countries wouldn't exchange them, so it kind of encouraged you to spend whatever you had exchanged. I kept a $5 note for a souvenir, as it's a bit different to anything I'd seen elsewhere. Mags and I had been hoping to get a hotel room for a night or two, but there were no vacancies – and they were probably way beyond our budget anyway. We'd have to wait for another port to indulge in that luxury again.

About twenty new voyage crew joined in Antigua, quite a few of whom I knew already – Martin and Ruth of course, from the Hawaiian voyage in 1999, and two others from that trip, Ivo and Paul. Ivo's wife was with him this time, so he'd obviously persuaded her to give the *Endeavour* a try. Another newie whom I knew was Peter, from Western Australia and the *Leeuwin*. He was coming on as voyage crew but would also act as ship's doctor, as that was his profession. He had been on the *Endeavour* before, as had quite a few of the other crew who were joining, although I didn't know them all – yet! The repeat offenders were definitely in the majority.

The *Tenacious* having already departed, the *Anson Bell* left the day before we were due to head off, which meant there was now enough space for us to berth alongside the dock properly. This made it much easier to get stores loaded on, not to mention new crew and their gear, and allowed us to open to the public and say, "Thanks for the hospitality". Mags and I got excused from the safety drills and training for the new crew, which gave us time to catch up with laundry ashore and phone home.

That was when we found out about the earthquake and tsunami that had affected Indonesia and many other countries on Boxing Day and resulted in the deaths of thousands and thousands of people. Indeed, the numbers we heard at the time would turn out to be hugely under-estimated. We didn't see any newspaper reports or television footage of the aftermath until we were in Panama, in fact, and didn't know for quite some time that the death toll was upwards of 200,000. We'd been having such a good time that we felt a bit guilty about not knowing of the tragedy. It certainly made my Christmas morning hangover pale into insignificance.

We sailed out of English Harbour on 27 December, with cannons firing again, and headed down through the Caribbean Sea past the island of Montserrat and several others. Montserrat still has an active volcano, and a huge eruption relatively recently completely wiped out the resort on the southern end of the island. That was where Princess Margaret used to holiday when I was a young girl, and I can remember thinking how exotic it looked at the time. The sun went down behind the island and created a spectacular sunset that evening, and then a little while later the moon came up over the opposite horizon. It was huge and orange, and its reflection in the water made it appear to have a teardrop hanging from it. It was just the most amazing sight. While we always enjoyed our times ashore, you don't see things like that from land very often. It was good to be back on the briny again.

It was also nice because we had a bit of a breeze. The warm weather, which we originally couldn't wait for in cold, wet, wintry England and the North Atlantic, had cranked itself up a few notches and it was now hot – very hot. The temperature below decks was over thirty degrees continually, and it was difficult to find any relief from it. I'd taken to setting up the dampened sarong system again, but often still had trouble sleeping. This would go on for many, many weeks to come, although we didn't realise we were in for so much of it at the beginning.

Our course took us in the general direction of the top of South America, as we were headed for the Panama Canal. Plan A was to anchor off an island near Curacao to spend New Year's Eve. Curacao. That rang a bell. I remembered my brother being there on oil tankers about forty years before. I mentioned this to the captain, and he confirmed that there was a huge oil depot and refinery there that had been operating for years. It's still going. Strange that all these years later I should be sailing past it. He lent me the binoculars to have a look as we went by, but I didn't see any tankers belonging to BP, my brother's old company. That would have been too much of a coincidence.

The weather and tidal currents were such that Plan A changed a bit, and we ended up dropping the anchor off Aruba for New Year's Eve. We didn't go ashore, but went over the side for a swim in the late afternoon, which was glorious. About 6 pm the fireworks ashore started. It wasn't even dark by then, but they started anyway and went on virtually all night. It would have to be one of the most amazing displays I've ever seen. We had some drinks on the deck while watching the fantastic fireworks, then got ready to do the countdown to midnight.

It's a naval tradition that, at midnight on New Year's Eve, the ship's bell gets struck sixteen times. (Note: you don't *ring* a ship's bell!) This is the only time that the bell is struck sixteen times, the normal maximum being eight. The oldest person on board strikes eight bells for the old year finishing and the youngest then immediately strikes eight bells for the New Year starting. The honour of seeing out the old year went to Martin, who was very thrilled to be involved in that way. Young Andy welcomed the New Year in. At sixteen he beat Clare, who had been the youngest on board to this point. This is younger than we would normally take voyage crew, but he had been allowed to sign on as he was travelling with his older brother. He was even more thrilled to take part than Martin, and he told me it was something he would remember for the rest of his life. So would I for that matter: in all the time I've been going to sea, that's the only time I've heard sixteen bells struck. It was now 2005.

Our next scheduled port of call was Colon, in Panama, where we were due on 9 January, so it was time to up anchor and head off again. We were allowed to go over the side for another swim first, which was again just glorious, and then we all got stuck into raising the anchor by hand, the way it was done in the old days. It's a challenging task, and takes virtually the whole crew about an hour's worth of sweat and effort, using the capstan. We could have done with the swim *after* that effort rather than before. Never mind, it was an achievement.

We settled down to the routine again, getting to know our new shipmates and continuing with the maintenance. At least we had finished refurbishing both sets of heads and the majority of the 18th-century deck before we'd got to Antigua. Our day-to-day living areas were now more congenial in spite of the fact that minuscule flakes of white paint were still appearing at random and with gay abandon. We told our new shipmates that we had stripped and painted the whole place on the way across the Atlantic, and many of them seemed quite impressed. A lot of the maintenance work was now on the weather deck and in the Great Cabin, which were more pleasant areas to be working in while coping with the heat.

Some of the new crew were going only as far as Panama, but others had signed on for the rest of the voyage to Australia. One of the supernumeraries, a lovely English gentleman called Dennis, was bored already. Oh dear! He had an awful long way to go yet. This trip had been his wife's idea: they were both going to visit their daughter in New Zealand, but she was flying. Dennis would meet up with her there. One or two of the others were a little disenchanted too: being at sea doesn't suit everyone. The classes and lectures were stepped up to keep people's interest and raise the motivation levels. That, by default, meant the time spent on maintenance was reduced somewhat. Those of us who had already been on board for a couple of months didn't mind at all.

One of the lads who had got on at Antigua had clicked straight away with Mags and me. As we got to know him better, Jason confided that he had recently and unexpectedly lost his mother. Mags and I immediately became two surrogate mums. She was SME (surrogate mum English) and I was SMO (surrogate mum Ozzie). We both became very fond of him and have kept in touch, still signing our emails to him SME and SMO. Jason was a bit bored as well, so he hooked up with the ship's engineer and helped out with the work that was being done in the engine room. Engineering being his profession, that sparked his interest a bit more than sanding blocks and chipping rust. It all still needed to be done before we got to Australia, but the intensity of the maintenance had reduced somewhat. I, for one, was grateful.

The watches were much improved now, as we had more people per watch. One of the new chaps in ours was a full bottle on astronomy, and had a laser pointer with him. It was brilliant on deck at night, as Bob could indicate stars with his pointer and give us an astronomy lesson. He knew many of the legends and stories attached to different constellations as well, and was generally very entertaining and informative. It was Bob, in fact, who told us about the Geminids when we mentioned seeing that huge meteor shower on the way across the Atlantic. He was very envious.

The wind had picked up again and the sailing was fantastic. There were flying fish everywhere, dolphins cavorted on the bow at times and the phosphorescence in the water at night was mesmerising. I spent many a happy hour on the helm, and particularly enjoyed it during those glorious starry nights listening to Bob's explanations about different stars and planets while keeping us on course.

One day while I was on the helm steering full and by, a sudden squall hit us, and I couldn't hold the course at all, due to the fickleness of the wind gusts and its general change in direction. The captain was at my side immediately and put me under helm orders. This is where the officer of the watch makes all the decisions, and you do *exactly* what he tells you – port five degrees, midships and so forth – and you turn the wheel in response to that order. The squall passed, he got me settled down again and gave me a course to steer before he left the deck to continue what he had been doing in the charthouse.

Just as he was backing down the companionway a rogue wave hit us and suddenly we were *surfing* sideways down its face. In about three seconds I was thirty-five degrees off course. All I could do was hang on, keep the ship as steady as I could and wait for it to pass. Meanwhile I could hear a lot of crashing and banging going on below decks as things got thrown around. The captain was at my side again immediately.

"Sorry Captain," I said, "that was me!"

"No it wasn't," he replied, "it was a wave that came from nowhere." I hadn't even seen it until it was upon me. He got me back on course once more and disappeared below.

Two minutes later he was back on deck complaining in a loud, mock-stern voice that he had no clean underwear left. "Come on, Chris", I said. "It wasn't *that* bad!" implying that he'd wet his pants with fright. It turned out that one of the crashes I'd heard below involved his chest of drawers. It had been wrenched off the bulkhead to which it was bolted and gone careering across the passageway. The body of the chest had come to a sudden halt at the doorframe of his cabin but all the drawers had kept going with the momentum. The end result was that all of his undies had been tossed out of the drawers and were now strewn all over the floor. We had a good laugh about it and I gained yet another reputation. By this time people were appearing from below and demanding that the "bloody woman driver" be relieved.

As we sailed on we passed some towns and cities on the northern coast of Columbia, which was on our port side. At one stage their coastguard called us up and warned us to be on the lookout for pirates and drug smugglers. This was almost the stuff of storybooks! We didn't see any, though, and continued on our way. Yet again the winds were so good that we were getting ahead of our schedule and looked like having another flat tyre before long. The San Blas Islands were selected and a new course was plotted. It was hoped that we could get ashore and have a barbeque and perhaps a cricket match on a beach somewhere.

We were also planning on holding a kangaroo court to decide who would be initiated by King Neptune when we crossed the line, which would be in the not too distant future, and who would be excused and on what grounds. We actually had three lawyers on board, so they started planning how the "court" would be conducted, while the shellbacks began plotting as to who would be the victims. You could just tell that this was going to be a lot of fun. Spirits lifted enormously, and there were no more mutterings about being bored – indeed these had already eased off considerably with the excitement of the rogue wave incident. Needless to say I kept getting teased about my "driving" …

17

 PANAMA

As we got nearer to the San Blas Islands, it became apparent that we would not find a good anchorage there. They were too exposed, the winds were too strong and the current was running too fast, so the idea was abandoned and we sailed on. But, rather than have us disappointed at not getting our barbeque and cricket match, Chris came up with another destination – Portobelo. This is a small settlement located not far from the port city of Colon, the place where we were to meet up with the pilot who would take us through the Panama Canal. As had been the case with Porto Santo in Madeira, I was blissfully ignorant of its existence. What an interesting little place it turned out to be.

During his fourth trip to the Americas in 1502, Christopher Columbus named it by exclaiming "Porto belo" (Beautiful port) when he entered the harbour. There's that following-in-Columbus's-footsteps feeling again. It's nestled in a delightful bay, with hills and lush vegetation all around, and one could easily understand him making the comment. However, it is the ruins of the Spanish fortifications surrounding the harbour and the history that attaches to them that make it an astonishing place to visit now.

In addition to Spanish conquerors, the English had been there too – Captain Henry Morgan, who would have to be one of the *real* "pirates of the Caribbean", and Sir Francis Drake, whose lead-lined coffin was put into the sea near a small island at the mouth of the bay. Despite the local legend that it's full of gold and other treasures worth millions and millions of dollars, it's never been recovered. One of the buildings in the township, which is now an art gallery and museum, used to be the customs depot in Spanish times, when it was reputed to have held over two-thirds of the known world's gold. We couldn't wait to get ashore.

After dropping the anchor, we were getting the last of the sails furled when we had unexpected visitors. Among the few yachts anchored in the bay, one belonged to an Australian couple who had been sailing around the world for a few years. When they saw our Australian ensign they scooted over in their tender to find out who we were and what we were doing there. We invited them on board and caught up with some news. They had been at Portobelo for a few days already and, having been ashore several times, were able to tell us something about the history of the place.

They also brought us up to date with news about the tsunami, and we learned of devastation in countries we hadn't known were affected. At that stage the death toll had risen to over 150,000, there were still thousands more unaccounted for and millions of people had lost their homes. We couldn't begin to imagine the scene, as we had not seen any newspapers or television reports of the event.

They told us that they had friends who were diving in the Maldives at the time the tsunami hit. They were actually under water in the middle of a dive and became aware of "something going on up there" when they started getting buffeted around by currents. Sensibly, they stayed down until the turbulence passed. When they surfaced, their boat, complete with local guide and helpers, had gone. They looked towards the shore, about a kilometre away, and saw that their hotel was gone and there was nothing left but devastation and debris. They had no choice but to dump their scuba gear and weight belts and swim for it. They made it ashore safely, and were able to contact friends and family somehow to let them know they'd survived. They had nothing left except the bathers and wetsuits they were wearing, but at least they were alive.

Some local people had arrived at the *Endeavour* by this stage, and we negotiated with them to ferry us back and forth to the shore for a very nominal cost. This would be much more efficient than unlashing the fizz boat and putting it over the side. We paid $1 a head, and about ten of us could get in their boat at a time. We hadn't yet cleared customs or immigration, as there weren't any officials around, so we were kind of "personae non gratae" – no-one knew we were in the country except the locals. The captain stressed that we must stay out of trouble while we were ashore; otherwise we would *really* be in trouble. "Us get in trouble?" we all chorused in feigned innocence. We got the message though.

There wasn't a lot to the township except for a small market, a few shops and tavernas, and a superb catholic church. Inside the church there is a black baby Jesus, one of the few in the world I understand. We would have liked to go in and see it, but it would have been disrespectful for Mags and me to enter dressed the way we were, in shorts. We contented ourselves with taking some photos of the church from the outside and paying our respects at the nativity scene that had been erected outside it. Then it was off to purchase a few trinkets at the market and find somewhere to eat. Yet another new experience awaited us.

We met up with some of the others from the ship and picked out what we thought looked like the best taverna in the street. They were all pretty simple, as the main reason tourists come to the town is to visit the church and see the ruins so they don't get thousands and thousands of visitors. Consequently, the menu doesn't really cater for western tastes. It was all in Spanish, and the waitress spoke only broken English, but we managed to order something for everyone – and I was pretty sure I'd ordered fish. Sure enough, when my meal came, fish it was. I felt reasonably safe with that.

David's meal was, however, a new dimension in dining – a barbecued iguana. He was brave enough to tackle it, and said that it was actually OK. He did fine until he got to the foot, when he let out a startled cry. "What's up?" we asked. He held it up for our inspection – a dear little foot complete with claws. Everybody dived for their cameras amidst groans of mock horror and laughter. The waitress couldn't understand what the fuss was about. He didn't eat that bit.

Afterwards we set off to visit the art gallery / museum, read more about the history of the place and explore the amazing ruins. There are actually several different sets of ruins of Spanish fortifications, complete with cannons, dungeons and large stone walls. There are three different forts straddling the hillsides, with the two upper sections offering terrific views of the bay and the town. The positioning of the cannons, which are all still there – although the gun carriages disintegrated long ago –

210

was such that anyone foolish enough to poke their nose into the bay would have been blown out of the water very easily. It was a fantastic defensive set-up. Then again, if the Spaniards had had two-thirds of the world's gold in the township, it would have needed a bit of defending. The ruins are listed as a World Heritage Site now, so hopefully they are protected forever.

Back on board ship it was decided that we would hold our kangaroo court that evening, while we were still at anchor. The trial was of the accused pollywogs who would soon be trespassing into Neptune's domain. What a funny night it was. One of the lawyers was the prosecutor, one was the defence and one was the arbitrator. Ruth, as the judge, looked resplendent in her wig (a string mop head) and cloak. Paco, the engineer, was the hangman. The noose was already swinging off the deckhead. There was a panel of shellbacks, those of us who had already crossed the line on previous occasions. "Bring forth the accused and we will hear their excuses and make judgments." The "accused" had already been selected – carefully!

First was Cian, our former shore manager from the UK. According to his defence lawyer he had already crossed the line during a voyage on another replica ship, the *Duyfken*. The prosecutor argued that it hadn't actually crossed the equator, and so his claims were false. Three of us on the panel agreed with the prosecutor – we were all from Western Australia and knew of the ship and the voyage in question, and that it *hadn't* crossed the line. "Done", said Ruth in her judge's capacity, and banged her gavel. "You will pay homage to Neptune in due course." Well, we all knew that would be the outcome anyway, irrespective of whatever defence the accused managed to put up.

And so the evening went on, amid much hilarity, dreadful overacting by everyone involved and some great excuses. Liam, the mate, and Malcolm, one of the captains o' tops, were both accused. They both *had* crossed the line previously, and had entries in their seamen's logbooks or other evidence to prove it, but the judge declared that the entries were faked. They would have to pay homage to Neptune too. They appealed to the arbitrator. The arbitrator conferred with the panel. The panel decided to reserve a decision on the appeal. We would get back to them in a few days once we had considered our verdict. We would make them

211

sweat! They were led away amid much protesting of their innocence and laughter all around.

Young Andy protested that, at sixteen, he was a minor, and should not be subjected to adult "punishment". He was happy to accept the charge that he was a pollywog and would be trespassing, but should be let off lightly. Hmm – that was a good angle, we thought. "Done", declared the judge again with another whack of the gavel. "Guilty as accused, but the court declares that a lighter punishment shall be carried out." Well, we'll see what happens when we actually cross the line, won't we. It wouldn't be for another couple of weeks yet, so we had plenty of time to cook up something suitable for him.

And then Clare's defence was presented. It was a beauty. She appeared wearing her shorts, with her belly stuck out and her hand in the small of her back, walking like a pregnant woman. On top of the shorts she wore a clingy singlet top, which revealed the most spectacular set of nipple bumps that could be imagined. She really did look pregnant! The "nipples" were actually the lids from Keelin's contact lens cases, but they sure looked realistic. While she also happily admitted to being a pollywog, the plea was that she should be excused from the indignities of paying homage to Neptune on the grounds that she was "with child". The physicality involved with the initiation rites might hurt the unborn baby. This was a very good defence strategy, but was she really pregnant?

"Have you examined this young woman?" the judge asked Peter, the ship's doctor.

"Oh yes, your honour, several times", replied Peter. Well, she was a good-looking, shapely young girl … His answer brought the house down.

Several other accused were brought forward and presented to the court, and of course all were declared guilty. The shellbacks had plenty of victims lined up and plenty of time to devise what we would actually do to them when eventually we did cross the line. We didn't actually get around to "hanging" anyone that night, but so much wine was consumed that we were all a bit "hung" (over) the next day. I thought there was a delicious sense of irony about that. We were staying in the bay at Portobelo overnight, and were going ashore again briefly in the morning, so it had been a chance to let our hair down, as there would be no requirements for sail handling.

What we did manage to do during the night, though, was drag the anchor and pick up an undersea electric cable in the process. Oops, perhaps this bay was not quite as sheltered as we had thought. There seemed to be no harm done, either to the ship or the town, so we quietly dropped the cable back on the seabed and re-anchored in another spot for the next few hours. The local authorities didn't appear with a large bill, so we could only assume that all was well.

We motor-sailed out around midday, past Drake Island, where the remains of Sir Francis, supposedly in full uniform complete with helmet, reputedly lie in that lead-lined coffin full of treasures. There are also supposed to be two galleons that were sunk with him. I haven't been able to verify the truth of this, and would have imagined that modern-day treasure-hunters and marine archaeologists would have been ferreting about looking for them long before now. It wasn't very deep here. If they were able, with today's technology, to find King Henry VIII's *Mary Rose*, in the Solent in England, and the Titanic, some six kilometres down at the bottom of the North Atlantic, why would they not have been able to find this treasure? It makes a good story though.

It wasn't too far to sail around to the port city of Colon, on the Atlantic side of the Panama Canal. We wouldn't be going ashore there, but we had to anchor and wait for our turn and for the Panama Canal Transit Pilot to come on board. The place was crowded with ships of all shapes and sizes, which I found very exciting. A couple of the voyage crew decided to get off: they'd had enough. When the fizz boat returned from taking them ashore, it brought back a few others who were joining us for the next part of the journey. One of them was Elaine, the American woman who had enjoyed herself so much between the UK and Madeira. She *had* come back. Also in this group was Ian, one of the *Endeavour* guides from Whitehaven, who had said upon our departure that he was intending to join us somewhere along the way. Fantastic!

The captain, using his wondrous diplomatic skills and silver tongue, had been able to gain the necessary approvals for us to do a daylight transit. This was great news, as we'd previously been told that we would probably have to go through the canal during the night. The canal operates twenty-four hours a day, but for safety reasons big ships are given preference for daylight transits. We would be going through tucked in behind another smallish freighter, so that both vessels would be in the same lock at the same time. We were scheduled to commence the transit early the next morning, and it would take the whole day before we came out on the Pacific side. I hadn't realised that it would take so long, and hunted out a book from the ship's library to learn a bit more about the canal.

I knew that the French builder of the Suez Canal, Ferdinand de Lesseps, had started construction in 1881, and another French group had taken over after his attempt had failed, due partly to formidable geographic obstacles and partly to tropical disease – it has been estimated that more than twenty thousand people died during the construction phase, mostly from yellow fever and malaria. The original intention had been to build a sea-level canal, but this was abandoned in favour of a lock-type canal. The second French consortium was unable to secure adequate financing for the project, and was eventually forced to sell its rights and equipment to the US Government. The Americans recommenced construction in 1903, but it wasn't until August 1914 that the canal opened for business. Since then it has accommodated more than 900,000 vessel transits.

The Canal itself is an eighty-kilometre-long waterway travelling north-west – south-east, and consists primarily of three sets of locks – Miraflores, Pedro Miguel and Gatun – the Gatun Dam and Gatun Lake, and the Galliard or Culebra Cut. It is now managed and operated by an autonomous Panamanian government body known as the Panama Canal Authority, its ownership having been transferred from the USA in the 1980s. Currently the PCA employs approximately nine thousand full-time and part-time workers, and it is the country's second largest employer.

Each lock chamber is exactly the same size, measuring about thirty-five metres in width, three hundred and five metres in length and twenty-four metres in depth. Approximately 750 megalitres of fresh water are added to or drained from each chamber every time a vessel is raised or lowered. It takes about eight minutes for this to happen. This water is gravity fed from Gatun Lake; no pumps are involved. It's an incredible piece of engineering when you think about it, particularly when you realise how long ago it was built. I was getting more impressed the more I read.

There is obviously a limit to the size of vessels that can transit the canal. As modern-day vessels get bigger and bigger, there are some that are too big to fit into the lock chambers. The books told me that some vessels have become so big that sometimes there is only ten centimetres on either side of the hull when it advances inside a lock chamber. What the books *didn't* tell me was that when you are sitting at the bottom of a lock in a small ship, looking directly at the walls towering above you on either side, you can clearly see lots of paint scrapes that have been left behind by ships that have been there before you. It's exactly like an enormous version of an underground car park, where cars have swiped the concrete columns and left some of their paintwork behind. I could hardly believe my eyes.

Very early the next morning the pilot came aboard. He wasn't too pleased with our location: we weren't in quite the right position in the "queue". The captain explained that we had dragged the anchor several times in the night, and had had to move and reposition the ship about eight times. We were now quite close to the actual pier at Colon, and noticed another tall ship had tied up alongside. It was the *Thor Heyardahl*, a German square-rig vessel that I'd seen before in Amsterdam. We fired our cannons at them (naturally!) as we passed by, and set off all the car and security alarms nearby. The pilot thought this was marvellous – his slight displeasure at our not being in the designated place in the queue immediately dissipated. He turned out to be a very nice man, actually, and was extremely helpful to the crew in many ways once we got to Panama City. He was thrilled at the opportunity to take an 18th-century sailing vessel through the canal: "I have done over four thousand transits, but I don't get the chance to do *this* every day!"

The queue began to move, and we shuffled our way, under motor, into the designated spot behind the freighter. Once you have entered the lock, the huge "mitre gates" are closed behind you and wire ropes from the shore are passed to the deck crew and fastened to something substantial on the deck. This presented us with a problem: the wire ropes would chafe our wooden rails so much that they might do horrendous damage. The captain convinced the pilot to allow us to do it the other way around, i.e. we passed our much softer 18th-century-type ropes up to the shore gangs, who secured them to the shore equipment in the form of electric locomotives at each side of the canal. These hold the ship in position in the centre of the lock. Each new loco costs in the order of $2 million, and each of the newer tugboats in the PCA fleet costs over $5 million. With such costs to contend with, this is a massively expensive facility to operate, especially as improvements, extensions and equipment replacements are ongoing.

The money to operate and improve the canal comes from the tolls payable and Government subsidies. The average price paid for a vessel transiting the Canal in 2002 was $47,461. The cruise ship *Radiance of the Seas* paid the most expensive toll on record on 12 April 2001, at $202,176.76. (Don't forget the $0.76!) The least expensive toll ever paid was $0.36 – in 1928 by a man called Richard Halliburton, who swam the length of the canal over a ten-day period. The toll was calculated against his 150 pounds weight. And then there are those of us who manage to get "mates' rates". Because we were tucking in behind another vessel in the same lock, and because our captain is extraordinarily skilled in negotiating these matters, the *Endeavour* wasn't charged as an ocean-going ship but as "Daddy's yacht", for a very modest fee. Needless to say we took great delight in calling Chris 'Daddy' instead of 'Captain' for a few hours.

And so the transit began. After we'd entered the first lock and been secured in position, the great mitre gates closed behind us and the chamber started to fill with water. It comes in from the bottom, so you are not really aware of it until you realise that the walls are not towering above you so much any more. This process continues until the ship is floating on top of the extra 750 megalitres of water that have entered the chamber, and you are now looking down at the people on the side of the canal again and waving to the donkey (loco) drivers. It really was fascinating. I'm sure that we had a much greater awareness of how it was all happening than would have been the case had we been on a large cruise ship. We had three locks to negotiate at this end of the canal, which would raise us some twenty-four metres above sea level to reach the height of Gatun Lake, so we could observe the process three times.

What was also fascinating was the effect of going aloft and working the yards with land, trees and other vegetation all around us instead of open sea. It was a very odd feeling indeed, but certainly a photo opportunity. As we got nearer to the Gatun Lake, the captain sent us aloft to ungasket sails, and loosen them so that they were hanging in their gear, "in case we get the opportunity to set them". Aha – what was he planning? We had already established with the pilot that this wasn't really allowed. However, in true Chris fashion, as the gates on the last lock before the lake opened, we set a couple of sails and sailed out of the lock with our cannons firing and much yahoo-ing, to the delight of all the donkey drivers and other canal employees. They were all rushing for their cameras as well. It certainly wouldn't have been an 'ordinary working day' for them.

It had taken about half the day to get to this point in the transit, which was where our pilot got off and went back to Colon. He promised to come and visit us in Panama City, with his family, when the ship was open for exhibition. The pilot who got on to take us through the rest of the transit seemed a bit sterner than the first one, or perhaps his English wasn't quite as good: I'm not sure. No-one told him that this was a non-smoking ship, and he stood puffing away on the poop deck next to the captain. I had the impression that no-one *dared* tell him not to smoke. The pilot is "boss cocky" at these times, and the ship's master takes on an advisory and guidance role only. So if he wanted to smoke, smoke he did.

Shortly after we entered the lake, which covers an area of 550,000 hectares (in other words it's *huge*), we became aware of something approaching us from the opposite direction, and it seemed to have some sort of escort. The binoculars came out. Oh my, it's an American submarine, on the surface, complete with a mini-armada of Panamanian escorts in small boats carrying armed military personnel. Well, this was too good to be true. "Ally," bellowed the captain to the bosun, "get the cannons readied for firing." Ally quickly went about the business of stuffing the cannons with newspaper and priming them ready to be lit. This was going to be fun. We dived for the cameras again.

The captain got on the radio to the captain of the US submarine and told him that we would be "firing a salute" to them as they passed us. (That's our excuse anyway.) They were fine with that, and even without binoculars we were now close enough to see that people were crowding into the conning tower – with cameras. We let fly as they were abeam of us, and got a great cheer from them. The only problem was that the submarine captain had not told his Panamanian escort that this was going to happen. As far as they were aware, the sub was suddenly under some sort of attack – in their country!

Two of the boats swiftly pulled out of formation and headed towards us with their military crew shouldering machine guns and pointing them in our direction. I ducked! A reflex reaction. The chippie was next to me. With a very wry smile on his face he said, "You realise that machine-gun bullets will go right through wood, Fran." Oo-er, no I didn't. After frantic messages had flown back and forth via radio, the boats veered away and rejoined their formation, much to our relief – but also our amusement. Now *there* was a story to tell your grandchildren – about an 18th-century sailing ship firing upon a 21st-century American nuclear submarine.

Chris and I were having a great laugh on the poop deck over this, as I had reminded him that it wasn't the first time the *Endeavour* had fired upon a US Navy ship. One day, a long time ago now, when the *Endeavour* was doing day sails out of Fremantle, a number of US Navy ships were coming in for a few days' R&R at the port. They used to come in with the crew standing at attention all around the rails of the ship, looking very smart in their whites – the modern-day version of dressing the yards, I suppose. As we were going out of the harbour and they were coming in, we fired a cannon at them, only on that occasion we had put a tennis ball down the barrel. The bang was so loud that several of the crew "hit the deck" in the same reflex reaction that I'd just had to the threat of machine guns. The only problem was that, in the process of doing this, one of them twisted his ankle quite badly and needed medical attention. That meant an incident report had to be completed.

We have since been told the report states that the sprain occurred to seaman so-and-so as a result of being fired upon by cannon from a foreign 18th-century sailing ship. We have also been told that this story, and a copy of the incident report, has percolated its way upwards through the ranks of all senior US naval departments, and has even got to the Pentagon and the White House itself. *That's* a yarn that will take some beating.

The rest of the transit passed relatively uneventfully. It was blistering hot and, being inland, there was no sea breeze. The Gatun Lake is fresh water so, although it was a bit murky, we started dropping buckets over the side to pour over ourselves and cool down, clothes and all. It was practical, if messy, and certainly helped to drop the body temperature. Below decks was pretty unbearable by now, so most of us stayed on deck, trying to find bits of shade where we could. We didn't really have any work to do, as we weren't sail handling and couldn't do maintenance, but had to stay alert for the "just in case" scenarios.

Near the Galliard or Culebra Cut, we could see that we were approaching a rather swish-looking modern suspension-type bridge that crossed the canal, so we asked the pilot about it. The books I'd been consulting hadn't mentioned it, and I now found out that was because it was new. It was called the Millennium Bridge, and had been built to celebrate the year 2000. It would cut the travelling time between the northern and southern towns and villages on either side of the canal enormously once it was in use. Interesting. Pardon? What did he mean by "once it was in use"? It transpired that the bridge, although it had officially been declared open, wasn't actually being used yet, as the approach roads to it on either side of the canal hadn't been built. Bureaucracy is alive and well even in Panama, it seems. Obviously the powers that be wanted to have the bridge finished for the new millennium, hence the name. The fact that no one could use it yet was neither here nor there. I liked the silliness of it.

By the time we came out of the last of the locks on the Pacific side, it was almost dark, so it had indeed taken us the whole day to transit. When you think how many weeks it would have taken to round the Horn in the old days, though, this was nothing. We had a big map of the world on the wall in the 20th-century mess. It was the type that has the Americas on the right-hand side of the map and Africa and Europe on the left, Australia and New Zealand being thus bang slap in the middle. (Most world maps that I've seen have Australia on the bottom right-hand corner.) Fastened to the map we had a little ship that we'd been moving during the voyage in accordance with our progress. As we completed our transit, the Aussies ran below to move it to the other side of the Panama Canal. The only major landmass in front of us now was Australia – we were definitely on our way home. We all cheered. There was still a long way to go, but it looked totally different on the map now.

We continued across the bay towards Panama City itself, where we would tie up at the Flamenco Dock for a few days before continuing on our journey. We would be open to the public, we would take on more stores, there would be another crew changeover, and hopefully we would get some leave. Mags and I were desperate to get off and find a hotel room for a few days. We longed to get out of the hot, sweaty conditions that we seemed to be in all the time now and find some air-conditioning and a bath. We needed to rest and recuperate in other words. This was where our first pilot turned out to be a godsend. He arrived early next morning and, as he "knew people who knew people", was able to make a few phone calls that got nearly all of us who wanted to booked into a divine, luxurious five-star hotel in downtown Panama for the most ridiculously cheap rate imaginable.

It was off-season (January), so that helped, but I'm sure his phone calls were a much bigger help. And then he insisted on driving Mags, Jason, Bruce and me into the city, some thirty kilometres away, right to the door of the hotel. It was brilliant. Mags and I hadn't originally planned on finding a hotel in Panama. We were a little nervous of some of the stories we'd heard about the place – muggers, drug runners, crime etc. etc. – but the pilot assured us we'd be fine as long as we didn't go up any back alleys at night. We hadn't had the opportunity to be in a hotel since Madeira, so we were more than ready for a break and thought we'd take a chance on it.

Our room was superb. It had the obligatory air-conditioning, huge beds, bath as well as shower and all the mod cons that you could think of. The hotel was very nice, with restaurants, bars, casino, swimming pool, Jacuzzi, gym, elegant shops in the basement arcade and staff that couldn't do enough for you. It was bliss. We were past caring how much it might cost and just revelled in the luxury. In fact we enjoyed it so much that it was two days before we left the hotel to go exploring – we just couldn't be bothered until we'd recharged our batteries and felt human again. We slept in, took long baths and showers, swam in the pool, ate leisurely meals in the restaurants and vegetated. It was absolutely wonderful.

Having discovered that there was a guest laundry, the four of us decided to tackle all of our dirty, smelly gear. We took it in turns to put loads in, adjourn to the pool, then check how things were going maybe twenty minutes later. Unfortunately, on one of the occasions when the machine was left unattended, something went awry, and when Mags and I went back to check on things we discovered Jason in the middle of a flooded laundry. It was located on the fifteenth floor, and the flood was disappearing downwards somewhere. We rang reception to report it and turned off the machine. Used to cleaning up after ourselves, we found a cleaning cupboard nearby and set to mopping up the mess.

The hotel staff was horrified at this when they arrived – we were *guests*! They didn't speak English too well, but a Puerto Rican girl called Yari, who was also a hotel guest and had been waiting to use the laundry, acted as translator for us. She was most interested in the fact that we were from the *Endeavour*, so we befriended her and invited her to join us for dinner that night. She was lively company, and as she spoke Spanish was helpful in translating menus, ordering food and sorting out the bill at the end of the meal. She was also very good at mental arithmetic and could work out who owed what very quickly. From that point on, whenever we were ashore somewhere in groups and a bill needed to be split up and sorted out among us, it became known as "doing a Yari". We kept in touch for a while by email, and she had a good laugh when we told her that. We never discovered where our disappearing flood had gone to, but presumably there was no damage or we would have heard about it.

Eventually Mags and I ventured outside the hotel to do a bit of shopping. We went off to find a department store looking for strappy tops and singlets that would be cooler to wear on board than the clothes we already had. We discovered to our amusement that a lingerie shop near the hotel had some very interesting items on display in the window – foundation garments with large amounts of padding in the buttocks area to "enhance your natural bottom" I think was the phrase. We couldn't believe it. And then when we found the department store we noticed that all the manikins displaying rather nice dresses all had very large bottoms. We cracked up laughing. There must be millions and millions of women in the world who at one time

221

or another have asked their friends, "Does my bum look big in this?" It seemed that in this part of the world a large bum was a desirable physical attribute. The shop assistant couldn't understand why I took a picture of a manikin, I'm sure. Then again, it was a good reminder to us that different cultures around the world have different values. We did laugh though.

Later on, and back in our foursome with the lads, we decided to go off exploring "Old Panama". The concierge cautioned us against going on our own, as the area is rife with pickpockets, bag-snatchers and other undesirables. It's one of the main tourist parts of the city, and crowds of visitors attract opportunists. The hotel organised a car for us, with a driver who spoke English. He took us to all the major attractions in the old city and we caught up with some more of the history of the area. The pirate Henry Morgan had been here, too, after he'd looted and pillaged Portobelo in 1668. Folklore has it that, thanks to some devious and heroic efforts by the priests, the Golden Altar of Saint Joseph's Church was saved from Morgan's looting, although he took other artefacts and valuable religious icons. The altar is breathtaking, and certainly rivals altars I've seen elsewhere. The whole church, in fact, was pretty spectacular.

Another place we stopped at that made a huge impression on me was the National Theatre of Panama, a beautiful building, outside and in. Dame Margot Fonteyn, the famous English ballerina, used to dance here. I'd forgotten that she had been married to a former Panamanian diplomat for many years, and in fact lived in Panama after her retirement. I had the privilege of seeing Dame Margot dance many years ago as a child, when my mum used to take me to Glasgow to see the ballet. It's a love that I have still, and in later years I used to take my mum to the ballet in Perth. I discovered that you could actually go onto the stage of the National Theatre, so up I went, the shoes came off and I struck an appropriate pose for the obligatory photograph. Then I suddenly remembered that I wouldn't be able to show it to my mum, as she was no longer with us, and became quite emotional. Jason picked up on it immediately; no doubt because it hadn't been that long since he'd lost his own mother.

When we went out again, we met up with a big group of tourists who were off the Queen Elizabeth II, which was anchored out in the bay.

Some of them got chatting to us, and we discovered that the QEII was heading for Fremantle. "You'll be there before me", I said to one chap, and explained that I actually lived in Perth. I told him to look out for the volunteer West Oz Welcomers when they arrived, as I was part of that group. It's a group that is associated with the Tourism Commission, and we "meet and greet" new arrivals at both the domestic and international airports in Perth and also at the seaport during the cruise-ship season. I described the uniform, which is pretty distinctive, mostly because of the Akubra hats, so he said he'd look out for them. I found out months later that he had, indeed, spoken to some of my West Oz Welcomers colleagues, and had taken great delight in telling them that he'd met Fran in Panama. It's a relatively small group, so we all know each other. Needless to say, they could hardly believe it. The world is definitely getting smaller.

After our few days in Panama City we felt refreshed, recharged and almost ready to head off again. We made our way back to the ship and discovered that some more new crew, both voyage crew and professional crew, had joined. Once again, I knew some of them already from previous voyages and some were new. The settling in and training began again, plus the usual loading of stores and spare parts for the next leg of our voyage. Galapagos Islands, here we come.

18

THE GALAPAGOS ISLANDS

We left Panama on 12 January, having ensured before we departed that we made some last-minute phone calls home. Apart from the fact that it would be a couple of weeks before we could be in touch again, we weren't entirely sure what sort of facilities would be available at the Galapagos. The majority of the thirteen or so islands in the group are actually uninhabited, and the whole place is a national park under the auspices of the Ecuadorian Government. We would have to wait and see when we got there. That's *if* we got there! – this was when the captain issued his challenge to Sarah to navigate the old-fashioned way. At that stage of the game we weren't sure how successful (or otherwise) that might prove to be.

But before the Galapagos, it seemed, we would be having another flat tyre. A Colombian television film crew wanted to charter the ship for a day or so and had approached the captain. They were going to be filming episodes of a new *Survivor* series for local TV, and they wanted the celebrities to be offloaded from "a pirate ship". The *Endeavour* fitted the bill beautifully. There is a group of islands in the Gulf of Panama called the Pearl Islands, and we would drop anchor at one of them, Isla Contadora, for the day. Most of the voyage crew got a shore day while the celebrities embarked and a bit of filming took place on board, with the island as the backdrop. We didn't mind that at all: it was another unscheduled stop that would allow some swimming and lazing around, culminating in a barbeque ashore in the evening. What made it even better was that the TV company picked up the tab for drinks.

We went ashore in the fizz boat, and then had to walk around to the other side of the island to where the resort was. As it's a small island, this wasn't a problem. It was very hot, with lots of mosquitoes and other biting insects around, but otherwise quite pleasant, and the beach at the resort was superb. We headed into the water as soon as we got there and spent the rest of the day lazing, snoozing and trying to stay in the shade while we watched from a distance what was happening on the ship. We could see the sails getting set, then getting furled, then getting set again, time after time. Those back on board were obviously having to do all this for the film crew. We felt a bit guilty, momentarily, then ordered another round of drinks.

Everyone came ashore at the end of the day, and we had a barbecue followed by a very large cake – it was Lucy's twenty-first birthday and Allan had risen to the occasion in the galley again. Liam insisted that there was an old Irish custom according to which "a young maiden" attaining the age of twenty-one had to sit upon a chair and receive kisses from twenty-one different gentlemen – in twenty-one different places! That sounded like fun, so we got Lucy set up in a chair, ignoring her protests. The guys from the ship lined up in a queue, with the captain at the head of it. One or two of the waiters who had been looking after us all day joined in as well.

Then we noticed that some complete strangers from the resort were lining up at the back of the queue to join in too, which poor Lucy got a bit embarrassed about. I think we managed to head most of the strangers off at the pass, and the evening ended with everyone getting flung in the pool, either in their bathers or in their clothes – it didn't matter much. It certainly would have been a memorable twenty-first for Lucy, and very different from what she might have enjoyed had she been back in England.

The next day we headed off in the direction of the other island where the contestants were going to be put off and marooned for the duration of the TV programme, about two months. As they were stars of Colombian television, they were not recognisable to us – except for Maradona, the famous South American soccer player of some years ago. They were all searched thoroughly by the TV production people, as they are not allowed to take with them any knives, tools or other implements.

225

They have to survive on their wits. Frisking completed, they were made to walk the plank, much to our delight. Some of the glamorous young ladies looked decidedly uncomfortable about the whole idea – and this was only Day One of their challenge. They then had to swim over to some rowing boats, climb in and row ashore. We have heard nothing more about them since, and can only presume that the series got made, it went to air, and there was a winner. We'll probably never know.

Now we were headed for the Galapagos. We would arrive in about two weeks' time. The ship had to settle into sea routine again, with sail-handling lectures and knot classes re-commenced, watches allocated and working, sails being set and trimmed as required and something new: helping Sarah with the 18th-century navigation. That was interesting, as us scurvy-dog sailors felt that we were contributing to the calculations by reporting what speed the ship was doing according to our log-line readings. Inevitably, the scrubbing and cleaning and tarring and maintenance resumed again too. Still, it was nice to be back at sea, although we certainly did notice the lack of creature comforts after our few days of indulgence in the five-star hotel in Panama.

In particular we noticed the heat, which had become relentless. One day when I was on the helm we had some unexpected and sudden wind shifts, and the rest of my watch had to scurry aloft to furl sails. They were busy for quite a while, and by the time I got relieved from the helm I had been there for about an hour and a half in the blazing sun. Immediately after the watch change we had a fire drill, which necessitated staying on deck in our life jackets at our muster stations, still in the blazing sun. I passed out. One of the guys told me later that he saw it coming: a classic parade-ground type of faint, he said. My eyes rolled, I went limp, and I just slid to the deck – "fairly gracefully", he was kind enough to add.

I woke up on the deck a few minutes later with *five* doctors around me. I'd never had so much medical attention in my life. There was a group of four doctors – friends from the same hospital – among the new voyage crew, and of course we already had Peter on board. Heatstroke and dehydration, they declared, and wouldn't let me get up until I'd drunk two litres of water with electrolytes in it. I kept saying I couldn't drink that much without having to go to the toilet, but they insisted I could because my system was so dehydrated. They were right. We were all drinking three or four litres of water a day, but still, it seemed, that wasn't enough. Jason, bless him, was very upset at this little incident: he thought one of his newly adopted surrogate mums had had a heart attack and keeled over. "I'm made of tougher stuff than that", I said. Nevertheless I was very touched by his concern, and my collapse made everyone more aware of the need to keep fluids up.

After my little "party piece" I found out that one of our supernumeraries had collapsed with heat exhaustion while we were in Panama, and had actually been hospitalised. Because we were off the ship luxuriating in our hotel we hadn't heard about it. I understand that he woke up in the intensive care unit of the hospital, packed in ice and with a saline drip in his arm. They put five bags of fluid into him before they would let him out of ICU, and then it was a couple of days before he was allowed back on board. No wonder I had created such a stir and got so much medical attention. With the little drama over, things carried on regardless, as they do at sea.

All of the 18th-century uniforms that had been used during the TV filming needed mending – again. They're not made from very substantial fabric, so they get ripped pretty easily during sail handling aloft, and now we of the sewing team had several days' worth of work ahead of us. Some of the other girls joined Mags and me around the mess table and the "stitch and bitch" sessions grew larger. Except for the heat it was quite pleasant work, and we chattered about all sorts of things as girls in groups are inclined to do.

The topic of making films for TV and movies came up, and someone mentioned a "fluffer". "What's a fluffer?" I asked. The eye contact among the younger girls flashed backwards and forwards, and then a couple of them burst out laughing.

"Don't you know what a fluffer is?"

"Nope, never heard of it", I said. Mags didn't know either. More laughter. Clare explained as delicately as she could that it's the name applied to young ladies (I use the term loosely) who are trying to break into the pornographic movie industry.

They start behind the scenes, apparently, and "prepare" the male stars before a scene gets shot. I think in polite horse-breeding circles they would be referred to as "teasers". I was shocked. I'm still not sure whether I was shocked at learning such an occupation existed or that a nineteen-year-old girl had enlightened me! And then my sense of humour kicked in. "I wonder if they have any occupational health and safety regulations in that job." "Are there fluff inspectors?" "I wonder what they write as their occupation on tax forms and passport applications." Oh dear, we did have some very ribald jokes about it. I was certainly getting an education that had nothing whatsoever to do with tall ships or the times in which they sailed.

And then they asked us if we knew about boiler tickets. "You mean a boilermaker's ticket?" I asked. More laughter. It seems that these days a young lad can be awarded a mythical "boiler ticket" by his mates if he meets the challenge of sleeping with a woman who is at least twice his age, i.e. "an old boiler" as opposed to a "young chick". My God, Mags and I were *really* getting an education here. Wait a minute: we could have some fun with this. We reflected that we would be more than twice the age of most of the lads on board, so that would make us eligible, if that's an appropriate word, to count in the awarding of a boiler ticket. We decided we would pick a victim, start flirting with him outrageously and see what happened. Of course we had no intention of actually *doing* anything about it, but it could be a laugh. We swore the other girls to secrecy and went off to confer with each other about which of the boys would be our victim.

We decided on a twenty-four-year-old lad called Timmy. He had a lovely sunny nature, was very obliging, and had already been voted the nicest person on the ship. We thought that if the joke backfired on us somehow, and it all went horribly wrong, he would see the humour in it and not really mind having been the victim. We both started flirting with him, and getting him to rub sunscreen on our backs when we were working near each other on the deck, and making comments about how nice he looked with a suntan etc. etc. He began giving us some funny looks. Remember, we were both old enough to be his mother. The flirting was obviously being correctly interpreted, and he didn't quite know whether we were kidding or not.

This went on for quite some time. Occasionally Tim would have a quiet word with Mags to the effect that he was getting a bit concerned about my behaviour; would she mind having a word with me? Then a few days later he would have a quiet word with me. "I think Margaret must be missing her family a lot: she's getting very affectionate." Mags and I would compare comments later and have a great chuckle. Poor Timmy; he was 99 per cent sure, I think, that we were just larking about, but that 1 per cent doubt made him rather wary of allowing himself to be in a situation where he was alone with either of us. At the St Valentine's Day dance a few weeks later one of the items on the fun questionnaire the girls had prepared was, "What's the sweetest thing that your date has ever done for you?" Timmy's answer was, "Save me from Fran!" Oh dear, I think this has gone on long enough. Everyone had a huge laugh about it, though, and he didn't get his boiler ticket before we got to Sydney. At least as far as I know …

We sailed on through what was turning out to be an interesting part of the world. Flying fish abounded in shoals of what seemed to be thousands at a time, and performed some fantastic skimming feats across the tops of wavelets, enabling them to "fly" quite a distance. We saw the occasional shark and sunfish, and lots of dolphins again. Disturbingly, we also saw lots of garbage in the water from time to time. I have come to absolutely hate plastic bags. There were lots of logs too, something that I'm not used to seeing around the Australian coastline. Then again, we were pretty close to rain-forest country. One day we hit one. It was actually more like a complete tree, minus foliage, than a log. It was big. We slowed down while the engineer tested the engines and the rudder and had a pretty close look at everything over the stern. All appeared to be in order, with no damage done. It was, however, entered in the ship's log (pardon the pun!) and the incident would actually prove to be useful later on.

Two things happened about this time. One was that we found ourselves in the doldrums, so had to put the engines on again, which the sailors of old wouldn't have been able to do. Because there was little or no breeze, it was stiflingly hot below decks and not much better on deck. We went over the side for swims when we could, had deck showers and even reverted to having buckets of water tipped over us to try and cool down. It wasn't very pleasant in all honesty. The description of the *Endeavour* in my journals had now changed from "my beloved ship" to "this bloody boat"! There were days when

I longed to be somewhere else – *anywhere* else – than stuck on a ship in the doldrums in the heat.

The other thing that happened – or rather was about to happen – was that we would be at the equator, so plans for the Crossing the Line ceremony began to get detailed. There had been buckets of leftover galley slops brewing in the engine room for a week or so, so they were obviously going to come into play. At one or two secret meetings at which the plans were being concocted, we shellbacks realised fairly quickly that there weren't enough of us who were big enough to subdue some of the pollywogs on board, if that became necessary. There were a number of quite big lads to be dealt with. It was decided that we would have to induct two or three of them early – and surreptitiously – and get them on "our side". Then they could help us deal with the rest of the pollywogs. Everyone knew that we were getting close to the equator (unless Sarah's naviguessing was *very* bad), so they were becoming very jumpy and suspicious about what plots were being hatched. And they were hatching counter-plots!

The captain came clean at a morning meeting and advised the date that we would be crossing the line and that, yes, there would be a ceremony. Those who had not already paid tribute to King Neptune on some previous occasion would be expected to pay homage on that day, particularly the ones who had already been found "guilty" at the Kangaroo Court held previously. This had everyone relaxing a little, as it was out in the open now. That was the whole point. Because the pollywogs had dropped their guard, that allowed us to "get" a couple of the bigger lads in their hammocks that night or while they were on watch on the deck. They got doused with their own individual buckets of slops. We now had the numbers to deal with everyone else should there be any resistance. It's all done in good fun of course, but like anything else in life it can get out of hand occasionally, particularly if someone resists *too* much.

Roles got sorted out. Big Gee, one of the captain's old compatriots, who has a wonderful voice and sounds like a BBC commentator, would be King Neptune. Chef Allan, who is just a naturally funny man, would be Queen Aphrodite, with the most outrageous pair of "falsies" imaginable, and Reg, another of the captain's old compatriots, would be the surgeon. Other crew members were Sweeney Todd the barber and the executioner. Ruth and I were "Neptune's nymphs", and the rest of the shellbacks on board would be Neptune's police, or the heavy gang. Ruth and I had to blindfold and bring people up from down below, two at a time, for them to get slathered in this wondrous organic muck and grovel at Neptune's feet to appease his wrath over their trespassing into his kingdom. That was the general plan anyway: we might have to wait and see how willing or otherwise the accused turned out to be.

We had told everyone who would be getting initiated to wear really old clothes, as it was likely they wouldn't ever be the same again. We all wear old clothes when we're tarring and doing dirty work anyway, but we told them to find the *really* old ones. They would probably get chucked overboard in the end, although not around here as the environment was a bit too sensitive. Someone made a comment about it being easier to rip off the old ones in order to get the "new shell" put on and become shellbacks. Very droll, we thought. The ship always seems to have lots of quick-witted people aboard.

The ceremony started with Big Gee on the PA system, his voice booming through the ship as he read an appropriate piece about those "who dared to trespass into my domain" and then calling out the names of the accused. Ruth and I would fetch them up on deck – unless they resisted, in which case we sent for the heavy gang. As the afternoon went on, everyone got dirtier and dirtier and the deck got messier and messier. The fire hose got used to clean it up a bit, but it didn't seem to be making a lot of difference.

The last two to be brought up from down below were from the professional crew and just *knew* they would cop the lot. Whatever was left in our buckets of slops had their name on it. One of them was Cian, our former shore manager from the UK. He succeeded in stealing the show – he appeared at the top of the steps completely naked, and said, "I'm all ready for my new shell!" There were shrieks from the girls, roars of laughter from the blokes, and cameras popping everywhere. Even the captain appeared to check out what was happening. Sensibly, he'd been staying out of the way of the melee – on the helm.

Everyone took it in good part, even some of the lads who were now sporting exceedingly strange haircuts. Big Gee was almost shaved, except

231

for a tiny little Mohawk running down the middle of his skull. Greg had half of his head shaved, along with the opposite half of his beard, so he was sporting a very asymmetrical look. Paco, the engineer, had been a bit worried about his treatment, as we'd been coming up behind him for weeks making ZZZZZZ noises like an electric razor. He had lovely auburn hair – thick and wavy – the kind most girls would envy. He had lost half of it on one side of his head only. Cian's haircut was the most inventive, however: it had been done in tufts, so that he looked a bit like a startled owl. All that missing hair would grow again, but the lads did look strange in the meantime. They had the last laugh, because *they went ashore* looking like that! I mean, it really doesn't matter what we look like at sea, but going ashore with their eccentric haircuts took courage on their part. The rest of us were suitably impressed (and amused).

All of us – even those who were already shellbacks – received a rather elaborate certificate to say that we had crossed into the royal domain on 20 January 2005, signed by Neptune Rex himself. We were pretty thrilled, and it's become another of my treasured trophies of the trip, even though I already had one from a previous *Endeavour* voyage. This one was a bit more special: this occasion could well prove to be the last time that the *Endeavour* crosses the Equator.

The Galapagos Island group sits almost *on* the equator, and in fact we crossed the line several times over the next few days, although there was only one ceremony. We were now only a day or so away from anchoring there and were getting pretty excited about going ashore. Some information in the Lonely Planet guide put a slight dampener on the excitement, however. It stated that landing charges and taxes are $100 per person, *plus* $200 per person per day if you come in by boat rather than by commercial aircraft. We were scheduled to be there for a few days, so it was going to be extremely expensive if that information was correct and current. The captain started making investigations by radio with the ship's agent.

It transpired that the $200 per person per day charge is aimed at people who arrive at the Galapagos on cruise ships or in their private yachts. Because they stay on board while they are there, and use those vessels to visit other islands besides the main one, Santa Cruz, they do not spend money ashore by staying at hotels, eating at restaurants or taking any of the available cruises to other islands, so the local economy gets little or nothing out of them. Tourism is their major industry these days, although tightly controlled due to the unique and sensitive environment. Monies earned from tourism go back into the local economy to help pay for wildlife rangers, radar equipment to monitor the surrounding seas and the like, so it's very important to keep the cash flow up.

When the captain explained that we would be going ashore and spending money there, and that we were working crew, the authorities took a different attitude to our situation and agreed to drop the $200 per person per day charge. They even reduced the landing fee to $10 per person. We heaved a collective sigh of relief. As the captain pointed out, there was another way of looking at the situation. We had to get some parts for the propellers due to hitting the large log (remember the large log?), so in effect we were shipwrecked sailors and had no choice but to remain there for a few days. I liked that version enormously.

Being on watch the night before we arrived at Santa Cruz was just magic. It was balmy and very clear, with thousands and thousands of stars to be seen, including lots of shooting stars again, although not as spectacular as the Geminids. The Southern Cross was directly ahead of us, as our course was due south, so the scenario took on the "star to steer her by" image, with apologies to John Masefield. We knew we were getting close to land as we had begun to see several varieties of birds. Sarah's 18th-century navigation had obviously been successful.

When I emerged from my hammock the next morning, land was in sight, three frigate birds were hitching a lift on our fore t'gallant yard and others were flying alongside the ship. The wildlife was prolific and the waters were very clear. Within an hour of being on deck, I'd seen more dolphins, a turtle, some seals, a manta ray, lots of fish and heaps more birds. Apart from the frigate birds there were fulmars, pelicans, blue- and red-footed boobies and other birds that we hadn't yet identified. It was like being *in* one of David Attenborough's nature documentaries.

Watching the blue-footed boobies feeding was nothing short of astonishing. They can hover like helicopters while they spot the fish they are after, then dive down into the water at amazing speed. They look like arrows being shot from a bow. Just before they hit the water, they fold their wings back like an F111 aircraft. If you can imagine dozens of them doing this together, you'll get some idea of the truly wonderful scene we were watching. And we weren't even *there* yet.

By late afternoon we had arrived at Santa Cruz, the most populated island and the one where most visitors arrive, it being the site of the only airport. To get to the Galapagos by air you usually have to fly to Quito in Ecuador first, and then fly from there to Santa Cruz. When you look at a world map, you can see that it's a pretty isolated archipelago, but that is what has given rise to its unique and diverse flora and fauna.

We dropped anchor in Angemeyer Bay, in Puerto Ayora, and waited for the officials to come aboard. Clearance to go ashore took some considerable time to negotiate, with several rather stern looking men surrounding the captain in the Great Cabin and Ros doing her best to translate when necessary. In due course we were all given the seal of approval, we paid our now modest landing fees, and smiles broke out all around. We were welcome!

It was quite late by this time, so we decided to have our Sods Opera on board that night, which would give us all the chance to go ashore the next day. Most of us who were going further got the opportunity to book off for a few days and decamp to hotels again. Quite a number of the voyage crew, including Elaine, our American lady, and one or two of the supernumeraries were getting off here and going on to separate adventures, visiting places like Machu Pinchu and Iguazu Falls on their way home. And a few new crew would be getting on.

We went ashore next morning, booked ourselves into modest hotels for a couple of nights and went exploring. We all wanted to see the famous giant tortoises and iguanas, and discovered a tour company that offered a trip to a recognised tortoise area in what's called the highlands. There is also a lava tube, left over from an old volcanic eruption, that you can walk through. As well, there were snorkelling trips that offered the opportunity to snorkel or scuba-dive with sea lions. Along with a few of the others, Mags, Jason and I booked one of these for the next day.

You don't have to look very hard for iguanas. They are everywhere, and we saw many during a walk around the township. There were lots of lava lizards as well, which are much like geckos. We came upon a spot where the local fishermen pull in to offload their catches. From the air, herons, pelicans and frigate birds were besieging them, trying to steal fish. While the fishermen were foiling the aerial attack, sea lions would take the opportunity to pop up from the water, lean into the boat and help themselves. They were obviously very tame. It was just enthralling watching this. The locals didn't think so, of course, as it's an almost daily occurrence. Our cameras clicked madly.

The tour the next day was fantastic, starting with the boat trip in the morning. The sea lions among which we swam and snorkelled were as tame as the ones we'd seen the previous day – and very curious. They would come right up to you, twirling and twisting like graceful ballet dancers in the water. A young one came right up to me and "kissed" me, whereupon I gurgled with delight, but discovered that's not a good idea when you're under water – I got a snorkel full of the briny. A little further away from the sea-lion colony there was a colony of blue-footed boobies nesting in the cliffs, and lots of marine iguanas swimming around, much faster than I'd imagined they could. The ones we had seen on our walk previously had been land iguanas, a slightly different species.

In the afternoon we climbed into trucks and got taken up to the highlands to see the giant tortoises, some of which are reputed to be over 150 years old. Most of those we saw were adults, about the size of coffee tables. There are a couple of different species, one of which is being bred with reasonable success at a tortoise farm on another of the islands. But of the other species there remains only one old male, christened "Lonesome George". They have been unable to find a mate for him, and it's thought that he's the last of his breed. Sadly, unless an as yet undiscovered female is found on one of the other uninhabited islands, that particular species will become extinct when Lonesome George dies.

Some of the group went horse riding up in the highlands. When those of us who hadn't participated caught up with them later that night, we of course asked them how it had been. "Marvellous", exclaimed Dennis. "But the horse I was on was a bit big for me, so when we got back to the ranch I dismounted using one of the tortoises as a step. They're just the right height." We were aghast. Then he burst out laughing – with his deadpan expression he had really sucked us in.

235

We also had all gone scrambling through the lava tube, which was pretty interesting, although difficult to negotiate in places. I took one look at it and deemed it to be "ankle-buggering country". Remember the ankle that got injured in Tasmania? It's never been quite the same since, and I have to be pretty careful with it. Jason and Ian came to the rescue, helping me over some particularly difficult bits. Jason even piggybacked me at one stage: it's nice having a surrogate son on hand at times. The Galapagos Islands are all volcanic in origin, and eight or ten volcanoes are still active today. One of them, the Sierra Negra, has erupted in fairly spectacular fashion since we were there.

After our few days on Santa Cruz it was time to head off to one of the other islands, Isabela, the largest in the group although not the most populated. It has only two villages, along with six active volcanoes. It wasn't far away from Santa Cruz, so we motor-sailed during the night and dropped anchor in the bay at Puerto Villamil the next morning. We were there only for the day, so virtually everyone went ashore to do some more exploring.

Some of the locals met up with us at the beach, and trucks quickly got organised to take us to various places of interest, including the ranch where they breed the giant tortoises. The five-year olds are about the size of "normal" pet tortoises. It's a very long term programme to rear and then repatriate them onto other islands, but hopefully it will prevent them from becoming extinct. It's amazing to think that some of these animals could have been there when Charles Darwin visited on HMS *Beagle* in 1835. One of the guides teased us with his contention that one of the old tortoises had been Darwin's pet. We wondered how anyone could know which tortoise had been the pet. It was a good yarn, but a bit implausible.

We got back on board to discover that we were going to visit yet another island, Fernandino, which is uninhabited. There was a BBC television film crew coming aboard, and they wanted footage of the ship with a volcano in the background. Apparently, this would be the best location to get such shots, so the authorities had granted special permission for the visit on the proviso that two of the Ecuadorian National Park rangers accompanied us. The rangers and film crew embarked, together with three goats that had been "borrowed" from

236

Isabela Island for the day to be used in the filming. We tethered the goats to a line on the deck that allowed them to move about a little. Alas, they were all seasick on the way to Fernandino. We tried to make them feel more comfortable. It was pretty obvious they were scared out of their wits and had no idea what was happening to them.

"We should give them names", Eefje said.

"That's easy", declared Allan, the chef with the black sense of humour. "Breakfast, Lunch and Dinner – they make good curry!" Eefje was horrified – until she realised he was joking. They would be getting off again at the end of the day, anyway, and taken back to Isabela on the BBC's chartered boat, which was following us. As we neared Fernandino, some of the crew got into the 18th-century costumes again to take part in filming. I could feel another sewing session coming on.

The coastline of Fernandino is absolutely awesome. We could see huge cliffs with caves all along the bottom of them where they meet the sea. Real pirate country. Appropriately, the boat that accompanied us was called the *Pirata*. The water was very deep here too, which allowed us to get into little nooks and crannies and bays, *very* close to the cliffs. We were allowed to go ashore in small groups accompanied by one of the rangers, who took us to a spot that just teemed with wildlife. There were land and marine iguanas, sea lions, manta rays, turtles, Sally Lightfoot crabs in their hundreds, brown noddies, storm petrels, hawks, frigate birds and the inevitable blue boobies, all in this one small bay. We felt so privileged to have had the opportunity to visit it. When filming was completed, the TV crew and equipment, the goats and the rangers all transferred onto the *Pirata* and headed back to Isabela, and we prepared to get under way again for our next long haul, to French Polynesia. One of the girls had a gadget on her watch that told us that it was eighty days since we had left Whitehaven. As it was eighty-one days until we were due in Sydney, the voyage was now at the halfway point.

237

19

SHIPMATES AND SHENANIGANS

In addition to our sail handling, maintenance work, cleaning, lectures and classes, we got up to all sorts of mischief to keep ourselves amused, particularly on the long hauls. The challenge was still out there for the lads to come up with something to beat the girls' aerobics routine – although they reckoned that they beat us every day anyway just by doing things "properly". Depends on your point of view I guess.

One morning, chef Allan, his cook's mate and Paco the engineer came up with a crazy session. We'd had the troll lines out again fishing, and for days and days had caught nothing, so they conjured up a "fish god" dressed from head to toe in shiny Alfoil. There was also a "mermaid" – Paco with his legs bound together in clear plastic wrap, flippers on his feet and a long blonde flowing wig. Allan completed the cast with a pot full of cut-out little cardboard fish. There was a song too. Each of us extracted a fish from the pot and dutifully danced around on the deck singing the fish song and waving our little fish in the air. You get a bit troppo on board this ship after a while. Then, at the appointed time, we threw them into the water amidst much laughter. You wouldn't believe it: almost immediately we got a strike and hauled in a decent-sized fish. The boys had definitely won round two of the morning exercise challenge.

On another occasion Jason was volunteered by the mate to lead the exercises the next day. Although he'd never been involved in anything quite like this before, he didn't mind doing it, but was a bit bashful about wearing his Lycra bike pants and top publicly. I said I'd wear mine too if it made him feel any better, and we could perhaps lead the exercises together. He was fine with that. What I didn't tell him was that I planned to enhance mine. We both emerged out of the hatch the next morning together, only I was holding my hat in an appropriate place and he didn't notice my "bulge". Captain's briefing over, we stood up to start the exercises.

"Has Fran got stuffing down her pants?" someone asked.

"I sincerely hope so", said someone else.

Jason looked around to see what everyone was tittering about, and found me leaning on the rail, scratching my crotch the way men do. He absolutely cracked up laughing, and immediately lost all his self-consciousness. Round three of the morning exercises divided equally between the guys and the girls.

Another morning exercise routine that was organised later in the voyage was "Dances from Around the World". We had Irish on board, so Keelin set about trying to teach us some Irish dancing, "Riverdance" style. That would have been funny enough in itself, but on a rolling ship it was absolutely hilarious. We were all losing our balance and falling about like skittles. In Irish dancing you have to keep your arms by your sides and the top part of your body still. It wasn't working, but it was good fun trying. We had Scots on board, so Mike and I (the two Jocks) press-ganged some others to make up a group of eight and demonstrated, and then had everyone try, a Scottish country-dance called an eightsome reel. What made *that* funny was that we were dancing to Irish music – it was the closest that we could find to the real (pardon the pun) thing.

But the one who stole the show that morning was George, my old Hungarian shipmate from previous voyages, who said that he would do a dance on his own. We expected something Hungarian, but what we got was a belly dance, George style. He's not a skinny man, and when he wants to he can shove his belly out in a really exaggerated manner. That was what we got – with a very large smiley face painted on it. It grinned and winked at you as he swayed his hips to the music and his stomach muscles moved. Everyone rushed for cameras again and declared George the best entertainment that morning. There weren't too many sit-ups done that day, but we all had sore stomachs from laughing so much.

I can't be sure, but it might have been George's effort that spawned another belly-related event, one that turned out to be quite superb. Because many of the permanent crew had their own laptop computers and digital cameras, we quite often got treated to some terrific slide shows of the places we had just visited. They would set the images to music and project them onto a big screen in the mess. The end result was very professional, and we could pass a pleasant evening discussing things that we'd just experienced.

That was what happened on this occasion, except that it was a Belly Button Competition. Dan had skulked around the deck during lay days and siesta times, and taken ten photographs of ten different belly buttons while people were lying around the deck sunbaking or snoozing. Then he had taken ten photographs of the owners of the belly buttons and put them all into a PowerPoint presentation, in random order, to the music from *Mission Impossible*. The idea was that we had to match up the correct belly button with the correct owner. It was a very inventive and amusing idea, and the presentation was very professional.

The captain offered a prize of dinner for eight in the Great Cabin – with the good Wedgwood dinner service and 18th-century cutlery and crystal – to anyone who got a perfect score. For the winner and seven of their best shipboard mates, that would certainly beat scoffing down their meal in the mess. Trying to catch people in the shower or some other revealing location in an attempt to sneak a peek at their belly buttons was most definitely out of bounds. We all tried and tried, but the best that could be achieved was seven correct answers. I mean, who takes any notice of people's belly buttons? So no-one got the prize, but we had a lot of fun trying.

One of the most elaborate diversions of the whole voyage was the St Valentine's Day dinner and dance. The girls who organised it excelled themselves with the arrangements, and had the whole of the 18th-century deck decorated with anything they could find that was red and/or white – flags, fire hoses and buckets, red tablecloths. Lots of cardboard cut-out hearts were strung from the deck head, and the place looked as festive as it had at Christmas. They'd also devised a fun questionnaire that we'd all had to fill out, anonymously. The idea was that the emcee would read the best answers at the dinner. A lot

240

of stifled laughter could be heard emanating from the locker room as our offerings were taken out of the ballot-type boxes where we'd been told to put them.

The organisers had paired us all up in dates, and had obviously had some fun with that too. The tallest girl (Mags) was paired up with the shortest man (the captain), the youngest with the oldest, the fattest with the thinnest, and so on. Some of the couples were the most unlikely of pairings imaginable. Inevitably there were more guys than girls – usually only about one-third of the crew is female – so quite a few of the lads had to go dressed up in drag to even up the numbers. There was much excitement as we all got dolled up for the night. It felt extremely strange wearing a dress again – I hadn't worn one in months.

The lads had to bring their date a flower, to be presented to them when they came to the "door" (the girls' locker room) to collect them for the date. What inventive people we had on board: the array of "flowers" was delightful. One was a whole bouquet, with the bud in the middle being a toilet brush (a new one thankfully!) surrounded by crepe paper flowers in bloom. Another was the lid of a paint pot, with all the little crimped bits on the edge flattened out to be the petals. Stuck on a stick and painted yellow, it looked like a sunflower. My date brought me a corsage, cleverly fashioned out of string and dyed with vegetable colouring, to wear on my wrist. It had obviously taken a great deal of effort: there were some very elaborate knots in it, one of which, he said, was a "maiden's knot". I told Greg I was a bit too old to be a maiden, but his effort had certainly bowled me over. It's another item in my "treasured mementos" collection.

The evening itself was great fun, beginning with a lovely dinner in the 18th-century mess. The answers to the questionnaire that the emcee read out were all pretty funny. The questions had all been related to one's love life and some of the answers were so outrageous I'm sure they must have been made up. I *hope* they were made up! That was the evening Timmy commented about his date "saving him from Fran", which had caused a good laugh. The lads in drag were superb, hamming it up as they "worked the room" in their wigs, frocks and full make-up. We'd had to share the locker room with them when we were getting dressed, as the *real* girls had had to do the make-up. All in all it was a

241

hilarious and very enjoyable evening. The next day was declared a lay day so that we could recover from all this debauchery.

Often on lay days a "scram bag" auction would be held. I mentioned earlier this old Royal Navy tradition, according to which you had to buy back your lost property and in the process help to build up a slush fund for spending in the next port. We had adopted this custom in principle, but always seemed to have a much bigger collection of stuff in our lost-property locker than would have been expected. We'd begun to realise that, as voyage crew got off, they left a lot of items behind – deliberately or otherwise. What's that old saying about one man's trash being another man's treasure? The auctions were great fun, as Liam always acted as auctioneer and his wisecracks about socks and jocks and other items were very quick-witted and funny. Sometimes he would model whatever it was that came out of the bag for auctioning. Liam in a black bra had to be seen to be believed.

Many of the items had been mislaid by someone currently on the ship – they were genuine lost property in other words. When one of those appeared out of the bag, there would be great yells of "Hey, that's mine; don't sell it" in indignant voices. But they had to buy it back, usually at a very nominal price, which helped to top up the slush fund for drinks in the next port. Liam was fair about this, though, and wouldn't let other people bid against the original owner. The bidding against one another for unclaimed items was, however, another matter, and sometimes it got quite fierce. What made it all the funnier was that, if someone had just paid $10 for an *Endeavour* tee shirt, more often than not the next item out of the bag was another *Endeavour* tee shirt, which someone else would get for a quarter of that price. It was just like a real auction, and Liam became very skilled at obtaining contributions for our slush fund. We told him that, if he ever got fed up being at sea, he could pursue another career as an auctioneer.

Another thing we always did on lay days was catch up with our washing. If there was enough fresh water available – that depended upon how well the reverse-osmosis equipment was working – each watch would be allocated a day per week when we could use the washing machine, although with approximately ten people per watch you were limited as to how much you could put in. Consequently we would often have a backlog of washing to do when we got the opportunity. We did it by hand in buckets of salt water on the deck, with perhaps a quick rinse out in fresh water in another bucket. Lines got strung up all over the place to hang the washing out. In the main we used normal spring-clip clothes pegs, and that's what started the "pegging".

One day, as someone walked past one of the washing lines, someone else clipped a peg onto his shirt without him noticing. It was hours before he discovered it, and in the meantime we all found it rather amusing. He decided to get back on the first person by doing the same to him – without him realising it of course. And so it began: a simple, almost childish, game that we got a great deal of mileage out of. Within a few days people were appearing for meals or coming on watch with pegs hanging off them in the most unlikely of places, without any knowledge of who had put them there or even that they had been pegged at all. So it just grew and grew. We all started keeping a few pegs in our pockets "just in case". The captain was of course the ultimate target, but he's a pretty wily and very sharp-witted fellow, and it took about three weeks before someone managed to get him. With the ultimate target pegged, the fun kind of went out of the game – until we got to another port, perhaps, or crossed paths with another tall ship somewhere.

Usually when we went over the side for a swim the fizz boat would be put in the water for safety, in addition to there being lookouts aloft on shark watch. We always swam on one side of the ship, and the fizz boat would scoot backwards and forwards beyond where we were swimming, parallel with the ship. We would also put a life ring over the side, with a long tether on it, so that if you felt the current was carrying you along a bit more swiftly than you were comfortable with, you could hang on to the life ring without actually needing the fizz boat to rescue you. It rarely got used, but we knew it was always there.

When we had the opportunity for a swim, more often than not we would dive in or jump in from the rail – or perhaps from half-way down the man steps. One day when the pool was declared open, we observed the cook's mate slowly lowering himself all the way down the steps so that he could slip into the water gently, rather than diving in and making a big splash. He still had his hat on. What was he up to? He was a very inventive young man – he had even managed to

243

make a banjo while on board, using the bottom of a cooking pot and a piece of ship's timber as the basis – so we *knew* he was up to something. He slowly swam over to the life ring, pulled himself into it, then waved his hands about a bit in the air to dry them off. By this time a lot of us were watching. Then he took his hat off, removed a packet of cigarettes from inside it and lit one. He instantly became every smoker's best friend, and we all swam over to beg a puff. We're not allowed to smoke anywhere on board on the *Endeavour* – but he wasn't on board! It was brilliant in its simplicity, its effectiveness and deviousness. Of course it reminded me of the occasion, years previously, when the actor had gone over the side at Geraldton, only this time around the strategy was successful.

Another big event that most certainly deserved the notation of shenanigans was our St Patrick's Day Parade. Everyone had to dress up in something appropriate, and again inventiveness was in evidence. Liam made the best leprechaun I've ever seen, although he did admit to more or less having the costume and carting it round in his luggage with him. There were a couple of Irish queens, both men, and Irish kings, one of whom was female. (Isn't it interesting how humans like to role-play and swap genders?) There were two Miss Irelands – again, both blokes – McNamara's band, Irish racehorses (the chippie's saw horses) with jockeys, Irish dancers and several saints and bishops. There was even the last potato in Ireland, being chased by a bunch of starving Irish peasants. This was a clever idea from one of the girls, whose nickname was "Spud": she wore a hessian sack and rolled along the deck like a potato. Everyone else was wearing green or orange, although you couldn't always tell what was being portrayed.

The saints and bishops stole the show, with George, as the Bishop of Blarney, and Jason, who was his altar boy, topping the list in my book. George had already taken a couple of small tumbles on the deck by this time, and we were a bit concerned about him falling over once he was in costume, as he had a long Bishop's smock (a sleeping bag liner) as well as the cardboard mitre that we'd made for him. He wanted to use a toilet brush and a small bucket of water to go around "blessing" people with holy water, which would mean he had no free hands to grab onto something if the ship rolled.

We came up with the idea of making a "bishop's staff" (broomstick), which he could use for stability, and dressing Jason up as an altar boy who could carry the bucket of water with the toilet brush in it. That would leave George a free hand, and it also meant Jason could take George's arm and steady him if necessary during his parade round the deck. George's costume was already well in hand, but what to do with Jason? We borrowed some bed sheets from Rachel, the steward, and made him a paper ruff for his neck. A small ice-cream bucket with a handle and a new toilet brush were sourced, and we were just about ready.

"How are you going to fix the sheets on me so that they look like an altar boy's surplice?" asked Jason.

"Oh, we'll just pin and peg", we replied. The irony of that wasn't lost on us – Jason was one of the main "pegging" culprits!

As we were all getting ready for the parade on the morning of St Patrick's Day, Mags and I went to get George and Jason sorted out and quickly realised that Jason couldn't really wear anything underneath the surplice – it would show through too much and spoil the effect. "Not a problem", said Jason. "I'll go commando." We draped and pinned in such a way as to preserve his modesty, then shot off to get ourselves ready. We were two parts of the Irish flag, she in orange and I in green, with another girl in white. Until we got on deck we hadn't realised it was quite so windy. Within a few minutes the breeze had caught Jason's surplice, and so much pressure was put on the pins that they popped open. They weren't the only things that popped open! Jason didn't realise that the sheets had opened at the back to the point where his bottom was clearly visible. Unkindly, I grabbed my camera and got a shot before we re-pinned him. Weeks and weeks later, when I got about twenty rolls of film developed, the first photo I looked at in the shop was the one that displayed some of Jason's bare bum. I just *had* to show it to the girls in the shop.

That evening we had another 18th-century dinner, at which Eefje appeared looking absolutely stunning. She was draped in the Irish flag and not much else. Fortunately, though, her pinning had been much more proficient than ours, and she maintained her modesty and dignity throughout the dinner. The fact that she was Dutch was neither here nor there, but Keelin, our Irish lass, was not to be outdone and shot off and found another Irish flag and reappeared wearing it as well. But she had a *pièce de résistance* – she also had a bottle of Bailey's Irish Cream. It was a fitting end to a really fun day.

There were lots of other little pranks and jokes that we got up to. You might find cling film across the toilet pan when you went to use it, or you'd find the paintbrush that you'd been using before lunch and had left soaking in turpentine had no hairs on it when you went back to the job, as a swap had been perpetrated. We wrote lots of messages and put them in bottles and threw them overboard in many different parts of the oceans. To the best of my knowledge only one has been recovered – on one of the South Pacific Islands. It was a thrill when we heard that the finder had contacted the Endeavour Foundation office in Sydney to let them know.

We kept on sailing, or motor-sailing depending on the weather, as we headed for French Polynesia, still navigating by 18th-century methods. The maintenance was ongoing, and still seemed to be relentless, as was the heat, especially below decks. We saw very little except the sea for days and days on end. Apart from the odd fun occasions such as those I've described, the routine was a bit unforgiving and the lack of sleep and constant heat were starting to get to me again. This haul between the Galapagos and Tahiti was going to take twenty-odd days. I had begun to think about getting off, even though I was, of course, booked to go all the way through to Sydney. Mags and Jason tried to cheer me up and jolly me along, but as the days went by I got more and more into a "stop the boat – I want to get off" frame of mind. And then Chris told us that, because we were well ahead of schedule again, we would be having another flat tyre: we were going to call in at the Marquesas. The news brightened me up no end.

20

FRENCH POLYNESIA

I knew roughly where the Marquesas were, but, as had been the case with some of the other places we'd already visited, didn't know much about them. One of the crew had a Lonely Planet guide to French Polynesia that we all took turns at borrowing and found very informative. The last few days' sailing before we arrived at these islands were very pleasant, especially as we had some rain. This brought down the humidity levels and the temperature below decks. The nights were balmy with lots of shooting stars and huge banks of phosphorescence in the water again, and I managed to get more sleep than I had in the previous couple of weeks on board.

The captain told us that we would be visiting two islands, Fatu Hiva and Hiva Oa. He'd been on the radio again and told us "festivities" were being arranged for our visit. As we approached our first planned anchorage at Omae Bay we could see spectacular razorback ridges and hills, all covered with lush vegetation. Like most of French Polynesia, these islands are volcanic and tropical. A seventeen-kilometre track runs from Omae Bay across the island to another village where our second anchorage would be, and some of the crew decided they'd like to walk it. We dropped them off ashore, and then motor-sailed around to our next stop, where we would all meet up again for the festivities.

As we approached our destination we could see many large phallic rock protuberances at the entrance to the bay. The Lonely Planet book told us that this place used to be called the "Bay of Penises", which horrified the early missionaries when they arrived. They added another *s* to the French name, which transformed it from "Bay of Penises" to "Bay of Virgins". Very clever, I thought.

It is a spectacularly beautiful place. A number of private yachts were anchored in the bay, so adventurers who sail this part of the world obviously know about it. The small village was dominated by a Catholic church, no doubt built and left behind by the horrified missionaries. It seemed the entire population of the village had been informed of our visit, as everyone had come out to welcome us. It was quite humbling. These are poor, simple people, and yet they had hand-made a beautiful lei for every crew member, they bestowed gifts of fruit on us and they had organised a welcome of music and drumming and dancing. All dressed in their Sunday best, so to speak, they made an enormous fuss of us. They have some sort of cooperative in the village and earn money from selling wood and bone carvings, beads and tapa cloth, which the ladies make, and a little tourism, but that's about all. My grumblings of the previous few days suddenly fell into perspective, and I realised how fortunate I was even to *be* there.

The group we had dropped off at Omae Bay rejoined us at the village in time to take part in the festivities. The walk had been absolutely fantastic, they said, if very hard going at times. Some of the photos they took from the top of the razorback ridges we'd seen from the ship are just amazing, all the more so because a tiny little ship (us) was down in the bay. This helped give perspective to the height of the ridges. Most of us joined in the dancing at various stages as the evening progressed, but the walkers were already absolutely exhausted. After an exchange of gifts we all headed back to the ship in small groups in the fizz boat and slept like logs for the rest of the night. Well, some of us did.

I woke in the morning to discover that the wind had got up in the night, we'd dragged the anchor and pulled over the coconut tree that we had an extra stern line attached to – and that there had been an "All hands on deck" during the night. They hadn't been able to wake me so I'd slept through the whole drama. Oops! "All hands on deck" *means* "All hands on deck". I felt a bit guilty when I was told, even though I thought they were exaggerating. But when I went up on deck I found that, sure enough, we were anchored in a different spot and there on the shoreline was a coconut tree with an extremely strange lean to it. I went to my captain o' tops and the captain to apologise for my absence, but it turned out that, in the urgency and drama of getting the ship safely anchored again, they hadn't even noticed I wasn't on deck. That made me feel a bit less guilty — I think.

It was time to move on, so we motor-sailed to Hiva Oa. It is considerably bigger than the island we had just been to, with a population of approximately 1800 people, whereas Fatu Hiva has only around 500 spread between the two villages. Martin and Ruth had been to Hiva Oa before on another sailing ship, and could tell us that Paul Gauguin had lived there for the latter part of his life and was buried there; also that, in addition to banking facilities, a post office, telephones and a few shops, the island has an interesting Gauguin museum. We'd had no local money (the Polynesian franc) at the other village, and had been unable to buy any of their artefacts — or anything else for that matter. While Fatu Hiva had been incredibly beautiful, this sounded more my cup of tea. I was in need of a little civilisation again.

We dropped anchor in Hanakee Bay late in the evening. Some of the crew went ashore and walked to the town, some three kilometres away, but Mags and I just had a stroll around the local area. We would tackle the village tomorrow, we thought. There was no public transport at night and we didn't fancy walking all that way in the dark when we hadn't been there before. Besides, all the biting things were out with a vengeance. We set off early the next morning and had barely walked two hundred metres when a woman stopped to give us a lift. This is the norm here, apparently, as most visiting boats anchor in this bay and the locals know the bus service leaves a lot to be desired, so they just stop and pick anyone up — very friendly and obliging. We tried out our schoolgirl French again, and managed OK. We changed some money at the main shop, explored what there was of the town, found the post office, then headed for the Gauguin museum. We never quite made it into the museum.

At the entrance we met up with a charming French gentleman who turned out to be the manager of a spectacularly luxurious bungalow-style hotel located high on the hill overlooking the bay where we had anchored. Gerard was extremely welcoming and friendly, but in reality was touting for business. "Did we know that a traditional welcome would be happening at the bay?" No, we didn't. "You mustn't miss that," he said. "It would be insulting to the local community." That made sense.

Several of the rest of the crew had arrived by this stage, so we all piled into his minibus and he drove us back to the jetty. Sure enough, another fantastic welcome took place, with mostly male dancers this time, the culture being a little different on this island.

While we were enjoying the drumming and dancing, Gerard was making friends with the captain and anyone else in white, i.e. the officers – probably the ones he thought most likely to become guests at his hotel. He had some vacant bungalows, he said, and would give us a special rate. Mags' and my antennae went up. Here was an unexpected opportunity. Virtually the whole crew went up to the hotel for lunch, and the view was spectacular. A swimming pool was perched on the edge of the cliff overlooking the bay, and the bungalows were huge, individual and luxurious. The *en suite* bathrooms looked like things I'd seen pictures of in magazines but had never actually been *in*. The rate was $110 per room per night. He had eight vacant bungalows. Not any more! Mags and I shot back to the ship to collect some gear and then decamped for two nights. So did quite a few others, including Jason and Dennis.

When Mags and I got into our bungalow we found hibiscus flowers placed throughout the room, including on top of our pristine white terry-towelling bathrobes, which were lying neatly across the beds. The bathroom was a riot of colour and aromas; in addition to the hibiscus there were frangipani and *tiare* flowers, not to mention all the French soaps, shampoos, lotions and potions. We pulled back the curtain to discover that we overlooked the bay and could see the ship. We hugged one another with glee, ordered some pina coladas from room service, sat on our balcony having a leisurely cigarette and drank in the ambience – and the pina coladas. It beat the hell out of a sweaty hammock in the 18th-century deck. This wasn't just civilisation – this was pure pampering in the fullest degree. We never made it back to the village: everything we wanted was here.

We swam in the pool and luxuriated. We had long, long hot showers and shampooed our hair using every conceivable bottle of stuff in the bathroom and luxuriated. We got dressed up and made up and met Jason and Dennis for dinner and drinks in the hotel and luxuriated. It was absolutely decadent – and absolutely wonderful. Most of the crew, including the captain, were still in the bar running up a tab. It was so big that the captain had to sign for it as guarantor until everyone got some money and sorted it out the next day. Gerard seemed quite happy to accommodate all of this on credit. (I'm sure if we hadn't paid up he could have had the local gendarmes arrest the ship or something.) Our credit cards all took a battering, but who cared? This was the stuff of dreams, and I figured it was extremely unlikely that I'd ever be back again. *Carpe diem!*

We slept late, and had actually needed to turn off the air-conditioning during the night – we were *cold*. My God, that was something that we hadn't been for months. A leisurely brunch around the pool, more swims, another long shower, and then we had to pinch ourselves back into reality. We were sailing at 5 pm, so it was back to the ship and our sweaty surroundings again. It was hard to believe that we'd been here at all, but I don't think either of us will ever forget it. One of the lads was so taken with the beauty of the place that he said if he ever got married he'd come back to this hotel for his honeymoon. He bought one of the towelling bathrobes that had been provided in the rooms and appeared in the mess wearing it on our next lay day, which absolutely cracked everyone up. They accused him of pinching it, of course, but Mags and I had seen the sale take place and could vouch for him.

Dennis had decided to change his plans, and got off the ship at Hiva Oa. He could fly from there to Tahiti, then on to New Zealand and meet up with his wife and family to spend some time with them before rejoining us in Gisborne. Jason was thinking about getting off, too, as he'd also had enough of the heat, the maintenance, the seemingly endless chores and the routines. However, he decided to stay on at least until Tahiti and would rethink once we got there. It was only a few days' sailing away, so at least it wasn't one of the long, long, almost monotonous legs of the voyage. Their unrest was unsettling me too, and I also began to think about getting off at Tahiti. Perhaps I'd bitten off more than I could chew.

With the sound of our cannons echoing grandly off the surrounding mountains, we sailed out of Hanakee Bay. A small group of locals had come to see us off, including Gerard, his wife and their delightful little girl, Calypso, who was about eight years old. She was jumping up and down with excitement at our cannons firing and stood waving and blowing kisses to us all shouting, "Au revoir mon amie, au revoir". It was very touching. It took us a couple of hours to put all the dirty, tarry anchor ropes and mooring lines away, by which time we were our usual filthy sweating selves again, and below decks was stinking hot and full of mosquitoes, midges and other biting things. The massive bunches of bananas that we'd been given at Fatu Hiva and hung from the deck head had ripened and were dropping off their bunches to make a squishy, smelly mess right in our hammocks. Our beautiful hotel was already but a memory. As the captain wryly said, "Welcome to the world of sailing".

We hit some nasty weather, with huge rainsqualls, periods of thirty- and forty-knot winds and big seas. We were up and down the rigging furling and unfurling sails, getting soaked to the skin with alarming regularity. Our route took us down through the Tuamotus, a low-lying group of about seventy-eight islands and atolls between the Marquesas and the Society Islands, only about half of which are populated. We had to keep particularly vigilant bow watches, especially at night: our radar wasn't working again and this area is fraught with danger because of outlying reefs and coral outcrops around the islands and atolls.

One night we thought we saw some lights, but as soon as we reported them to the officer of the watch they were gone again. He went to consult the chart – no lighthouses around here. We peered into the distance through the gloom again. "Quick! – There! – Did you see that?" He had this time. Maybe it was a vessel? Without our radar we couldn't really tell. We resumed the watching – very, very intently now. We didn't want to run into anything, and there was *definitely* something out there. It puzzled us for about an hour, until we began to discern the outline of the land and could see a bit better. We were getting near one of the bigger islands. And then we realised what we had been seeing – car headlights, out here, in the middle of the Pacific Ocean! It was one of the spookiest things I've encountered at sea. We had a laugh about it once we realised what the lights were, but they had really had us stumped for a while. It's just not something you would expect to see in such an isolated area.

After sailing on through the Tuamotus uneventfully, we arrived at Matavai Bay, Papeete, on 26 February, 237 years after Captain Cook was there. I was back in "stop the boat, I want to get off" mode again: the maintenance had resumed with a vengeance, I'd been soaked to the skin umpteen times – my wet-weather gear had rotted with the heat and given up the ghost – I'd been on the graveyard watch all week and I was exhausted. To top it all off, this was Ken's birthday, we were thousands of kilometres apart, and it would be a few weeks yet before we saw one another again.

Mags and I were among a group invited to the Great Cabin for drinks and a buffet to celebrate our arrival in Tahiti. I didn't feel like celebrating; Chris picked up on it pretty quickly. "What's up?" he asked. Inevitably I broke down, not for the first time on this trip.

"I think I'm going to get off in Papeete", I sobbed. "I've had enough." Chris let me have a little weep, and then reminded me that I'd flown all the way from Australia to join the ship and be here, and that I'd never forgive myself if I wasn't on board when we sailed, triumphantly, into Sydney Harbour.

"You're exhausted," he said. "We're in Tahiti for a week. Get off, get into a hotel and get some rest. Bugger the sightseeing! You'll come back a new woman." That made sense: I was far too emotional to be making decisions about whether I stayed or not. I'd decide before the ship sailed from Tahiti. Jason was still muttering about getting off too, but funnily enough he'd now started trying to convince me that I must stay on.

In the meantime we would be taking part in a huge welcome at Venus Point the next day. This was the spot that Captain Cook, Sir Joseph Banks and the rest of the party from the Royal Society had come to in the original *Endeavour* to observe the Transit of Venus in 1768. A monument and a plaque remain at the spot where "Fort Venus" used to be, but there is nothing left of the wooden stockade, which would have long since rotted away. Although she had been sailing since 1994, our *Endeavour* had not been here before, so the local tourism people had planned a massive welcome for us. This was quite a historic visit, but not everyone was happy that Captain Cook had been here, so it might prove to be a little controversial.

253

Early the next morning, canoes and other boats started gathering around us, helicopters were hovering overhead, a TV crew came out in a boat to interview and film, and the excitement began to build up. This was going to be another huge day. I'm not sure why, but I was one of the crew who was interviewed – in English, but for the French-speaking television station. We had a huge laugh at the idea of my Scots-accented answers being dubbed in French before it was shown locally.

Some of the lads were a little disappointed when they realised that the absolutely beautiful dusky maidens who were arriving by the score to greet us weren't topless. These days, although still in grass skirts, with leis and floral wreaths or frangipani in their hair, the girls are all quite respectable and don't have bare breasts. "The missionaries have a lot to answer for", muttered one of the lads. We told him he'd been watching too many Hollywood movies. Of course the girls wouldn't have bare breasts – it would be politically incorrect now, and they would run the risk of being charged with indecent exposure or sexual harassment or something. Besides, they probably all worked in offices or some other "normal" jobs now. Oh, how times have changed.

We all got into our best uniforms and went ashore in batches, courtesy of the TV crew's boat – except for the captain. He would be rowed ashore in the ship's pinnace and then carried from the boat onto the beach, as Cook probably was all those years ago.

"Drop me and you're dead", Chris said to Ally, the bosun, who was in charge of the rowing party.

"I didn't drop the other old goat", replied Ally, referring to the goats that we'd had on board at the Galapagos. Good one, Ally.

The day was obligingly sunny and pleasant, and the event promised to be quite memorable. I had cheered up already, especially as I could look forward to another few days off. Mags and I started plotting our break, but we would have to wait until the festivities were over and we were in Papeete itself. We didn't know it then, but during the day we would meet some tremendous Tourism Board people who would go out of their way to help us enjoy our stay in their lovely land.

The welcome was memorable. Elders from local communities presided over a very solemn ceremony; there were gift exchanges; then the music and dancing started. And the dancing! There were several different groups of girls in wonderful costume who danced in slightly different styles, some of them joined by men and some not, but all to the fantastic rhythm of Polynesian drumming. It was very hard to stand still. We got the opportunity to join in the dancing a little later, the captain being one of the first invited onto the floor. That man has hidden talents – he made a very good job of it, dress uniform and all. There were lashings of local delicacies provided for us: iced coconut milk and many exotic fruits, some of which I'd never seen before, all of them delicious. Some of the dancers turned out to be Tourism Commission staff, and they told us to drop into their office later in the day. They could arrange all sorts of things for us.

After the ceremony we returned to the ship and sailed across to the other side of Matavai Bay, where the city of Papeete is located and where we would berth for a few days. Papeete is the only city in the thirteen thousand kilometres between Panama and New Zealand. But it *is* a city. Our ears weren't used to such traffic noise and general hubbub, and it all seemed very loud at first. True to his word, the captain booked me and Mags off for the week, and we went in search of the tourist office. We decided to spend three days in Papeete and the rest of the time at Moorea, another island about half an hour away by ferry. After her stay in Papeete the ship would be calling there for another change of crew, and we would rejoin her there.

After some phoning and emailing, we had to get ready for a cocktail party that the entire ship's company had been invited to. When we got back down to the dock to meet up with the rest of the crew for bussing to the party venue, we discovered that many of the oncoming crew had arrived already, including two of my former *Leeuwin* shipmates – George, my old Hungarian buddy, and Heather, a girl I'd sailed with on a couple of *Leeuwin* trips and with whom I'd become friends. With about fifteen new crew joining, the ship was going to be *very* full between Tahiti and Sydney. All the more reason to enjoy our time off, we reasoned. That's if I stayed on – I hadn't quite decided yet.

It's amazing what a good night's sleep can do. After the party, we retired to our hotel and slept another of those sleeps of the dead – undistinguished, with no watches to get up for and no biting insects to contend with, in air-conditioning. By the time the next morning came I was already feeling like a new woman. We set off exploring, first visiting the markets and drooling over the famous black pearls. Purchased individually, they range in price from about $5 to whatever you like. Or they can be bought as a piece of jewellery, already set. "We can't be in Tahiti and not buy a black pearl", we thought, but decided not to do it on the first day: we'd look around first. The pearls were everywhere, we discovered, and it made selection very difficult.

We also visited a wonderful museum – the Museum de Tahiti and her Isles – and spent the whole afternoon there absorbing the history and culture of the place. I found it very interesting that there were many similarities between the canoes, woodcarvings and evolving history of Tahiti and what I'd already seen and learned in both Hawaii and New Zealand. Our taxi driver – a wonderfully chatty fellow, with excellent English – brought us up to date on current happenings in Tahiti, which happened to be in election mode. There were two schools of thought on whether they should become independent from France or remain as a French Overseas Country. We showed him over the ship as a thank-you for his courtesy, and he was absolutely astonished "that two English Mesdames such as you could tolerate living here for so long".

Margaret and I had a good laugh at that. "He should see us when we're working," we muttered to each other. "He wouldn't call us English ladies then."

We'd arranged to do a four-wheel-drive safari tour up into the mountains the next day – to see something more than the city-side of Tahiti – so had an early night. When we arrived at the tourist office in the morning we were pleased to find that a few of the others had booked as well. Jason wasn't among them, as he'd decided to fly to Bora Bora and was off on his own for a couple of days, while various others had scattered to other spots around Tahiti. Some of the permanent crew were on duty, as the ship was open to the public on exhibition.

It was a great day. We saw some spectacular waterfalls, went swimming in crystal-clear pools and rivers and lunched at a hotel on the edge of a volcanic crater with the guide telling us about the native plants and local customs. Then he took us to a Tahitian *mare*, where we learned how the elders were mummified when they died, and how their *mana*, or spirit, left them and was imbued into standing stones and

256

other objects nearby. Those stones, containing their *mana*, would then be moved to create the beginning of a new *mare* elsewhere. I was struck again by the resemblance to Maori cultural beliefs. To demonstrate the early communications system that the Polynesians used, he banged on a *mape* tree with a big rock. Because it has a hollow trunk, we could hear the sound echo a long way down the valley. Then he laughed and said, "Nowadays we use mobile phones".

We had one more day in Papeete, so stocked up on the girly things again and in the process discovered how expensive day-to-day items are in Tahiti. We came out of the chemist, each with our little polythene bag of goodies, and stood on the pavement looking at them going, "Bloody hell, that cost almost $100". It made us wonder how the locals managed. This wasn't a touristy shop: we'd paid just the normal prices. Finally we went back to the pearl market – we couldn't help ourselves – and both indulged, but in fairly modest necklaces. We left the 5,000,000-franc items for the rich people.

We planned just to chill out in Moorea, Papeete being too busy and noisy for that. The smaller island is only about eighteen kilometres north-west of Tahiti, but it's almost another world. Just sixty kilometres in circumference and lightly populated, it has been described by many people as the most beautiful place on earth. It would certainly have to be among them. One of the features that make it so striking is the array of jagged peaks and spires that give the island its unique profile. Geologists speculate that thousands of years ago the northern rim of the volcano either fell into the sea or was blown away by a huge volcanic explosion, leaving the heart-shaped island of today. The girls at the tourist office had helped us select where we would stay – Bali Hai on Cook's Bay. There's a romantic name for you. Margaret and I commiserated with each other that it was only we who would be there together, our menfolk being thousands of kilometres away. C'est la vie!

It was another of the bungalow-style hotels that abound in this part of the world, this one being situated right on the beach at Cook's Bay. Of course Cook's Bay was named after the famous captain, even though the original *Endeavour* had actually anchored in the neighbouring Bay, Opunohu. From our bungalow we could see glorious white beaches and a lagoon, as well as jagged peaks that were very reminiscent of scenes from the movie *South Pacific*. Indeed, local lore has it that some of those scenes were shot here; hence the name of our hotel complex. Then again, I'd heard the same story in 1999 when I was in Kauai in Hawaii. Either way, it was beautiful – and quiet – and so just what the doctor ordered. We spent a day or so doing absolutely nothing but laze by the side of the pool, read and snooze. Soon we were refreshed.

"Have you decided whether you're going to sign off the ship yet?" asked Mags.

"Sign off? No way: I wouldn't miss sailing up Sydney Harbour for quids." She laughed. That was what everyone was expecting me to say. I had just needed some space and rest to recharge the batteries again. The captain, as always, had been absolutely right.

We did a little sightseeing the next day. We'd bumped into one of the new crew members, and we decided to hire a car and set off. It didn't take long to travel around the whole island, stopping at one or two villages along the way. We went to a fantastic lookout spot high up on one of the ridges, which overlooked both Cook's Bay and Opunohu Bay. Good Lord, wasn't that the *Endeavour* coming into Opunohu Bay? She wasn't due here for another couple of days. We wondered if plans had changed, and drove back down to the bay to find out.

The story was that the captain had chartered out the ship to another film company. They were making a documentary about the French explorer Bougainville's arrival here and wanted to film in the bays at Moorea. The crew still on board were all in 18th-century costumes again so that their "arrival" would look authentic. It certainly did. All the maidens in the canoes welcoming the ship this time were topless – they were all actors, but the lads wouldn't have cared. They thought all their Christmases had come at once; cameras and video recorders appeared from nowhere. Someone told us afterwards that Ruth stole Martin's glasses so that he couldn't "perve" on all the young lovelies. "The camera has automatic focus", she said. "You don't need to be able to see". I'm sure the tale had been exaggerated somewhat, but it certainly made an amusing story.

After filming was completed, the ship moved around to Cook's Bay, which made things very convenient for us when we rejoined it a couple of days later. More of the crew got off for a day or two, and also booked

258

into the Bali Hai. Jason re-appeared, having come back to Papeete from Bora Bora to discover the ship had gone. As he had also decided not to get off, that was momentarily alarming for him. He hopped on the ferry and came over to Moorea – too late to catch all those topless maidens, much to his chagrin. We had another couple of days in this idyllic place, so made the most of it. We were determined to enjoy doing little or nothing before our next long haul – to New Zealand.

21

COOK ISLANDS

When we left Moorea, on 7 March, we had another long stretch of sailing in front of us – about twenty days of it – before we could expect to reach our next scheduled port of call, Gisborne, in New Zealand. Once again we had to settle down to ship's routine, get to know the new crew members, adapt to the change of watches, go through the safety drills and so forth. The sadness at having said our farewells to Big Gee, Reg and a few of the others was tempered for me by the pleasure of seeing George and Heather, from Perth, and Gil, whom I'd met in Darwin previously. George and Gil were both going through to Sydney and Heather would be getting off in Gisborne. We hadn't yet discovered how far the rest of the new people were going, but what we were acutely aware of was that, for the time being anyway, the ship was very crowded. The officers had had to vacate their cabins for the extra ten supernumeraries on board, and there wasn't a spare hammock point to be had anywhere.

Maintenance resumed – with a vengeance. We were now running out of time to complete it, as there were only about forty days of the voyage remaining until we were due to arrive in Sydney. Still, much of it had been done, and the new crew members were happy to get stuck into it with great gusto: they hadn't been doing it off and on for four months already. Even those of us who had been got back to work with renewed enthusiasm, as we'd just had a good break. So the chipping, and sanding, and painting, and varnishing went on. We had to have all the ship's make-up on before we sailed into Sydney Harbour.

Inevitably, there was more mending to be done after the filming at Moorea. Most of the 18th-century pants, in particular, needed fixing up yet again, so the sewing team regrouped, and Mags and I and a few others got going on it. Then we found that a lot of little private jobs were sneaking in to the mending as well. We charged a pina colada at the next port for those! Rachel had also presented me with a new challenge. From within her curator's Pandora's box of goodies she produced a bolt of new fabric, in an old-fashioned weave, and a pattern for an 18th-century shirt. Could I make a brand-new shirt? Before we got to Sydney? By hand? The ship didn't have a sewing machine, but of course in the 18th century it would have been done by hand anyway.

Normally not one to turn down a challenge, I said I would have a go. It proved to be more difficult than I'd anticipated. In the first place there seemed to be an awful lot of pieces when I'd cut it out, and as the job progressed I thought it was rather a strange shape. The captain reminded me that in the 18th century people were generally shorter, and ordinary seamen would have been short, stockily built men with great barrel chests. Just as well, as that described the person this shirt would have fitted by the time I finished it. I tried to find someone on board who met this description to model it, but it still didn't look quite right. Everyone very kindly said that the stitching was very neat, so I suppose I could take some satisfaction from that. I've no idea what happened to it in the end – whether it's now part of the museum display or whether it's remained in Rachel's Pandora's box.

Given that we had just left Tahiti, it was almost inevitable that somewhere along the line morning exercises would turn into a Tahitian dance extravaganza – and, indeed, one morning they did. Banana leaves and coconut shells had been acquired at the last stop, and were now adorning a number of the girls – and Allan and Greg – in appropriate places as clothing. Allan had also brought up on deck two wooden spoons from the galley: he was the drummer. What made it very amusing as the dancing progressed was that you couldn't help but notice the coconut shells came in various sizes, and they had been judiciously distributed according to the girls' various bosomly endowments. Allan started playing the drums – that is to say he started banging on the coconut shells with his wooden spoons and, much to our amusement, we became

WIND IN MY WINGS

aware that the resulting tone depended on the size of the coconut shells being struck, just as would be the case with a proper set of drums.

The days rolled by, very pleasantly in the main. As we were heading away from equatorial latitudes now, it was starting to get a little cooler in the evenings. Most of us were looking forward to leaving the heat and humidity behind, except for the occasions when we got the chance to go over the side for a swim. On one such occasion the sea was about four and a half kilometres deep and the water was flat calm, with just a gentle swell, and the colour of blue ink. It was glorious, although again I couldn't help but think of what else might be in there looking up at those splashing legs and wondering if toes and other bits might be worth eating. It didn't pay to dwell on such thoughts for too long, so we pretended to have the ocean to ourselves and just enjoyed the swimming. Sometimes we put the fizz boat in the water to allow for opportunistic photography of the ship under full sail. She looked magnificent.

Flying fish were back in huge numbers again. We often saw other sea creatures like turtles too, but the flying fish were the most fascinating to watch. They provided endless entertainment and were extremely clever. With just tiny flicks of their tails on top of a wavelet, they could keep their momentum going and "fly" another metre or so to the top of the next wavelet, and then do it again. Suddenly, they would all be gone again. There were lots of dolphins around at times too, cavorting on the bow wave and vying with one another as to who could jump the best and who took the lead position in the group at the bow – or so it seemed to us anyway.

Night watches were pleasant, too, with lots of nights when the stars seemed endless. On many occasions we saw shooting stars with tails of different colours, like pink and green and blue, in addition to the "normal" white ones. Sunrises and sunsets were spectacular almost on a daily basis. While we were enjoying this lovely weather pattern, we were also keeping an eye on three low-pressure systems that were forming to the north of us. There had already been several cyclones in the area during the season, and it wouldn't do to get caught up in one of those. Although Captain Cook's claim that "no sea can hurt her" was a phrase most of us knew, we still didn't fancy being out in a little wooden ship in a cyclone.

There were rumours going around that we might call in at the Cook Islands for a day or two, partly to run for shelter if we needed to get out of the way of an impending cyclone, and partly because the captain was considering another flat tyre. That would certainly break up the long haul between Tahiti and New Zealand. At morning meetings he kept us briefed about what was happening with regard to our planned arrivals in New Zealand and Sydney and about weather in the area. Then, sure enough, the rumours proved to be true – we were going to call in at Rarotonga, in the southern Cook Islands. This was good news, except that it presented the second mate with a bit of a problem – we didn't have a Cook Islands courtesy flag. It's normal when sailing in foreign waters for a ship to fly a smaller version of the flag of the host country as a mark of respect, and part of the second mate's responsibility on the *Endeavour* was to ensure that courtesy flags were available for all the countries she would be visiting. But we hadn't been planning on visiting the Cook Islands so, not unreasonably, we didn't have one.

The sewing team got assembled again, this time under the supervision of the second mate, Eefje. We consulted appropriate maritime manuals to determine what the Cook Islands flag actually looked like. On a navy blue background, there's a Union Jack in the top left-hand quadrant and a circle of fifteen white stars, representing the fifteen islands in the Cook group. A navy pillowcase was examined: too small. A bed sheet was examined: too big. A mattress cover from one of the supernumerary bunks was examined: it had distinct possibilities. The pinnace jack was about the right size and could perhaps be incorporated into the design. Eefje and Margaret started cutting out thirty white stars from a damask tablecloth (fifteen for each side of the flag) and I dismembered the pinnace jack and the mattress cover and started sewing – furiously.

The flag began to take shape. We didn't have a lot of time. The port was getting closer. When we were only a couple of hours away from the harbour it was decided to glue all the stars in place, as we'd run out of time to hand stitch. We raided the chippie's store for glue that might work, and a hot iron helped to do the job. About twenty minutes from the harbour the flag was raised to the top of the mizzenmast, to a great cheer from the crew. We felt quite proud of our creation, at the same time being relieved that it was far enough up the mast to preclude a close examination of the workmanship.

Alas, our misgivings proved to be well founded. It rained during the night, and the moisture must have had an effect on the glue. We awakened to find there were no longer fifteen islands represented on the flag, as some of the stars had blown away – one or two were floating in the harbour and one had been picked up by Martin and pocketed as a souvenir. This latter discovery immediately prompted a chorus of the old Perry Como hit "Catch a falling star and put it in your pocket" from those of us old enough to remember it. The locals didn't seem to notice and/or mind, however, that our flag had a few stars missing. One or two to whom we spoke on the dock seemed quite impressed that we'd even bothered trying to make it – and enjoyed the humour about the Perry Como song.

We had a couple of days to spend in Rarotonga. I could remember trying to find Rarotonga on a world atlas when I was a child. Like most kids, I used to collect stamps, and had bought some very colourful stamps at some schoolboys and schoolgirls exhibition when I was about ten years old. They were from Rarotonga, and I had absolutely no idea where to put them in my stamp album: I don't think they actually indicated that Rarotonga was part of the Cook Islands. Mum and dad wouldn't tell me where it was (I wonder now if they even knew), but made me find out for myself by looking through books and atlases until I managed to locate where this strange-sounding place was. And now I was actually here – isn't life interesting?

We discovered that the islands had already borne the brunt of four cyclones in the previous eight weeks, and that there had been a fair bit of damage done – mostly to crops, but to some buildings as well. Thankfully, there hadn't been any deaths or injuries. The population was, however, somewhat subdued it seemed, and the cyclones had certainly had an impact on their tourist trade. The captain decided that we would open the ship to the public at no charge as a small way of saying thank you for having us and to give the local children something with which to brighten their day. "Raro", as the locals call it, might have a relatively small population, but I think every one of them came to see the ship – we were busy! It seemed to cheer everyone up, though, so it was very worthwhile.

Those of us who wanted to do a bit of touring were collected from the dock by a couple of guides in four-wheel drive vehicles. We set off up into highland areas and discovered huge similarities to Tahiti and the Marqueses, with lush vegetation, volcanic peaks and lots of waterfalls. The guides told us many stories of their culture and legends, and again the similarities between Hawaii, Polynesia and New Zealand struck me. And of course, in terms of our British history and culture, we were still following in Cook's wake.

One of the things I found really interesting was the number of graves that were virtually in people's private gardens. Given that there was a large church and cemetery, and missionaries had obviously been there, this struck us as curious. We asked our guide about it and he explained that, because each family had been given a piece of land when the tribal feuding stopped, they owned it outright now. They are therefore allowed to bury family members on their own ground, although the Christian church hadn't actually consecrated it. He also commented wryly that, in modern times, the fact that a family grave exists on a property helps to prevent one sibling selling it off, or leasing it out, against another's wishes. Sibling squabbles – now there's something that happens in *both* our cultures!

The Cook Islands are still known for their stamps and currency, so when we got back downtown we set off in search of the post office and a bank to investigate what was available. To my delight I discovered a first-day cover set of stamps from the 1986 Australian International Philatelic Exhibition that had been held in Adelaide. It depicted Captain Cook, his landing at Botany Bay, *Endeavour* careened at Cooktown, and Cook's Cottage in Melbourne. Naturally I had to buy it for my collection of "trip treasures". I've also kept a couple of the local coins – they are extremely unusual shapes – and a Cook Islands $3 note, which is legal currency. The bank people told me it's the only place in the world that has a $3 note, so that was another "must have" curiosity.

The Antipodeans amongst us recognised instantly that there were branches of the Westpac and ANZ banks, and the local supermarket even stocked some familiar brands of biscuits and other items. We were definitely getting closer to home. Some of us stocked up on favourite goodies that we hadn't seen for months, never mind eaten, in addition to making the usual purchases of shampoo and moisturiser. Our lockers ended up being stocked with little private caches of nibblies, some of which would come back to bite us in due course, although we had no forebodings at the time.

For a lot of the time we were there it poured with rain, no doubt associated with the low-pressure systems that we had been watching, and it put a bit of a dampener on more touring around. Our last day there dawned sunny and bright, however, so a bunch of us headed off to the local sailing club, which was situated at a rather nice beach inside a lagoon. It might be one of the last chances for a swim at a beach, certainly a tropical beach, for a long time, we thought. We spent most of the rest of that day just relaxing there. We were sailing the next day, as the cyclone threat had now passed and we still had our schedule to keep. Next stop New Zealand.

22

ON TO NEW ZEALAND

Just before we left Rarotonga we took on one more voyage crew member as a special favour and more or less gave him a lift to Gisborne. He was a Maori chap, a master wood-carver who had been visiting Raro. During the voyage to Gisborne he spent time carving out a shield – "The Tiare Shield" – which would be used as a trophy in a junior football competition. It was fascinating to watch him at work, which he was quite happy for us to do. He told us woodcarving was a bit more difficult on board ship: at home his workbench didn't move around. Nevertheless the shield turned out to be a lovely trophy, inlaid with *paua* shell.

Something else came on board at Rarotonga – uninvited. The 'flu. As you can imagine, in the close confines of a small ship the disease can spread through the crew pretty quickly. A few days after we left, the first of the sniffles and sneezes started, and pretty well everybody succumbed over the next ten days or so. "Doctor" Liam went about dispensing Lemsips and paracetamol, and most of us had to take to our hammocks for two or three days. If you've ever been absolutely miserable with the 'flu at home in bed, you should try it in a hammock in a ship at sea. It truly adds a new dimension to the definition of miserable. One or two people developed nasty secondary chest infections and had to be dosed up with antibiotics until we arrived in New Zealand and they could get themselves checked out thoroughly, but the rest of us bounced back relatively quickly. We'd had virtually an illness-free voyage the whole way from England, and only one or two minor injuries, so we had been pretty lucky.

As we sailed on towards Gisborne the weather started to cool down. Almost unbelievably, after the months and months of heat and humidity, the jumpers and thermal underwear started getting dragged out from the back of sea chests and lockers. On the first lay day after Rarotonga most of us took the opportunity to have a clean-out and re-sort of clothes. In the process a pong engulfed the girls' locker room. We thought it must have been coming from the shoe rack, so we dragged all the shoes up on deck, scrubbed them out and left them to air; we also scrubbed and disinfected the shoe rack. But the pong was still there the next day. Strange. We'd have to investigate further.

We started going through every single locker, asking their respective owners to empty them out, scrub them and disinfect them. The smell of the disinfectant was starting to mask the pong, but it was unmistakably still there. What on earth could it be? Eventually we discovered that the culprit had come on board after our little raid on the supermarket in Rarotonga. Most of us had bought biscuits or nuts or other things that didn't need refrigerating to stash away in our lockers for midnight attacks of the nibbles, but someone had bought some "Laughing Cow" cheese – and most of it was still in the locker. That cow certainly had the last laugh: the cheese was so ripe it nearly walked out the door and mooed at us.

Life continued in the usual, simple way of being at sea, with the maintenance now well under control and the painting well in hand. My 18th-century shirt was starting to take shape, albeit a rather strange one to my eyes. And the yarning continued. On board this leg of the voyage we had several repeat offenders who had been on the Horn voyage, fifteen of them in fact if you included the permanent crew. The yarning that went on in the mess was really interesting to listen to, although each time I heard the same yarn from a different person it was a slightly different version, with the waves bigger and the winds stronger. Well, of course they would be – we're sailors, and that's one of the things we're known for. Liam, who'd never had the opportunity to sail around the Horn, was getting a bit fed up with all these tales of derring-do and declared the topic off-limits for further discussion in the mess, amidst good-natured booing and hissing from the Cape Horners. Still, they got the message and piped down a bit. Secretly of course, the rest of us were envious of their accomplishment.

As we sailed into more southerly latitudes, in cooler weather and closer to New Zealand, the marine life started changing again. There were not so many flying fish, but we saw huge pods of dolphins at times and the albatross had rejoined us. There were two or three different varieties, and some of the bigger ones had great wingspans. I recalled having seen one in the Te Papa Museum in Wellington that had a wingspan of about two metres. There's a photo of me standing in front of it with my arms held out on each side at maximum stretch. The bird's wings are visible on each side beyond where my arms stop – now that's *big*!

None of these were quite that size, but all of them were the most fantastic flyers, and they entertained us for hours on end with their aerial acrobatics. They would wheel and twist and then swoop down and hover so close to the wave tops that you would think they must surely crash into them, but they never did. Their judgment was unerring – and awe-inspiring. When they did choose to settle on the water, it was just as entertaining to watch them take off again. It's hard to imagine how the same bird that lumbered, flapped and struggled to get airborne, looking like a miniature Hercules aircraft trying to get off the runway, could exhibit such grace and control in the air.

Gisborne – and Easter – were fast approaching. Preparations were under way for our Sods Opera, planned for the night we would be at anchor before we sailed into the port. I happened to comment to someone that it would be the first Easter ever that I wouldn't be getting an Easter egg – my mum had always bought me one and Ken had kept the tradition going after she'd passed away. The comment obviously didn't go unnoticed, although I didn't think much of it at the time.

One of our watch members, Tony, who was very active in amateur theatre, had written a little skit for our watch to perform at the Sods Opera. It had a role for every watch member, but the only line we had to remember was "Aaah!" said in a variety of ways to illustrate what was happening at that moment. We all read the script and thought it was very clever, but would definitely need rehearsing. Another of our watch members, Jesse, was a trained actor, so we decided to put him in charge of directing the skit. We needed somewhere to practise away from the prying eyes of the rest of the crew, though, or it would lose all its impact.

We borrowed the Great Cabin on Easter Sunday afternoon to rehearse. While this was going on, amid much laughter and many retakes as the skit unfolded, we became aware of some other hilarity coming from the deck. Then into the Great Cabin bounded the Easter Bunny, alias Liam, carrying a basket full of Smarties, which he'd been dispensing all over the deck. He'd raided the ship's store after overhearing my comment about having no Easter egg, but it was his get-up that was causing the hilarity. Fittingly kitted out with some cardboard buckteeth painted white, he had a beanie pulled down tightly on his head and ears that flapped from it every time he hopped. These turned out to be a couple of sanitary pads. It was very effective, if somewhat unconventional – you learn how to make do with all sorts of makeshift items when you're at sea. Smarties distributed, we chased him out of the Great Cabin and continued with our rehearsals.

Another amazing and varied array of talent entertained us for the evening. Thankfully most of it was funny, as we were all starting to get the feeling of sadness that creeps in when the adventure is fast coming to an end. Those wretched goodbyes were staring us in the face again.

"Land ho", came the call on 29 March – New Zealand was off the starboard beam. Our arrival at Gisborne was imminent, and I was very much hoping that Adelia, my old pal from the 1995 voyage, might be there to meet us. I also looked forward to seeing our shipmate Dennis, who'd got off at the Marqueses and should be rejoining us. But first we would have to go through the business of clearing immigration, customs and quarantine once more. And that was where our little raid on the supermarket in Rarotonga *really* came back to bite us.

The officials and pilot boarded just before we sailed past the limestone cliffs at Young Nick's Head, which Captain Cook named in honour of the young lad who first sighted them in 1769. The pilot boat also brought out some former *Endeavour* crew who now live in New Zealand. Old friendships were quickly renewed, and immigration and customs were dealt with fairly speedily. Then it was quarantine's turn. They had to isolate or confiscate all the food on board. And I mean *all* the food on board. New Zealand quarantine regulations are very strict, as there are many pests and diseases endemic in other parts of the world that don't exist there. They inspected the galley, the fridges, the freezers and the dry store, confiscating a few items that they were suspicious of. With that done, they sealed everything up, not to be used again until after we left New Zealand.

And then a call came over the PA system. "If anyone has any foodstuff in their lockers, please bring it up on deck so that the quarantine people can inspect it." Our little private stashes were about to be gone over with a fine-toothed comb. Thank God we'd already got rid of the Laughing Cow cheese: that would really have upset them. Alas, most of our private larders went into the big yellow bin.

"Oh no, not the nuts".

"Sorry, you can't bring them in here."

"But look at the packaging – they went from New Zealand to the Cook Islands in the first place!"

"So they did. Sorry, you're still not bringing them in here."

"Oh no, not my Tim Tams! They're Australian, they must be all right."

"Sorry, the packet's been opened – into the bin please."

And so it went on. No amount of wailing and pleading on our part made any difference. We did manage to keep some boiled sweets, but that was about it. Welcome to New Zealand.

We were virtually alongside by this time, so I had started scanning the faces in the waiting crowd on the dock. I was disappointed that Adelia didn't seem to be there, and it turned out she'd been in hospital shortly before and hadn't been able to make the trip from Auckland down to Gisborne, which is about a ten-hour drive, I discovered. But I did spot Dennis, with his family, looking very excited. His grandson particularly was agog: he simply couldn't believe that his granddad had sailed on this *pirate* ship! He was about eight years old I think, certainly at an age where that would have impressed him.

Everyone in the Gisborne area knew that the *Endeavour* was arriving, so people had come from all around to be there when she docked. As we moved in closer I heard someone shouting my name. Who could this be? Blow me down: there was Glennis, one of the original mizzenmast mongrels from the 1995 trip. We had lost touch over the years, as we'd both moved house, so it was just fantastic to see her again. And then I spotted Donnamarie from the Hawaiian voyage in 1999, complete with her husband and twin babies – oh my! And then, to top it all off, there was Marian, my friend and fellow *Endeavour* guide from Fremantle … what on earth was she doing in Gisborne? I could understand Glennis and Donnamarie being there – they live in New Zealand. But Marian? That was another story. It wouldn't have surprised me too much to see her in Sydney, but I certainly hadn't expected her to turn up in Gisborne.

When we got ashore I discovered, after much hugging and carrying on, that Marian had made a conscious decision *not* to be in Sydney when the ship came in, as she thought it would prove to be far too sad an occasion: she'd been involved with the ship even longer than I had. She and her partner had been planning a trip to New Zealand, so they decided that it would just have to coincide with when the *Endeavour* would be there. That way she could say her goodbyes to the ship while they were enjoying themselves on holiday. Hopefully, that would take some of the sadness out of the occasion. That made sense to me, but it didn't alter the fact that she'd become a bit of a legend with regard to the number of places where she'd popped up when the *Endeavour* "just happened" to be there – Sydney, when we were leaving on the first voyage to New Zealand in 1995; Whitby, on that first voyage to England in 1996; Cooktown, when an *Endeavour* arrival re-enactment was taking place; and now Gisborne. There's no doubt about it: Marian is definitely an *Endeavour* junkie too.

She had brought with her a little *Endeavour* booklet that she'd had all the crew of the maiden voyage sign in October 1994. There was a party on board that first evening in Gisborne, and she went around and got all the crew from this voyage, which many of us felt might be her last, to sign it too. It is probably the only book in existence with all of those signatures in it. One day it might be quite valuable historically. I'm proud to say that my signature is there from both of those occasions, 1994 and 2005. I've got the same book, and had also collected all the initial signatures, but hadn't had the foresight to bring it with me on this voyage to do it again. Good thinking, Marian. The party was sheer nostalgia, as so many old shipmates from earlier voyages attended, and there were copious conversations that started "Do you remember the time that …" taking place all over the deck. Donnamarie's twins got passed around everyone for a hold, with even the captain getting in on the act. It was a very nostalgic and fun night.

Next day, Mags, Heather and I went in search of a hotel, as we were going to get off for a couple of days' respite again. At least Mags and I were: Heather came along with us, but she'd actually signed off the ship as she had to fly back to Perth to meet her work commitments. We found a convenient cheap hotel in the middle of town within walking distance of everything we needed. Later that night we discovered why it was so cheap – it was opposite the public toilets and above a Chinese restaurant and a pub that had karaoke nights. A bit different to our exquisite bungalow in the Marqueses. Never mind, it was clean and handy. Earplugs proved to be useful though: there were some dreadful acts on during the karaoke sessions. Our Sods Opera talent would have beaten them hands down.

The following day there was a social cricket match between the *Endeavour* crew and the local cricket club, so a bunch of us went along to support our team. What a hoot. Liam, being Irish, had never played cricket before, but had been in a hurling team when he was young, so he wielded the cricket bat in much the same way as one would a hurling stick. The end result of that was that he fired off several sixes all over the pitch. Rachel discovered that she couldn't run very well with pads on, so she adopted the same tactics and whacked sixes and fours at every opportunity. We got well and truly beaten, but the general consensus was that we hadn't disgraced the ship. At the end of the match, inevitably, we adjourned to the pub for some camaraderie, drinks and storytelling.

Thinking it would be our last port of call before Sydney, we had a pleasant, laid-back couple of days in Gisborne. But when we got back on board we discovered there was going to be one final flat tyre – at Picton on the South Island. We had the time, and the captain had some old friends there who had extended an invitation for the ship to visit. It would also allow us the opportunity to call in at Ship Cove in the Marlborough Sounds area, a spot that Captain Cook had used several times during various voyages to "water and wood" the original *Endeavour*. How could we pass that up?

A few new crew had got on at Gisborne for the last leg to Sydney, quite a number of them in the "mature age" group. One of them was Elaine, our American friend, returning for her third leg of this voyage.

273

What a woman! She had loved it so much before, and so badly wanted to be on board when the *Endeavour* did the triumphant sail up Sydney Harbour, that she couldn't stay away. We were all greatly impressed by her determination.

One "newie" that came on at Gisborne was an English lady called Sheila, who was one of the original guides in the UK. I had met her before in Fremantle, when she was a fantastic help to me during my time as Guide Coordinator in 2001. She was on as a supernumerary rather than voyage crew, a small concession to the fact that she'd recently had both her hips replaced and thought she "probably shouldn't climb aloft"! Who was it that said "After two hips there's always a hurrah"? Sheila was certainly doing a "hurrah", much to the consternation of her family back in England. Like me, though, she said that she wouldn't have missed this opportunity for quids.

We didn't actually realise how many "mature-age" group people we had on board until some American visitors on the dock asked us, "Is this some kind of elder-care outing for the day?" Sheila and I laughed like mad at that.

"No," we responded indignantly, "we're the crew." We then had to explain about the ship and how it had come about that we were all on board. It appeared there were still a lot of people who know very little, if anything, about the *Endeavour*, in spite of the fact that she'd done two world voyages by this time. Of course Captain Cook doesn't figure as much in American history as he does in British or Australian versions: they're more *au fait* with Christopher Columbus.

There was a last little run on the local supermarket to stock up on goodies again, although we Aussies warned everyone not to buy things that weren't going to get eaten before we arrived in Sydney. Australian quarantine regulations are just as strict as New Zealand's rules, and if there were any errant cheeses, nuts or the like they'd end up in a bin.

To get to Picton meant that we had to sail down the east coast of the North Island, through Poverty Bay, past Cape Kidnappers and Cape Palliser, and through Cook Strait. Cook Strait can be a very rough passage at times, and it didn't let its reputation down on this occasion – as soon as we rounded Cape Palliser we hit some rough weather. We all watched Sheila like hawks every time she appeared on deck, and made sure there was always something for her to hold on to or sit down on when the ship started rolling. It wouldn't do her new hips any good at all if she took a tumble.

The lifelines went up, we were all back into thermals, boots and wet-weather gear, and we had sixty-knot winds across the deck at one stage. Though it was absolutely exhilarating, it wasn't much good for actual sailing as the wind was blowing the wrong way. We spent much of one day going sideways and barely making any headway at all, but eventually managed to win out by putting the engines on, and arrived at our destination unscathed, if late.

Picton is a picturesque small town deep in the Marlborough Sounds, and is the link for all road and rail transport between the North and South islands of New Zealand. It's also the port where the inter-island ferries from Wellington berth. The sail up Marlborough Sounds was very tricky, as there are lots of little islands and headlands that have to be navigated carefully, particularly if it's done in the dark, as was the case with us. It was quite challenging being on the helm, and Sarah's 18th-century navigation had to be abandoned for safer 21st-century practices. Charts of the area are peppered with potential hazards.

It would be a short stop but a very pleasant one. The captain met up with his old friends and a barbeque was organised for the next day at Ship Cove, one of the idyllic spots in the Sounds. Meanwhile we all went ashore at Picton itself and set out exploring. Some of us went to the Edwin Fox Maritime Museum, where the remains of the *Edwin Fox*, the ninth-oldest ship in the world, are being restored – to a certain extent anyway – by the commendable efforts of a group of volunteers.

The museum is brilliant. The *Edwin Fox* carried 279 convicts from Plymouth in England to Western Australia in 1858 on a voyage that lasted eighty-nine days. According to the ship's documents that were on view, most of the time they would all have been confined below decks. And we thought we'd had it tough at times on our voyage! I noted with interest that there was a "Taylor" among them – transported for stealing sheep, as many of them were in those times. Perhaps he had been an early ancestor. In recent times it's become very fashionable in Australia to have a convict in one's family history.

We found a great place to eat that night, and had lots of fun dancing and bopping to really old fifties and sixties music coming from a proper old-fashioned jukebox in a place whose décor matched the era. Some of the younger ones weren't familiar with a lot of the music, but we "mature age" people knew them all and were mentally back at high school or church-youth-club dances. Every now and then we'd burst into noisy singing, but fortunately none of the other diners seemed to mind and the whole thing ended up being one big party.

Next day we boarded many invited guests and set off down the Sounds for Ship Cove. Our departure was later than had been intended, as we had woken to a thick fog, and there was no way we could attempt to sail through the myriad nooks and crannies until it lifted. At 7.30 am we could see only about twenty metres to the end of the jetty. We didn't want to meet the inter-island ferry coming in the other direction, so we waited an hour or two. As usual, Ally fired the cannon just as we were pulling away from the dock, and there was a fantastic echoing effect off the surrounding hills. But what made it different this time was the perfect smoke ring that came out of the barrel. We'd never seen that before. The stillness that comes with a foggy morning allowed the smoke ring to hold its shape while it floated upwards for a moment or two. Most of us weren't quick enough to grab cameras and get it on film, unfortunately. It will just have to remain in the "camera" in our minds.

As we sailed down the Sounds to Ship Cove we could see the beauty of the area for the first time, as we'd arrived in the dark. It would have to be one of the prettiest places that I've ever seen – not in a tropical way like the Pacific Islands we had visited previously, but all around the hills were so green and the waters so blue and calm that you could understand why there is a large flotilla of small boats at marinas in Picton. It would be an amazing place to sail such craft and picnic on some idyllic little beach that you could have entirely to yourselves.

Indeed we virtually had Ship Cove to ourselves when we arrived there and dropped the anchor. A couple of boats had accompanied us, and they would take our invited guests back to Picton at the end of the day, as we would be heading straight out to sea again. Cook and his men visited this place some five times during various voyages, for rest and recuperation and to water the vessels from the freshwater stream

276

that runs here. I'm pretty certain he would never have had a barbeque, though, particularly with fresh local lobster and beer. It was a very pleasant afternoon, and a great send-off from New Zealand shores. This would be our last stop before arriving in Sydney ... but there was one more surprise yet to come.

While he had been poring over charts of the area, Liam had discovered a spot in Marlborough Sounds called "Cape Horn". He had produced certificates on the ship's computer that stated so-and-so had rounded Cape Horn, *twice*, on 6 April 2005, and issued them to all of us on board who hadn't rounded the real Cape Horn. We could now all claim to be Cape Horners, he said. The real Cape Horners were less impressed than the "fakes" but enjoyed the joke, took the hint and stopped gloating about their voyage quite so much. Yes, Liam had at last quietened them down. That certificate is another item in my treasures collection.

And so it was time to leave the Land of the Long White Cloud and head out into the Tasman Sea for the very last leg of our voyage. It was hard to believe that the trip was coming to an end.

23

HOMEWARD BOUND

While we were in New Zealand Captain Chris was in touch with the Endeavour Foundation and the National Maritime Museum people in Sydney to find out about the arrangements for our arrival. He called us all together to brief us. As I had suspected back in October when I first heard that the ship was going home, it wasn't all good news.

We were due into Sydney on Sunday 17 April, and a huge welcome was being organised for our arrival – "bigger than Ben Hur". Chris hadn't been wrong when he'd used that phrase before, and I was sure he wouldn't be wrong this time either. A flotilla of tall ships and naval vessels was being organised, and harbour tugs would fire off their water cannons and lead us in. Sydney people always turn out in huge numbers for these occasions, and we could expect hundreds of private boats to come out and thousands upon thousands of spectators to cram vantage points all around the fantastic harbour.

A large marquee was being erected on the dock at the Maritime Museum in Darling Harbour, which would be the venue for a reception at which some three hundred VIPs were to be present. Entertainment would be provided by bands, sea shanty groups and the Qantas Children's Choir, which would sing, "I still call Australia Home." I had tears in my eyes already just thinking about it. Quite possibly there would be a gun salute as we sailed past Mrs Macquarie's Chair and the Opera House – that had happened when the *Endeavour* sailed into Sydney the first time in 1994 – and there would be TV and other media people in helicopters and boats. Who knew who else might be there?

We would anchor somewhere sheltered the night before, probably in Pittwater, a large inlet north of Sydney Harbour, and take on a number of VIPs early in the morning. These would include members of parliament (there were even rumours that the Prime Minister might be among them), the chairman and other directors of the Endeavour Foundation and many Sydney notables and media people. They would sail with us up Sydney Harbour to the berth at the Maritime Museum in Darling Harbour. It all sounded very exciting. That was the good news.

The bad news was that, as of midnight on 18 April, the HM Bark Endeavour Foundation would cease to exist and the ship would belong to the Australian Government, with the National Maritime Museum appointed as its custodian. The permanent crew on board would be out of work. Everyone would have to be off the ship by 8 am on 19 April, together with our belongings. The ship would be opening to the public in permanent static display mode at the museum the next day. While not exactly surprised, we were devastated to hear the news officially. We immediately started organising a petition to present to whomever was the most important of the VIPs, with a view to having the ship keep on sailing.

We also started making plans among ourselves as to who would get the "honour" of pegging the VIPs, not to mention the pilot, customs, quarantine and immigration personnel. Remember the pegging nonsense? This was going to be too good an opportunity to miss. Mags and some of the other English people thought that perhaps we shouldn't do it, because the visitors would be all officials, or important, or both. That just made them a more appealing target to us irreverent Aussies. Bring them on! The captain told the permanent crew not to be involved with this in case some of the VIPs took offence: it wouldn't look good for the ship. But there wasn't very much he could do about the voyage crew and volunteers. Put us off, perhaps? We were all getting off anyway. We rubbed our hands with glee, and decided that we should all have pegs in our pockets to whack on whomever as opportunities presented themselves.

The Tasman Sea can be rough at times – and unpredictable – but for this final leg of the *Endeavour*'s final trip the winds were slight, the seas were fairly calm, lots of stars were out at night and the albatross were still following us throughout the day. The last of the maintenance was done, the 18th-century shirt was finished and we had to start thinking about packing. Some of the permanent crew had been on board for three years, and for them this would be a huge task.

During the whole voyage the permanent crew had been making an inventory of all the ship's equipment and goods and chattels. This would become part of the documentation that would be handed over to the Government at the transfer of ownership. It had been a monumental task and, with whatever spare time we had left, we all threw ourselves into helping them complete it. Cupboards and sea chests were emptied and double checked to make sure all the contents were listed properly.

There started appearing from the bowels of the ship some very strange things that had been collected over the previous eleven years. "Where on earth did this polar bear come from?" It was a life-size upright cardboard polar bear wearing sunglasses. None of the current crew knew how it had got on board – but I did! It's an advertisement for Bundaberg Rum that we'd pinched from a pub in Bundaberg in Queensland one night in 1995. I'd had no idea it was still aboard, tucked away in some cranny all those years. I'm sure the captain remembered the night it got smuggled on board, but he took the diplomatic stance and claimed that he didn't recall. I didn't ask him about the White Ensign that had been purloined from an Australian Navy ship on the same night, but I'm positive he wouldn't have recalled that either.

I don't think the polar bear made it onto the inventory. We'd started a pile of things that were to be disposed of into a shoreside dumpster, and I'm pretty sure he would have ended up in there. As cabins were emptied and belongings got packed or put on the pile, the mood below decks changed noticeably. There was an air of disbelief that the trip was finally coming to an end – and despair at the idea that this wonderful, glorious ship might never sail the seven seas again. Sydney was getting closer – there were only eight hundred kilometres to go. We had one more Sods Opera to take part in and enjoy, and one more invitation "to enjoy the last drinks in the Great Cabin" – *ever*. It was very, very sad.

At the Great Cabin drinks, the long-term voyage crew and supernumeraries were presented with a hand-made wooden necklace with some nautical flavour, like a fishhook or whale tail or seahorse.

They had been secretly made for us by some of the permanent crew from a small piece of the *Endeavour*'s wood sourced from the broken timberheads. They had been filing and sanding away at them for days to have them ready for this last function. It was very touching. As well, each of us received a certificate to verify that we had undertaken the voyage. Margaret and I were the only ones to get one that stated we had "crewed aboard this vessel, joining at Whitehaven, England, and disembarking at Sydney, Australia, from 8th November 2004 to 17th April 2005". Needless to say we were very proud of those.

Sods Opera, quite possibly the last one ever to be held on the ship, proved to be more memorable than usual. Aside from the talented performances and funny skits that always seemed to appear, the whole thing was presented on this occasion as though it were an Oscar's presentation, Clare and Greg acting as emcees. There were some very strange and very funny "Oscars", each of them blatantly tongue-in-cheek and generally presented to an officer or crew member for an inglorious stuff-up that he or she had perpetrated at some point in the ship's life. Most of them would be positively defamatory if discussed here in any detail. Suffice to say that each one prompted lots of laughter and nostalgic storytelling. Clare and Greg must have done an enormous amount of homework to devise them all.

As we got closer to the coast, advice came through that there had been a change of plans. We were now going to Botany Bay, south of Sydney Harbour, as Pittwater was an inconvenient place for the VIPs to get to. Given that Botany Bay was where Captain Cook first dropped anchor in Australia, it seemed a particularly appropriate destination for us — we were still following in the great man's wake. The wind had dropped almost completely and we were now under motor again — somewhat ignominiously, perhaps, as it would have been far more fitting to sail into Botany Bay just as Captain Cook had. He didn't have our schedule to maintain, however — with all the arrangements that had been made for our arrival, it was inconceivable that we could be late.

As we headed south to Botany Bay, those of us familiar with the coastline began to pick out headlands and landmarks despite the darkness. Before I came off my watch for the night, we had been able to discern the famous Sydney Heads. Indeed, as we passed the entrance

281

to Sydney harbour, there was a spot where we'd been able to see, very vaguely, the outline of the Harbour Bridge in the distance, mostly because of the red aircraft warning light on its top. I called Elaine and Mags over to the rail to point it out, and they were quite excited. I don't think they'd realised until they looked at the chart that we'd had to sail past the entrance to Sydney Harbour in order to get to Botany Bay. We arrived at about 6.15 on the morning of 17 April, and dropped anchor about twenty metres away from where Cook had anchored in 1770. There was something uncanny about being there, so close to where he had been all those years ago.

Coastguard personnel came out in a small boat and directed their fire hose at our hull to knock off some of the copious amount of weed growing there. "You should have brought the lawnmower," shouted the captain to them, as we waited with lots of pegs in our pockets. In due course the pilot arrived. He was pegged as he climbed over the capping rail. Then immigration, customs and quarantine came along. I managed to get the customs people, and other shipmates must have got immigration and quarantine, as we noticed pegs hanging off the backs of their shirts as they went about their business. All the goodies that had been bought in New Zealand must have been either eaten or adjudged legal this time around, as we didn't get the grilling from quarantine that we'd experienced in Gisborne. The officials left once their business was completed – some of them still with pegs hanging off them. We giggled with glee. We had been cleared and were now formally *in* Australia.

Spirits were quite high at this stage. The VIPs and invited guests were gathering at a small jetty at Kurnell, near the oil refinery – in contrast to Pittwater, Botany Bay is an industrial area. From there, they would be transferred across to the *Endeavour* in small craft. Meanwhile there were large oil tankers coming and going from the oil refinery, various other vessels were approaching us for a look, and the tide had changed. We picked up the anchor and from time to time had to do a bit of manoeuvring, under motor, to get out of the way of large tankers.

We began embarking the VIPs and invited guests from the tenders that were running them over from the jetty. This entailed getting them out of the smaller boats and up over the capping rail of the ship using the man steps and ropes on our hull. This is not an easy manoeuvre if the boat you are getting out of is bobbing up and down on the waves – it can actually be a fairly daunting task for a landlubber, as many of these VIPs were. Chris manoeuvred the ship so that the small boats would be in our lee, thus affording some protection from the current coming in through the mouth of the bay. Various crew members were on hand to assist them over the capping rail as required – and peg them at the same time. It wasn't long before many of the guests and VIPs were mingling on the deck, ooh-ing and aah-ing over various aspects of the ship, totally unaware that they had clothes pegs hanging off their clothing, hats or bags. A federal senator and the chairman of the Foundation had been particular targets (of course!) – each had about four hanging off him, much to our delight.

It took some little time to get everyone aboard, as there were about fifty guests and the boats could carry only about a dozen people at a time. In the meantime crowds were gathering on the nearby shoreline at Frenchman's Bay, La Perouse and Kurnell, where the Captain Cook monument stands. A group of splendidly uniformed "soldiers" from a local musket club had formed a guard of honour and fired off their muskets into the air. We responded with cannon fire, inevitably. Quite a number of small boats were buzzing around us, and the tide was still changing. The whole place was a hive of activity, with newspaper photographers and cameramen from television stations snapping everything and anything. At last the crew were sent aloft to loose the sails in preparation for getting under way and sailing out of Botany Bay.

Suddenly there was a shudder and a jolt, and we came to a grinding halt. We had run aground, or as we preferred to phrase it "touched bottom": running aground conjures up far more dramatic images than what had just happened. Nevertheless, call it what you will, we were well and truly stuck and weren't going anywhere. We had just spent 160 days at sea, crossed sixteen time zones, visited eight countries and sailed approximately 14,500 nautical miles virtually unscathed, and we had run aground in Botany Bay barely a stone's throw from where Captain Cook had anchored. Great balls of fire! He would either be turning in his grave or having a huge laugh. Our high spirits evaporated as we realised that, while not in any danger *per se*, we were certainly in a bit of a predicament. And there was a *very* tight schedule to be followed if we

283

were to meet the obligations of the arrival celebrations. This did not look good at all. The media people on board couldn't hit their mobile phones fast enough.

We were all called back onto the deck, so abandoned our work of undoing gaskets and loosing sails. Hurried consultations were being held on the poop deck between Chris and the pilot – who was now back on board – and the other officers and Foundation directors. Charts and tide tables were being examined. Local knowledge was being gleaned from the pilot and others. Meanwhile some of our landlubber visitors were displaying a fair bit of alarm and consternation. "No madam, we're not in danger of sinking", I said to a lady who asked me the question. "When a ship sinks, it normally goes to the bottom. Our problem is that we're already *on* the bottom".

It was decided to apologise to the guests and offload them. After all, we were fifty-plus people heavier than normal. One or two of the Foundation's directors stayed on board, but the rest got taken back to the jetty from whence they had come. The engineer pumped out the fresh-water tank to lighten the ship a bit more – we were almost home and wouldn't be needing ten tonnes of fresh water. Unlike Captain Cook when he'd run aground on Endeavour Reef in Queensland, we couldn't start throwing cannons and other heavy things like that overboard: it wasn't the 18th century and we were in a very busy bay! Engines were put into various configurations of forwards and backwards and sideways to try and "jiggle" the ship off the reef or sandbank or whatever it was that we were stuck on – to no avail. Time was ticking by. We were going to be late … very, *very* late as it transpired.

After an hour or so of our own ineffectual attempts to free ourselves, it was decided to call in tugs to pull us off. It took about two hours of nudging and shoving, and pushing and pulling before we finally floated free. During this exercise some grumblings and groanings had been coming from the hull, and part of the sacrificial keel had broken off and floated away. It looked more alarming than it actually was: as the name implies, the purpose of this keel, an outer layer if you like, was to be sacrificed – to Toledo worms in the tropics on the original ship, certainly not to chunks of rock in a Sydney suburban bay as had been the case here. The fact that there had been any damage at all meant that we had to call in divers from the Australian Maritime Safety Authority (AMSA) to inspect the hull and clear it as being safe before we could leave Botany Bay and sail up the coast the short distance to Sydney Harbour. This of course, took more time, and made us even later.

Once we were given the all clear by the AMSA divers, we motor-sailed (alas!) out of Botany Bay to journey our last few kilometres. Though it had lifted a little, the mood was much more subdued than it had been earlier in the morning. It was all a great shame, and had certainly spoiled the expected "bigger than Ben Hur" arrival. Chris was devastated and spent hours, indeed days, apologising to us all. Irrespective of the details of what had actually happened, being the captain he of course took full responsibility for the incident and the outcome. It was heartbreaking to us, who had spent several months of our lives with him, seeing how upset he was on our behalf. "These things happen", we said. "Don't worry about it – it's only one day. We've had many grand welcomes and months of fun." Of course we *were* a bit disappointed, but what could we do? At the very least we could, and did, totally support our captain.

It was just getting dark by the time we went through the Heads, and we could see that there weren't any tall ships, naval escorts or those hundreds of boats and thousands of people waiting for us. We were about six hours late, after all, and it had been broadcast on both radio and television that the *Endeavour* had run aground in Botany Bay. All the official celebrations had been cancelled. The bands and shanty groups, the kids' choir, the helicopters, the VIPs and the spectators had got tired of waiting and gone home – except for a stalwart band of Endeavourites who came out to meet the ship and escort us into Darling Harbour in water taxis. They yelled and yahooed and buzzed around the ship, bobbing on the water in those tiny little boats, calling out people's names and waving madly. Our spirits lifted again.

A group of guides from Fremantle was yelling out for me to wave back to them. Another group from England, many of whom had seen us off from Whitehaven almost six months before, was also yelling out to me. When we finally arrived at the National Maritime Museum dock in Darling Harbour, there were more people shoreside, many of whom had been crew or staff previously, waving and yelling out for me. Elaine could hardly believe that all these people were welcoming me, and seemed impressed. "Hang on a minute, Elaine", I said, laughing. "It's not *me* that they've come to see, it's the ship. I just happen to be on it. I've been involved with her for so long that I've met all these wonderful people." Indeed, it suddenly dawned on me that the only two people who were on board now who had been there at the beginning were the captain and myself. This wasn't the end of a voyage, or even the end of my biggest adventure yet – this was the end of an era.

There was still some media presence at the dock, with TV cameras in evidence. As soon as the gangway was secured, I shot off to go and say hello to my friends on the dock and to phone Ken to let him know that all was well. I thought that, given the time difference between Sydney and Perth, I could reassure him that I was fine before he turned on the TV news. I was too late – his sister had already been on the phone from Tasmania (which is also two hours ahead of Perth) to tell him the news and to find out if I was all right. He hadn't known anything about the incident until she phoned, and was expecting a call from me a little later. Who was it that said, "Bad news travels fast"? His dry sense of humour kicked in again as he asked me "Were you on the helm at the time?"

"No, I bloody wasn't!"

Inevitably, there were still speeches to be made, the senator still blissfully unaware that there were pegs hanging off his jacket, and a formal handover of the ship to take place, but certainly without the pomp and ceremony that there would have been if we'd got there on time. The reception had gone ahead without us – it would have been a tremendous waste of food and drink if it hadn't – but everything else had been cancelled. We decided that the reception must have been all right: there was absolutely nothing left. They hadn't even left us a token bottle of champagne. There was nothing else for it but to adjourn to the pub. We would have done that anyway, after the formal reception, but instead of it being a celebration it turned into more of a wake.

Mags and I, along with Jason and a few of the others, had booked into nearby hotels from the day of our arrival. We could have stayed on the *Endeavour* for two more nights, but I'd had previous experience of being alongside at this berth while still sleeping on the ship. Gates were locked at midnight, I recalled, and you couldn't get back on board without climbing over the fence, which meant that you almost certainly got caught climbing said fence on surveillance cameras. (I hadn't worried about it too much back in 1995, though, as the captain had been climbing over the same fence a bit further along!) So if we'd planned to sleep on the ship that night we would have had to be back on board before the gates were locked or climb the fence. Having decided to book into a hotel, we could party on for as long as we liked. We checked in and dumped our gear at the place we were staying and headed for the Pyrmont Bridge Hotel – the *Endeavour* crew's local watering hole when she was home in Sydney. And she was home – possibly for good.

24

EPILOGUE

I never did manage to "go to sea" in a professional capacity, but feel that I've more than made up for it with my adventuring on various tall ships. Perhaps it was just as well that I couldn't get into Maritime College when I was young: I'm not sure that I would ever have got my head around celestial navigation! It's certainly been very satisfying seeing all these young women coming through the ranks over the years, ending up with captain's tickets in many cases, especially when I remember the disdain, nay ridicule, with which my adolescent ambitions were met some forty years ago, just because I was a girl.

But I never did let go of my dream of going to sea, and I'm grateful to have had the chance to fulfil it to a very large degree. I recall a young psychology student I met many years ago saying to me, "Not many people *have* a dream; even fewer get the opportunity to do anything about it if they do have one." I definitely had the dream, and I've certainly had the opportunities – and have taken advantage of them whenever possible. As a result of that I've visited some amazing places, had extraordinary experiences and met some wonderful people, many of whom have become lifelong friends. "Carpe diem!" is a great motto that I believe in wholeheartedly and try to apply to life.

The *Endeavour*'s motto is "Be excellent to each other", and, while this was not the meaning attributable to the motto in the first place, she's certainly been excellent to me. There was a young, joyful lad of about eighteen on the construction crew back in the late 1980s who used to say this frequently. Tragically, he was killed in a road accident, which stunned everyone at the time. Someone came up with the idea of using his saying as the ship's motto, so the woodcarver made up a plaque that was erected in the 20th-century mess to remind us of Patrick and his philosophy. It's been there ever since, and hopefully will remain there.

Are my sailing days over? Perhaps the long, foreign-going voyages are. I still have the *Leeuwin* nearby, and she sails from Darwin in the Northern Territory to Esperance in the south of Western Australia in multiple short voyages all year round. There are other tall ships around the world that are now accessible, thanks to the Internet. Somehow, though, other ships don't seem to have the magic that the *Endeavour* has. It's almost as though all of the people who have worked on her, guided on her and sailed in her have left a little bit of themselves behind, and the ship is imbued with the spirit of all of these multiple souls – the *Endeavour* family's souls.

Craig Todd, one of the voyage crew on the 1996 trip to the UK, captured the feeling beautifully in Richard Polden's book *Endeavour – A Photographic Journey* when he wrote, "Thus comes the final day. And we went out in style, friends that have shared a bevy of experiences that can only be summed up as 'we few, we lucky few.' Now below decks there is darkness where there once was laughter and light. It is no longer our ship. But in our hearts those nights of dolphins and comets are still with us, and every sunrise will remind us of the beautiful light on the morning watches in the doldrums. I miss you already. We are different people now and our dreams have changed – ordinary lives will not be tolerated. May Neptune bring us all our desires and a life that is remarkable."

I had received the book as a Christmas present that year, and shared it with my mother, who was by then relatively frail, with failing eyesight. She loved to look at all the exceptional photographs in it, however, and I explained different details about the pictures and read to her the captions underneath. I was never able to read Craig's comments aloud to her: I just got so choked up with emotion it overwhelmed me. It still does. Indeed, during the writing of this book there have been several occasions when I have had to stop because my tears were fogging up my glasses and I couldn't see the computer screen. At other times I have found myself laughing out loud at particular memories – many of which

I couldn't possibly write about! Such is the love and affection attached to this remarkable ship.

At the time of writing *Endeavour* is alongside at the Australian National Maritime Museum in Darling Harbour, Sydney, on display in museum mode. There's an old saying that says, "It's being in port wot rots ships and men". How true. All of us who have sailed in her (we few, we lucky few!) fervently hope that she will ply the seven seas again and give other people the opportunity to taste a sailor's life and visit exotic places, and not just be a floating museum. She has done one or two short voyages since coming home, and I understand plans are in hand for her to continue voyaging under the management of the ANMM which gladdens my heart. I somehow think that my sailing days on her are over, however, as I see myself as part of "the old guard". I should probably leave well alone and not try to re-create all of my amazing memories.

If all the farewells at the end of each leg of the voyage previously had been bad, the one in Sydney was nothing short of agonising. On my final day in Sydney I went down to Darling Harbour one last time to say farewell to my ship and anyone else who happened to be around. There was no-one I knew: we had scattered to the four winds already. The ship had lots of visitors on board, and some museum staff was in attendance, but that was all. Already I felt as though I didn't belong here any more. Strangers who, whilst admiring of the ship, had no idea what we had all just shared had invaded my home. I gave the carrick heads one last hug and ran down the gangway, tears streaming uncontrollably down my face. I hurried away from Darling Harbour, still weeping, and couldn't bring myself to look back.

There's a hole in my heart where the ship used to be. I don't know if it will ever heal, as I live on the other side of the country from where she now resides, some four thousand kilometres away.

I have no idea if I will ever see her again.

GLOSSARY

Abeam:	At right angles to the centreline of the ship.
Aloft:	Up in the rigging or on the yards.
Bear away:	To steer the ship away from the wind.
Belay:	To make fast a line around a cleat or belaying pin.
Bend:	To secure a sail to a spar or yard.
Block:	A pulley in a wooden case consisting of a sheave around which a rope runs.
Bosun:	Short for boatswain. The officer in charge of a ship's boats, sails, rigging, cables, anchors etc.
Bunt:	The middle part (or body) of a square sail.
Buntlines:	Lines attached to the foot of a square sail to haul it up or down.
By the wind:	A method of steering a ship.
Capstan:	Device for hauling up heavy objects, lines or the anchor.
Carrick heads:	End-pieces holding the windlass, often adorned with carvings.
Channels:	Strong flat timbers projecting from the sides of the hull to which the deadeyes, lanyards and shrouds are attached.
Cleats:	Pieces of wood, often fixed to the rigging, which lines are fastened to.
Clew:	The lower corner of a sail.
Clewlines:	Lines attached to the clews, which haul the sail up or down.
Cock-bill:	To adjust the yards so that they are at an extreme angle vertically.
Course:	The direction in which the ship is steered, usually given in degrees.
Cringle:	A rope loop, found at either end of a line of reef points. An eye in a sail.
Deckhead:	The ceiling.

291

Deadeye:	Circular wooden block with a groove around the circumference to take a lanyard, to tighten a shroud.
Destore:	Removing all the stores from on board the ship.
Earrings:	Small ropes to make fast the upper corners on square sails.
Fid:	A conical, tapered pin or spike used in splicing rope.
Fiddles:	Guard rails around the edge of a stove or table.
Fighting top platform:	A platform some distance up the mast, from where marines used to fire their muskets at the enemy.
First/second mate:	Deck officers, first and second in line to the captain.
Fizz boat:	Fast rescue boat.
Flaking:	Laying out rope or line in such a manner as to permit it to run free without becoming tangled.
Fo'c'sle:	Short for forecastle. The forward, raised part of the upper deck.
Footrope:	A rope fastened to the underside of a yard for crew to stand on.
Full and by:	Steering by ensuring the sails are kept full by the wind.
Furl:	To make fast the sails to the yards, or masts, by the gaskets.
Futtocks:	Short shrouds from the outside of a top to the mast below, making it necessary for crew climbing the rigging to hang backwards at this point.
Galley:	Ship's kitchen.
Gasket:	A piece of plaited rope used to tie the sails to the yards.
Grommet:	A protective eyelet in a hole that a rope or cable passes through.
Halyard:	A line used to hoist and lower sails, yards, flags, etc.
Hanging in their gear:	To have the sails ungasketed and hanging in their position on the yard, ready to set.

292

Hard tack:	A type of biscuit.
Hatch:	An opening in the deck that gives access to the interior of the ship.
Headway:	The forward movement of a ship through the water.
Heads:	Toilets.
Heeling:	Leaning over to one side.
Helm:	The ship's steering mechanism, or the act of steering (on the helm).
Jackstay:	Rail or wire running along the yards. Useful as a handhold, and the point to which a safety harness is secured. Sometimes used to secure the square sails.
Lanyard:	A short line attached to an object, such as a knife, with which it is secured to another.
Lee:	The side of the ship opposite to where the wind is coming from.
Lee rail:	The rail on that side of the ship.
Lee-boarder:	A type of boat which has a moveable keel on both sides of its hull, enabling either one to be lowered into the water as required by wind and current.
Leech:	The side edges of a square sail, or the after edge of a triangular sail.
Lifeline:	A wire or rope rigged around the deck that crew can clip onto for safety.
Log:	1. An instrument for measuring the ship's speed and distance travelled through the water.
	2. To record in a book the details of a voyage.
Lubber:	A sailor who does not know his duties.
Man steps:	Steps attached to the side of the hull that allow people to ascend the hull.
Manrope:	Rope which hangs adjacent to the man steps to assist the person to ascend.
Orlop deck:	The lowest deck of a ship.
Pin or fife rail:	A rail containing belaying pins to which halyards, sheets and other lines are secured.

Pinnace:	A ship's boat, usually for the captain's use.
Pollywog:	Person who has not yet crossed the equator at sea and undergone an initiation ceremony to be accepted into Neptune's domain.
Poop deck:	The section of open deck from where the ship is steered, often the domain of the officers.
Ratlines (pronounced ratlins):	Short pieces of rope tied between shrouds to act as rungs for climbing aloft.
Reef:	To reduce the area of a sail by folding and tying it up to the yards using reefing points affixed to the sail.
Roband:	A loop used to attach a sail to a yard.
Rope:	In general, a rope on a ship is referred to as a line.
Running rigging	All the moving lines, such as sheets and halyards, used in setting and trimming the sails.
Scow:	A type of sailing vessel.
Seats of ease:	Holes cut in the timber rail at the head of the ship to serve as toilet facilities.
Serve:	To wind a light rope around another rope to prevent chafe.
Serving mallet:	Tool with a grooved head, used when serving a rope to keep the twine at a constant high tension.
Shellback:	Person who has crossed the equator at sea and undergone an initiation ceremony.
Shrouds:	Ropes or wires, usually in pairs, led from the mast to deck level to prevent the mast falling sideways; part of the standing rigging.
Slop chest:	A slang term for a ship's collection of confectionery etc. for sale to people on board. The money collected from such sales.
Spar:	Horizontal piece of wood from which the sails hang.
Splice:	To join ropes or wires by unlaying the strands and interweaving them.
Spritsail:	A sail that is set on the bowsprit.
Standing rigging:	The shrouds and stays that are permanently set up and support the masts

Stay:	Wire or rope that supports the masts in a fore-and-aft direction, part of the standing rigging.
Stunsails:	Extra sails set on boom extensions to the yards, used only in light winds.
Tack:	1. The lower forward corner of a sail; a line used to trim that part of the sail. 2. To turn the ship through the wind by the bow so that the wind blows on the opposite side of the vessel.
T'gallant (topgallant):	One of the highest yards on a ship.
Tiller:	Timber beam that controls the rudder, connected by tackles to the steering wheel.
Tops:	Platforms on masts for observation and spreading the shrouds.
Trireme:	A 13th-century vessel propelled by oars as well as sails.
Voyage crew:	Amateur crew who pay to sail on a voyage, but who work as opposed to being passengers.
Watch:	Division of a ship's company that keeps the deck; a period of time that that group of people is on duty for.
Wear:	To change course by putting the stern of the ship through the wind (called gybing in yachting).
Weather deck:	The deck of a ship (often the top deck on a sailing vessel) that is open to the weather.
Weigh anchor:	To raise the anchor from the bottom.
Windlass:	A winch with a horizontal shaft and vertical handle, used to haul up the anchor chain.
Windward:	The side from which the wind is blowing.
Worming, parcelling and serving:	A system of protecting a line from chafe, using yarn and tarred canvas.
Yard:	Horizontal spar fixed across a mast, normally used to support a sail.

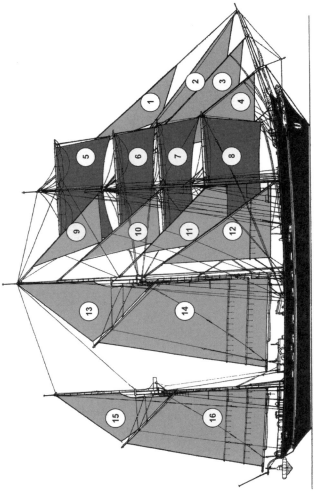

STS *Leeuwin II* simplified sail plan (drawing courtesy Ross Shardlow).

1	Flying jib
2	Outer jib
3	Inner jib
4	Fore topmast staysail
5	Topgallant
6	Upper topsail
7	Lower topsail
8	Fore course
9	Upper staysail
10	Middle staysail
11	Nock staysail
12	Main staysail
13	Main gaff topsail
14	Main sail
15	Mizzen gaff topsail
16	Mizzen sail

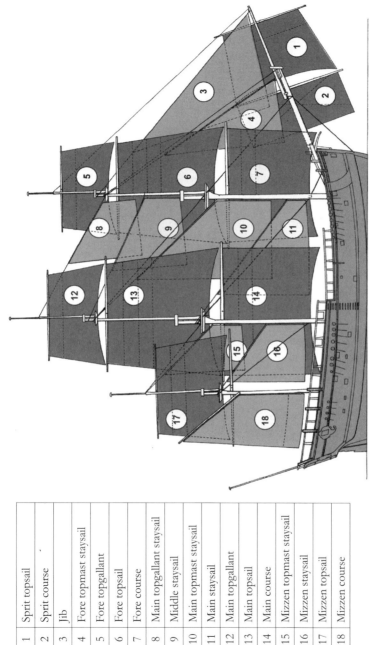

HM bark *Endeavour* simplified sail plan (drawing courtesy Ross Shardlow).

1	Sprit topsail
2	Sprit course
3	Jib
4	Fore topmast staysail
5	Fore topgallant
6	Fore topsail
7	Fore course
8	Main topgallant staysail
9	Middle staysail
10	Main topmast staysail
11	Main staysail
12	Main topgallant
13	Main topsail
14	Main course
15	Mizzen topmast staysail
16	Mizzen staysail
17	Mizzen topsail
18	Mizzen course

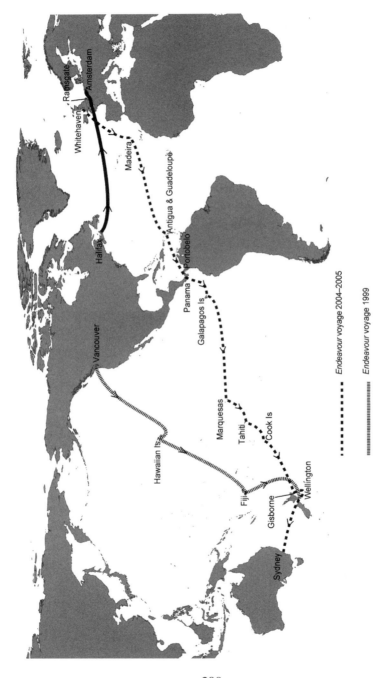

Ramsgate
Amsterdam
Whitehaven
Madeira
Antigua & Guadeloupe
Halifax
Portobelo
Panama
Galapagos Is
Vancouver
Marquesas
Tahiti
Cook Is
Hawaiian Is
Fiji
Wellington
Gisborne
Sydney

Endeavour voyage 2004–2005
Endeavour voyage 1999
Europa voyage 2000

International voyages by the author.

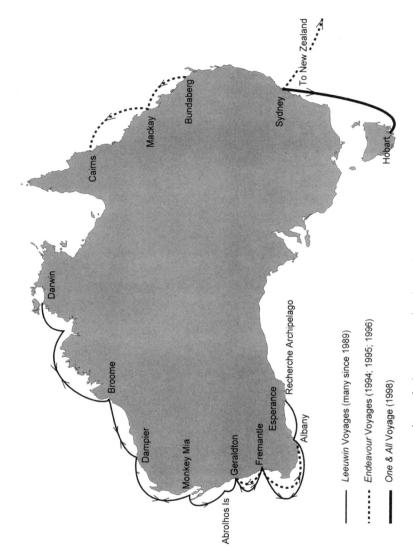

Australasian voyages by the author.

Leeuwin Voyages (many since 1989)

Endeavour Voyages (1994; 1995; 1996)

One & All Voyage (1998)

SELECTED REFERENCES

Cain, Roxanna (editor). *Panama*. Bogotá, Panamericana Formas e Impresos, SA, for Latin Publications, SA, 2003.

de la Harpe, Maureen (editor). *Leeuwin – A Maritime Heritage*. Perth, The Western Australian Museum, 1987.

Fabbri, Patrizia (editor). *Madeira – The New Millennium Collection*. Florence, Casa Editrice Bonechi, 2003.

Forty, Sandra. *Disasters*, Defining Moments series. Hoo, Kent, Grange Books, 2005.

Hedges, AAC. *The Voyages of Captain James Cook*. Norwich, Jarrold Publishing, 1983.

Heinzel, Hermann & Hall, Barnaby. *Galapagos Diary – A Complete Guide to the Archipelago's Birdlife*. Berkeley, University of California Press, 2000.

HM Bark Endeavour – Voyage Crew Training Manual.

HM Bark Endeavour Replica Handbook for Volunteer Guides. Sydney, Maritime Heritage Press, 1994.

Hooper, Rosanne. *The Sailor's Handbook*. London, Pan Books, 1983.

King, Dean. *A Sea of Words: A Lexicon and Companion to the Complete Seafaring Tales of Patrick O'Brian*. New York, Henry Holt, 1995.

Leeuwin Ocean Adventure – Voyage Crew Manual.

Lefroy, Mike (editor). *The Replica of HM Bark Endeavour – A Pictorial Record of the Building of the Replica of HM Bark Endeavour,* 1994.

Macarthur, Antonia & Longley, John. *Endeavour – North American Tour*. Hadlow, Kent, Ticktock Publishing, 1997.

Moore, Wm. *Reed's Seamanship and Nautical Knowledge*, 13th ed. Sunderland, Thomas Reed and Company, 1952.

Petroff, Peter & Ferguson, John. *Sailing Endeavour*. Sydney, Maritime Heritage Press in association with Halstead Press, 1994.

Polden, Richard. *Endeavour: A Photographic Journey*. Fremantle Arts Centre Press in association with the *Sunday Times*, 1998.

Server, Dean. *Tall Ships – The Magic of Sail*. New York, Todtri Productions, 1999.

Stannard, Bruce. *Aboard Endeavour*. Gosford, Ashton Scholastic, 1995.

Woodruff, John (editor). *Philip's Astronomy Dictionary*, 2nd ed. London, George Philip, 1999.